Burden  —  John Fowles - John Hawkes - Claude Simon

# EPISTEMATA

WÜRZBURGER WISSENSCHAFTLICHE SCHRIFTEN

*Reihe Literaturwissenschaft*

Band V — 1980

Robert Burden

# JOHN FOWLES – JOHN HAWKES CLAUDE SIMON

## Problems of Self and Form in the Post-Modernist Novel

## A Comparative Study

Königshausen + Neumann
1980

*Umschlaggestaltung: Charles D. Knights*

**CIP-Kurztitelaufnahme der Deutschen Bibliothek**

**Burden, Robert:**
John Fowles, John Hawkes, Claude Simon : problems
of self and form in the post-modernist novel ; a
comparative study / Robert Burden. — Würzburg:
Königshausen und Neumann, 1980.
    (Epistemata : Reihe Literaturwiss. ; Bd. 5)
    ISBN 3-88479-027-7

© Verlag Dr. Johannes Königshausen + Dr. Thomas Neumann, Würzburg 1980
Druck und Bindung: difo-druck, Bamberg
Alle Rechte vorbehalten — Printed in Germany
ISBN 3-88479-027-7

## ACKNOWLEDGEMENTS

Thanks are due firstly to those who supervised
my post-graduate work at the University of
East Anglia, Norwich: Professor John Fletcher for
his initial enthusiasm and assistance; and Professor
Malcolm Bradbury for his continual advice and his
criticisms of my writings. Furthermore I wish to
record my gratitude to Walter Bachem, currently
teaching at the Ruhr University Bochum, for the
many fruitful discussions on the literary and
philosophical issues raised in this study. Aspects
of the structural analysis of narrative and
'point of view' theory are largely indebted to
discussions with Professor Roger Fowler at the
University of East Anglia. An earlier draft of
Part Three of this study was read by Professor
Guido Almansi, and the conclusions enabled a
slightly different version to be published by
Edward Arnold LTD under the title,'The Novel
Interrogates Itself: Parody As Self-Consciousness
In Contemporary English Fiction' in The Contemporary
English Novel (London, 1979). Finally I should
like to thank Barbara, my wife for her unstinting
support throughout the genesis and eventual
completion of this work.

## Zusammenfassung

Angeregt wurde ich zu dieser Arbeit von der hart-
näckigen Weigerung der englischen Literaturkritik, sich
mit der narrativen Grundlage des Romans zu beschäfti-
gen. Will man versuchen zu beschreiben, wie eine Geschich-
te erzählt wird, so bedeutet das, daß das Wesen des
Narrativen ernsthaft untersucht werden muß. In letz-
ter Zeit hat sich der Einfluß des französischen Struk-
turalismus in der Literaturwissenschaft außerhalb Frank-
reichs in der einführenden Studie Cullers,Structuralist
Poetics (1975), und - auf einer philosophischeren Ebene -
in Jamesons The Prison House of Language (1972) be-
merkbar gemacht. Ich befasse mich mit diesem Bereich
der Literaturwissenschaft, um die Möglichkeiten der
formalistischen Analyse des Narrativen in einem wei-
teren Horizont zu bestimmen.

Ich habe das Prosawerk von John Fowles, John Hawkes
und Claude Simon ausgewählt, weil sie beispielhaft zei-
gen, wo der postmoderne Roman innerhalb der vorherr-
schenden Traditionen der englischen, amerikanischen
und französischen Literatur an die Grenzen des narrativen Diskurses stößt. Das Ziel dieser vergleichenden
Studie ist ein methodologisches und interpretatives.
Meine komparatistische Vorgehensweise muß als solche
von der Voraussetzung ausgehen, daß die Unterscheidungs-
merkmale eines jeden Textes aus den verschiedenen Möglichkeiten dessen, was unter einem Roman zu verstehen
ist, erwachsen, die wiederum in der literarischen Tradition jedes Landes verhaftet sind. Damit stellen sich
dem vergleichenden Literaturwissenschaftler Fragen,
die die Grenzen eines jeden kulturellen Nationalismus
überschreiten; Fragen, die auf eine universale Poetik
des Narrativen abzielen. Und was noch mehr ist, die
Fragestellungen sind sowohl formalistischer als auch
historischer Art: Gibt es heutzutage eine universale
Ästhetik des Romans? Gibt es ein universelles Menschen-
bild? Haben Literatur und Philosophie Anteil an gemein-
samen metaphysischen Voraussetzungen, die deren über-

greifende Problematik unmißverständlich aufzeigen würden? Es wird sich herausstellen, daß das Verständnis des "Ich" einerseits und die formale Frage nach dem Realismus in der postmodernen Ästhetik auf der anderen Seite den wesentlichen Problemkomplex dieser Arbeit bilden.

Meine Argumentation zielt darauf ab, über die formalistischen Grenzen der französischen strukturalistischen Analysemethode des Narrativen hinauszugehen, um Historizität wieder als Voraussetzung für das Textverständnis zu verankern, indem ich seinen ideologischen und ästhetischen Status durch die Analyse von Charakter, 'Struktur' und Selbstbewußtsein des Textes (z.B. Parodie) verstehbar machen will. Daher stellt meine Analyse des Ich in Part I einen Bezug her zwischen Problemen in der Philosophie der Sozialwissenschaften und unseren Vorstellungen die Kohärenz von Charakteren und erzählendem Subjekt betreffend.

Die ideologischen und epistemologischen Implikationen der Werke von Fowles, Hawkes und Simon werden dann als Auslegungen ihrer eigenen formalen Probleme sowie der der formalistischen Analyse selbst innewohnenden Grenzen deutlich. Damit beschäftige ich mich in Part II. Der letzte Teil der Arbeit ist dem Selbstbewußtsein des postmodernen Romans gewidmet, besonders den Elementen Parodie und Pastiche, mit denen der Roman seine angestrengte Suche nach seiner eigenen Form genau zu einem Zeitpunkt aufnimmt, an dem das intellektuelle Klima viele der konventionellen Schreibweisen unterminiert.

# CONTENTS

## PREFACE

This study is prompted by the need in English literary criticism
to deal more fully than we have with the narrative basis of the
novel.    One critic has recently drawn attention to this necessity:

> Critics of the novel have recently begun to devote
>
> a good deal of attention to the nature of
>
> narrative.   It is hardly surprising.   For with
>
> the honourable exception of Scholes and Kellogg's
>
> The Nature of Narrative the subject has been more
>
> or less neglected.   Oddly so, one feels, since
>
> trying to account for how the telling of a tale
>
> is done and the effect it has on the reader ought
>
> to be a fascinating and rewarding task.[1]

Anglo-American criticism indeed largely justifies this lament.
But, more recently, there have been signs of a change.   The
influence of French literary structuralism has been felt outside of France;   in Anglo-American criticism we might note the
influence of such an introductory study as Culler's Structuralist
Poetics (1975), as well as of a more philosophical critique like
Jameson's The Prison-House of Language (1972).   In what follows,
I engage in this whole area of discourse in order to determine
the possibilities for the formalistic analysis of narrative
within both a comparative and a historical perspective.   In
this respect, mention could be made of John Fletcher's recent
comparative analysis of Claude Simon's work in relation to other
contemporary writers of fiction, Claude Simon and Fiction Now
(1975), and also of Raymond Federman's comparative anthology of
essays on trends in contemporary American and European literary
fiction entitled, Surfiction, Fiction Now and Tomorrow (1975).

Both these books serve in different ways to indicate the
fundamental problems of a comparative analysis, either by
remaining on the level of a brief introductory study as in
Fletcher's case, or by the overproliferation of typologies of
apparent trends and characteristics in American and European
novelistic practice without any thoroughgoing analysis of the
texts themselves. Notwithstanding the intentions of these
particular works of criticism, I intend to go further into the
methodological and critical problems involved in a comparative
analysis of the contemporary novel. That is to say, the analysis of the narrative basis of the novel inexorably leads to the
common ground of universal properties. Furthermore, the discussion of marked individual differences within the broader
spectrum of universal properties, enables the rationale for
comparative analysis to be self-evident. This, then, allows the
critic to transcend the bounds of the type of thematic approach
which characterizes Fletcher's book which never quite manages to
clarify the rationale for such comparisons in a book on Claude
Simon's work. I am concerned in this study with contemporary
writing which challenges both the conditions of writing and the
problematics of contemporary reality, and I have selected the
narrative fiction of John Fowles, John Hawkes, and Claude Simon
as examples of the bounds of narrative discourse for the post-
modernist novel as these arise within the dominant, and different
national traditions of English, American, and French writing.
The aim of this comparative study is, then, both methodological
and critical. My comparative method (as, indeed, any such method)
proceeds under the initial assumption that distinguishing characteristics of any one text are 'rooted in different ways of thinking about the novel, which in turn are deeply embedded in the
literary tradition of each country'.[2]    However, questions then

arise for the comparatist which transcend the bounds of any
cultural nationalism; questions which encroach on a general
poetics of narrative. Such questions are necessarily both
formal and historical: Is there a common aesthetics for the
novel today? Is there a common image of man? Are there shared
metaphysical presuppositions in literature and thought which
would clearly define an abiding problematics? There is a danger
of localism in the study of contemporary literary fiction. As
Josipovici has complained, the nouveau roman has been separated
from the Western literary tradition, 'giving outsiders the impression that it is a phenomenon that must be treated on its own, with
perhaps a few esoteric references to Mallarmé and Roussel'.[3]
Perhaps the inward-looking attitude of many practitioners and
theoreticians of such experimental writing may well be largely to
blame for this state of affairs. But larger references and international comparisons are of great importance now. The contemporary critique derives in part from aspects of the Modernism of
the late nineteenth and early twentieth century, and this was
itself an international tendency, though with distinct national
variations. The different national responses to the implications
of Modernism, and the evolution of consequential modes of narrative,
hence offer the critic a grounding for comparative analysis. The
broad situation can be simply stated. But the discourse which
serves to justify such statements is lengthy and complex, as the
following interplay between literary criticism (the analysis of
texts), literary theory (the search for underlying principles and
presuppositions), and the philosophical arguments which serve to
rationalize contemporary epistemology, will demonstrate. As
Jameson perceptively claims:

> What is accessible to the theoretician is the
> relationship of the individual philosophical
> position or idea to the essential model or
> problem-complex on which it is based; the work
> of finding the model behind the idea is what
> Derrida has called a 'deconstruction'.[4]

In what follows, not only will the works of Fowles, Hawkes, and
Simon be 'deconstructed' in order to extrapolate their underlying principles of coherence, but also they will be related to
an essential problem-complex which, firstly, concerns the problem
of the 'self', and, secondly, concerns the formal question of
realism in a post-Modernist aesthetics.   These questions, and
their significance for such matters as the representation of
'character' in contemporary literary fiction, will thus form a
crucial part of my analysis.   For, indeed, the whole question
of 'character' as an aesthetic and a social concept has been
neglected too often.   In the light of the French Structuralist
metaphysical presupposition of the priority of the signifier
(language, the text) over the signified (character as individual
Subject, for instance), and this in relation to more properly
sociological analyses of contemporary reality, more naive, traditional concepts of character with their notions of consciousness
and stable views of the world, do indeed need to be re-examined.
The historical analysis of the social and intellectual conditions
in which the novel today is written, and through which it becomes
intelligible, is effected by the critic through relating concepts
and presuppositions to literary structures.   Thus, in discussing
the 'self', one questions precisely what can be known and claimed
about the world, about the limits of reason, and about the

viability of the Cartesian and Sartrean Cogito as the epistemic
foundation of the mimetic novel. These are questions about the
cognitive basis of literary texts, and they can be explored
philosophically. However, as meaning is always processed through
the form which expresses it, a formal analysis would seek to
characterise the principles on which the inner coherence of a work
is grounded. In this sense, 'structure' is defined as the developing unity of a work, the relationship of parts to the totality
of the artistic phenomenon; and, therefore, in analysing the
narrative basis of the novel, the basic problem to be accounted
for is, 'the diachrony or sequentiality of narrative discourse.'[5]
Narrative structure is perceivable and intelligible by describing
and making sense of narrative logic. My argument in this study
aims to go beyond the formalist limitations of the French Structuralist analysis to reintroduce History into the understanding of
narrative, by characterising the ideological and aesthetic status
of any text in terms of the reading of character, structure, and
self-consciousness. Inspired by Barthes's sophisticated methodology in S/Z (1970), this study aims to go some way towards
examining the formalistic possibilities for analysing the intellectual and aesthetic foundations for the novel today by pointing
to:

> ... some deeper ambiguity in the very structure
> of the literary work itself, to something in the
> verbal construction of literature which allows
> it to be assimilated to, and even perhaps to
> serve as a paradigm for, other, more properly
> sociological sign-systems.[6]

Thus the analysis of the 'self' in Part One of this study argues
for the coherence of characters and narrating Subjects in the novel
to be more systematically grounded in crucial debates in the philosophy of the social sciences.  For both novelists and social
scientists alike are involved in the complex issues surrounding
the social and psychological causes of the crisis of identity and
the understanding of modern consciousness.  Such questions are
crucial to the re-examination of the conventional concept of character based on a stable and knowable ego.  The belief-systems
and the underlying epistemology in the works of Fowles, Hawkes,
and Simon are then seen to explain the formal problems themselves,
and also the inherent limitations of a formalistic analysis.  This
will be the concern of Part Two.  The final section of this study
deals with the self-consciousness of the post-Modernist novel, and
especially with parody and pastiche, which will be seen as examples
of the way that the novel foregrounds its anxious quest for form
precisely at a time when the intellectual climate has apparently
undermined many of the conventional modes of writing.

It is precisely within the crucial argument between realism and
modernism that I characterize the post-war narrative fiction of
Fowles, Hawkes, and Simon as post-Modernist.  That is to say, they
all, in some way or another, define their aesthetic and philosophical
principles in relation to the kind of questions raised by the
Modernist art and literature of the late nineteenth and early
twentieth century.  The problematical status of modes of authority
(bourgeois values, the Church, the State; but also the author, and
his narrator surrogates, and language itself) in such art and
literature, has apparently generated two types of aesthetic response.

One is a return to (or continuation of) a realist-aesthetics in
the novel, often arising as a reaction against the 'élitist'
position of offering high art as an answer to the world's chaos.
The other is a return, with new premises involved, towards
Modernist problematics themselves.[7]  The post-war period, and
particularly the period since the late 1950s, has indeed witnessed
a resurgence of interest in Modernism, and a return in the novel
towards some of its experimental premises.  Thus, in the sense
that the works of the three writers in question embody the resultant anxieties and syntheses, and can be characterized as coming
after what one critic has called, the 'coupûre épistémologique'
of Modernism,[8] then they are truly post-Modernist.

There is, however, another meaning attributed to the idea of the
'Modern' which also offers a sense of continuity in our reading
of the literature of the nineteenth and that of the twentieth
century.  Weisstein points out that 'what is called modern is
always seen in contrast to the ancient, the familiar or the
classical'.[9]  'Modern' texts are, therefore, by definition,
critical of established conventions of writing.  The post-Modernist novel, as exemplified differently in the works of Fowles,
Hawkes, and Simon, reinvokes the profound drive of Modernist art
and literature towards a renewal of our perception of the world.
But this drive is also manifest on the aesthetic level in the very
play on narrative structures, on the logic of narrative, and on
our conventional literary expectations.  This can be seen as 'an
assault on our conventionalized life patterns, a whole battery of
shocks administered to our routine vision of things, an implicit
critique and restructuration of our habitual consciousness'.[10]

Given this idea of the 'modern', and the consequent historical
catergorization of a post-Modernist novel, the rationale behind
the organizing areas of concern for this study may be simply
explained.  Character, structure, and self-consciousness (parody
and pastiche), offer us modes of analysis which demonstrate not
only the intellectual questioning of conventional presuppositions
of a historical and social kind, but also the manner by which the
very idea of the novel is perpetually re-examined in novels where
form becomes content in their attempts to interrogate their narrative
bases.  This challenge offered by the novel is intelligible as part
of a total and determinate historical situation.  Furthermore,
because of the persistence of realism in popular, as well as in
many less popular, novels in this century, and despite the lessons
of Modernism, texts which question such aesthetics are likely to
be poorly received because of their unfamiliarity.  In this respect,
John Fowles is widely read;  John Hawkes in comparison is hardly
known;  and the work of Claude Simon continues to be read only be a
relatively small 'university' public, and this largely thanks to the
commitment of the publishing house of Les Editions de Minuit.  The
amount of realism in any one novel is proportional to the extent of
its readership.  Be that as it may, the persistence of the formal
and epistemological character of what Bradbury has called the
'modernist impulse', with its marked loss of stability for the
literary text,[11] may best be understood through Barthes' ideal models
of the 'classical' and the 'modern' which he postulates at the
beginning of S/Z (1970).  For this distinction is grounded in the
enabling notion of what is precisely readable, given our conventional
reading habits, and what is intentionally unreadable in relation to
those habits.  This will be elaborated in some detail below.

In the final analysis, the theoretical framework of my study on problems of self and form in the post-Modernist novel, which I have placed under the rubric of the logic of narrative (with all its formalistic implications), aims to account for those 'comparable historical pressures /which/ shape form'[12] in the novel.

PART ONE

THE DISCOURSE OF THE SELF AND THE
INTELLIGIBILITY OF CHARACTER

Tout roman exprime une conception de la personne
qui dicte à l'écrivain de choisir certaines formes
et confère à l'oeuvre son sens le plus large et
le plus profond; si cette conception se modifie,
l'art du roman se transforme.

Michel Zéraffa.

## INTRODUCTION

The creation of people in literature, in the form of individual
characters, has always enabled readers to relate the text to their
ordinary daily experience.   My claims here are based on the assumption that character in literature, grounded in both cultural and
social models, is a fundamental aspect of the logic of narrative:
the manner by which the reader makes sense of the literary text.
Because of the traditional referential identification of character
with historically available models of social coherence, the particular understanding in fiction of the self, and of what precisely
identity is, not only allows the reader certain kinds of expectations
concerning the plausibility of characters, but also enables writers
to devise strategies in which to encapsulate the problems involved
in defining the self;   problems of order, knowledge, perception,
memory, and relation to other minds.   The manipulation by novelists
of historically pertinent models of man, and the commensurable
problematics of the self, permit the critic to explain recalcitrant
phenomenon not only in relation to conventions of literary form, but
also to crucial debates in the philosophy of social science, itself
concerned with understanding concepts of the self, and with devising
models of reality from particular paradigms.

There are two principal aspects of character which cause certain
expectations to arise in literature.   Firstly, character serves,
conventionally, as an instrument of the perception of a whole world of
action based on our models of persons, behaviour, and the structure of
society.   Secondly, characters are often comprehensible in terms of

literary stereotypes. They are not just grounded in our social
but also in our traditional literary knowledge. As Northrop Frye
has argued:

> All lifelike characters, whether in drama or fiction, owe
> their consistency to the appropriateness of the stock type
> which belongs to their dramatic function. That stock type
> is not the character but it is as necessary to the charac-
> ter as a skeleton is to the actor who plays it. [1]

Heroes, villains, and picaresque protagonists, for instance, all
presuppose a certain structural coherence based on a conventional
archetypal logic of narrative plot. The structural analysis of
the folk tale and other analogous formulaic stories, deriving
from Propp, relies heavily on the type of logic and predictability
invested in stereotyped characters.[2] It is precisely because of
the inherent simplicity of these models of character that the
French structural analysis of narrative has exposed its fundamental
inadequacies in dealing with character.[3]

The Formalist and Structuralist theory accounts for characters
solely in terms of what they do in a story, not what they are.
Characters are defined as 'actants', participants in spheres of
action. In this respect, they are reduced to the demands of plot
sequences, where the abiding aim of the structuralist would be to
derive a typology of stereotyped roles which might then provide a
general, universal structural principle for describing all narratives. As I shall argue, the attempts in functionalist sociology
to define the self are as limited to such surface phenomena as role
and functional relations amongst the social actors as the French

structuralists are in the analysis of character in literature. In
more sophisticated literary works, this minimalization of understanding breaks down, and the text demands an account of idiosyncracies of personality in apparently heterogenous characters whose
qualities and motives may facilitate a clearer understanding of
actions in plots. The broad generalizations of the so-called
'actantiel' model of character may provide a useful typology of
the common origins of formulaic tales, but it must be rejected in
the face of the more complex and enigmatic protagonists of literature. Although character does rely on conventions of character in
the history of literature, describing those conventions is not
sufficient in itself to make the total phenomenon intelligible.
Our comprehension of this complexity often depends radically on
knowledge from non-literary discourse: our ordinary assumptions
about society and the individual, as well as, nowadays, current debates in
the philosophy of social science, have always aided our reading of
character in literature. As recent debate has clearly shown,
assumptions about man, and the necessary further assumptions about
society, have never been more problematical. One crucial approach
to the post-war novel is precisely to investigate the extent to
which texts respond both thematically and formally to this crisis
of the self. The works of Fowles, Hawkes, and Simon all offer
various instances of this crisis for the novel.[4]


The limitations inherent in the very methodology of the French
structural analysis of narrative are clearly recognised by Barthes.
For, although the original project of such an analysis may well have
been to, 'extraire de chaque conte son modèle, puis de ces modèles
nous ferons une grande structure narrative, que nous reverserons

(pour vérification) sur n'importe quel récit', Barthes rightly concludes that this is a 'tâche épuisante...et finalement indésirable, car le texte y perd sa différence.'[5] Thus, the difference of one text from another is more crucial than the search for the confirmation of universal narrative properties in the historical intelligibility of literary texts. The transcendence of the bounds of the structural analysis of narrative universals is effected by Barthes in S/Z (1970). His typology of the possible meanings of social and cultural signs enables Balzac's story Sarrasine to be characterised as readable and to be clearly comprehensible within a given model of reality. What is important is the historical difference between Balzac's text and its worldview, and the consciousness of the reader today.[6] Barthes devises a set of codes which enable the reader to appreciate the network of references, and pointers, that characterise the ideological sub-text of Sarrasine. Barthes demonstrates how the reader, himself a cipher of codes from his knowledge of both literature and the world, approaches the coded text. In this respect, psychology need not be seen to be in characters as such, but rather in the reader's perception of a certain 'effet de texte'. Balzac's realism encodes the vraisemblable of a culture.[7] The semiotic methodology, of which Barthes' S/Z is an example, would want to claim, therefore, that the notion of character is as much a reconstruction by the reader as a construction of the text itself. Deriving from Barthes' replacement of claims for realism as a viable aesthetic with the notion of 'reality-effect', and given that character functions as such an effect, Hamon, in his 'statut sémiologique du personnage', talks in terms of the character-effect of the text.[8] The

signs that refer to the external world of history and society are
referential codes, and if the enigmatic presence of mysterious
characters gives narrative an impetus towards revelation and
acceptable knowledge, then the least that can be said is that such
knowledge, especially for Barthes and the semioticians, is clearly
available in the appearance, actions, relationships, and thoughts
of characters. Once again, French theory evinces its willingness
to remain only on the level of the relationships between textual
manifestations and the reader's expectations. We do, however,
deduce from surface structures precisely what lies beneath the
text, so to speak. And such connotations are the evidence of worldview and
history, as Barthes clearly argues in S/Z.

The knowability of character in literature depends on the projections onto the text of reader-expectations. A Balzac-text exploits
a clearly defined readership, grounded in the crucial historical
intelligibility of models of man and cognate assumptions about the
nature of society prevalent in the mid-nineteenth century. The
relationship between individuated protagonists and stable societies
in eighteenth and nineteenth century novels underlies their models
of persons and conditions the expectations of their reading community. This would be confirmed by a now orthodox argument deriving
from Watt's The Rise of the Novel (1957) which claims that the novel's
genesis and initial development is grounded in the emergent ideology
of bourgeois individualism. This itself has been a useful interpretive model.[9]

Founded on the vexatious interplay between hero and society,

character was perceived as an individuated, psychologically knowable
entity.    Anxieties could always be resolved by relying on the
authority of society.    The novel achieved coherence in proportion
to the successful portrayal of richly delineated characters who
were clearly recognisable for both their typicality and their attempts
to be individual.    What D.H. Lawrence rejected as the emotive poverty
and 'surface' individuality of 'the old stable ego' of character,
much twentieth century literature has declared unknowable.[10]    For,
if implicit models of social and psychological coherence indicate what
levels of plausibility are available for constructing the literary
texts around characters, then the reliance on predominantly nineteenth
century models may well undermine the claims for a work's modernity.

That is not to say that there is no continuity with nineteenth
century debates about the self.    For many of the substantial arguments
which evolved in and from the nineteenth century enabled the 'crisis'
to be discussed, in this century, in the discourse of the philosophy of
the social sciences.    Mandelbaum, in his study of nineteenth century
thought, entitled History, Man and Reason (London, 1971), describes the
great conflicts between metaphysical idealism and positivism, the rise
of historicism, the epistemological questions about the limits of
reason, and, most significantly for this study, the concern with the
malleability of man.    The arguments about the self as either free-
caused or socially determined arose in nineteenth century debates
about human nature and social conditions, and, through the work of
thinkers like Marx and Durkheim, they brought about the foundation
of modern sociology.    Two most prominent twentieth century tendencies

which can be seen to be directly influenced by nineteenth century
thought are the doctrine of authenticity in recent existentialist
thought (crucial in Fowles' work), and the epistemological doubt
placed on the Subject, evident especially in recent French literature
(as I shall argue in relation to Simon's narrative fiction).  The
nineteenth century belief in Progress, and the essential rationality
of man and his world, is encapsulated in many novels of that era,
and is fundamental to any explanation of the character of nineteenth
century realism.  But also, as such beliefs, so close to the centre
of the novel, fall into doubt, so literature will take on a more
critical role.  The stable view of society and man's world progressively
moved towards the critique effected by, say, Nietzsche, Conrad and
Kafka.  The questioning of all types of authority became the staple
formula for the Modernism of the late nineteenth and early twentieth
centuries.  The effect of such questions on character and the models
of man on which it may be grounded is important for the literary
critic in his analysis of recent, post-modernist narrative fiction.

One crucial method of problematising outmoded notions of character
in twentieth century literature has been the undermining of the
emphasis on names as indicators of individuated and knowable persons.
Kafka's K is a well-known example.  More recently, the anonymity or
uncertainty of the 'single letter' character, has featured in Robbe-
Grillet's La Jalousie (1957);  and Claude Simon's 'O' in La Bataille
de Pharsale (1969), is another example.  Simon's confusions of 'il'
and 'je' as narrative perspective also exemplify the recording of a
loss of certainty about identity and about the epistemological status
of the Subject.  The stability of names is ironized in Robbe-Grillet's
La Maison de Rendez-vous (1965), where not only do characters' names

change through a play on their spelling, but also actions and attributes are established only to be swiftly denied.[11] For Pynchon, in V (1963) the letter of the title reaches an ultimate point of ambiguity with the proliferation of its symbolic meanings. These various attacks on the notion of the singleness of an identity as the basis for character radically fracture the traditional attributes of the Balzacian character. The monopolization of the proper name has traditionally contributed to the unity of identity.

The persistence of conventional approaches to the intelligibility of character in the novel can be exemplified in the successful attempts to recuperate a strangely dislocated text through rationalizing its strangeness in terms of psychological deviation. The jealous husband-narrator of La Jalousie is a case in point; and Booth's notion of the unreliable narrator is enabling in this respect.[12] Texts which remain within the bounds of conventions in some degree or other, no matter how radical their critique, must always be susceptible to a normative understanding. The extremes of recalcitrant avant-garde art always defy explanation within a normative poetics. I shall describe in this study precisely where Fowles, Hawkes, and Simon fit into this ongoing and crucial relationship between the norms of conventions and degrees of their critique.

The Realist-aesthetic of a Balzac established individuated essences through naming, describing physical appearances, and creating a psychological picture through action and thought. The individual character could be rationally explained. The dominant bourgeois

ideology expected the emphasis to fall on questions of the acqui-
sition of wealth, property, and the primacy of the family unit.
Barthes, in S/Z, explains the dominance of this ideology in Balzac's
work. The cultural code reinforces the status quo and lends the
text its historical relevance. The text of Sarrasine amasses
apparently incontrovertible information about life in a didactic
and pedagogic voice. In Barthes's words:

> Une Rhétorique et un recueil de maximes et proverbes concern-
> ant la vie, la mort, la souffrance, l'amour, les femmes, les
> âges, etc. Quoique d'origine entièrement livresque, ces codes,
> par un tourniquet propre à l'idéologie bourgeoise, qui inverse
> la culture en nature, semblent fonder le réel, la 'Vie'. La
> 'Vie' devient alors, dans le texte classique, un mélange
> écoeurant d'opinions courantes, une nappe étouffante d'idées
> reçues: c'est en effet dans ces codes culturels que se con-
> centre le démodé balzacien, l'essence de ce qui, dans Balzac,
> ne peut être (ré-)écrit.13

The traditional notion of character as individual is cognate with
the rise of the novel in the eighteenth century, and the great
achievements of nineteenth century Realism, especially in France,
England, and Russia. The aesthetics of Realism were grounded in
the belief in the direct representation of reality. Balzac saw his
task as to observe his society and then to portray it in a series of
novels which produced a valid scientific typology, given the available model of the natural sciences: empirical observation, then
classification. The apparent simplicity of such an interplay
between literature and society, between reality and expression,has
become the target for much of the 'theory' behind the Nouveau Roman
in France, and its more radical version in the ideological critique
centred around the journal Tel Quel. On a more philosophical level,

Jean-Marie Benoist has characterized the historical divide as a
'coupûre épistémologique', consisting 'de la diffraction du sujet.'[14]
The idea of Cartesian man, a giver of order and sense to the world,
is epistemologically problematical.  This relation of man to the
world is replaced, for Benoist, by the differential, structural,
and semiotic relation, which articulates the signs that confer
meaning.  It is within this intellectual climate  that twentieth
century literature has progressively questioned the very idea of
the primacy of the Subject.  Recent French theory, and the literature
it largely subscribes to, has effected the most extreme radicali-
zation of this problem on the form of the novel.  The work of
Claude Simon will be seen to be intelligible in this way.  Writers
elsewhere have often remained within the reach of conventional form,
and their analysis of this problem usually depends on further, more
explicit, assumptions about the nature of modern society.  These
narrative texts are comprehensible within a referential context.
Fowles, and Hawkes to a lesser extent, exemplify this aspect of the
post-war novel.

French structuralism, then, takes an ideological stand against the
primacy of the Subject as psychological entity, or as an epistemological focus.  Many of the theoreticians of recent experimental
narrative fiction in France refuse the transcendence of meaning,
the referentiality of the text.  The text is a linguistic, self-
referential phenomenon.  But the unresolved contradiction remains
in the analysis of character.  The 'actantiel' mode of analysis
demonstrates the recalcitrance of the concept of character for
this method.  As Jameson rightly argues,

> ...it is hard to see how the structural analysis of
> narrative can make any further theoretical progress
> without attacking this particular problem, which may
> be described as that of the stubbornly anthropomorphic
> nature of our present categories of character.[15]

Barthes's S/Z goes some way towards solving the methodological

problem, as he shows clearly how the idea of the person is

historically determined. Jameson's conclusion must receive

wide recognition:

> ...clearly, the problem intersects with the vaster
> philosophic one of the historical nature of the Subject
> itself.[16]

The intellectual foundations of the debate in literature about

character correspond to a highly complex ongoing discourse in

the philosophy of the social sciences. It is precisely here

that currently available models of man are to be found in conjunc-

tion with assumptions about the nature of modern society. A

brief outline of debates about the self in current thought will

enable us to assess precisely to what extent the works of Fowles,

Hawkes and Simon engage in this contemporary intellectual climate,

and, eventually (in parts two and three of this study), how far

the cognitive content of their works enables us to understand the

formal narrative problems.

Arguments about modern identity in the philosophy of social

science tend to ground their assumptions on a distinction between

the modern and pre-modern society:

Because of the plurality of social worlds in modern
society, the structures of each particular world are
experienced as relatively unstable and unreliable.
The individual in most pre-modern societies lives in
a world that is much more coherent.  It therefore
appears to him as firm and possibly inevitable.  By
contrast, the modern individual's experience of a
plurality of social worlds relativizes every one of
them.[17]

What is specifically modern in modern consciousness?  Modern

consciousness, it is argued, is pecularly aware of itself, where

not only is the outside world under continual scrutiny but also

the precise identity of the self is subjected to an anguished

search.  The stability formerly accorded to and offered by society

is no longer the case in a pluralistic modern world:

Stable identities (and this also means identities that
will be subjectively plausible) can only emerge in reci-
procity with stable social contexts (and this means contexts
that are structured by stable institutions).  Therefore,
there is a deep uncertainty about contemporary identity.
Put differently, there is a built-in identity crisis in the
contemporary situation.[18]

For modern man, identity ceases to be a given fact.  Instead, it

becomes the elusive object of a vexatious search:  man is forever

in search of himself.  This quest is to be clearly distinguished

from the quasi-religious efforts of Romanticism in late eighteenth

and early nineteenth century literature.  For this loss of a clear

sense of self is attributable to the state of modern life which can

be described as highly segmented.  The pluralization of social

realities is manifest both in society (its institutions) and in

consciousness.  The relationship between institutions and conscious-

ness is crucial to a thesis which posits a dialectical relationship

between, 'objective givenness and subjective meanings.'[19] The
linkages between established institutions and institutional
processes form the specific base for structures of consciousness.
In this respect, specific 'fields of consciousness' deriving from
given institutions found well-defined 'social life-worlds'; there
are, consequently, as many life-worlds as there are institutions.

The self, defined within the bounds of this argument, is apparently
experienced through its identification (or to put it less optimisi-
cally, through its anonymization) with the diverse components of
its social life-worlds. The self, therefore, is experienced only
in a partial and segmented way: 'indeed, it becomes a componential
self.'[20] Any attempts to describe a total self will be faced with
a plurality of fragments, a 'bricolage' of the self.[21] Inevitably,
doubt is cast on the possibility of ever describing a total self
without simplifying and obscuring the situation. It remains to be
seen precisely how Fowles, Hawkes and Simon, respond to this
'bricolage' of the self in their narrative fiction.

Modern society is characterized by two major forces which serve to
shape consciousness: technological production and bureaucracy.
They are primary carriers of consciousness, and they produce certain
intrinsic relations between consciousness and institutions: 'Clusters
of consciousness' are seen to be 'intrinsic properties of certain
modern institutions.'[22] This is fundamental to the crisis of the
modern urban experience. Modern society determines, precisely in
this manner, the available realities which consequently reduce the
subject to the object of 'abstractly normed behaviour.'[23]

Assumptions about the nature of modern man are related to such
assumptions about society. In order to construct, albeit in
abstract terms, a context in which self-actualization may indeed
take place, a shared frame of reference may be invoked under the
rubric of the 'symbolic universe' of modernity:

> The symbolic universe of a society is a body of tradition
> that integrates a large number of definitions of reality
> and presents the institutional order to the individual as
> a symbolic totality. In other words...
> the Weltanschauung of modernity.[24]

However, such a quest for a symbolic evocation of the wholeness
of a totalized perspective conflicts with the highly segmented
mode of social life. As the multiple realities of social life
are a 'constant and probably necessary feature of human consciousness,'[25] then pluralization itself problematizes the creation of
any overarching symbolic universe. One may conclude from this
argument that not only is a total, unified view of the modern
social world impossible, because of the assumptions which found
the theory of modern society described above, but also the self
is only knowable in its social manifestations, which results in a
pluralization of identity.

Sets of assumptions about the nature of modern society are a
priori to further assumptions about the nature of man in modern
sociological theory. According to Dawe, the history of sociology
has been grounded in two antithetical methodologies, both claiming
to deal with man and society.[26] A sociology of social system is
in conflict on every level with a sociology of social action.

They posit opposing models of man and relationships between the
social and the individual:

> The first asserts the paramount necessity, for societal
> and individual well-being, of external constraint; hence
> the notion of a social system ontologically and methodolo-
> gically prior to its participants. The key notion of the
> second is that of autonomous man, able to realize its full
> potential and to create a truly human social order, only
> when freed from external constraint.[27]

Society either creates its members, or it is their creation. A
tradition stemming from the Enlightenment, developing through
J.S. Mill, and Marx, culminates in the popularized versions of
Existentialism and the plea for a more 'subject' sociology in
post-war literature and thought;[28] this stands against the tradition deriving from Hobbes, Comte's positivism, Durkheim, and
persisting in sociology through functionalism, and specifically
the concept of socialization and its moral and political implications in social conformity. Both these sociologies produce ideal
models of reality, and from these models,'they derive their meaning
and their use; they are, indeed, doctrines.'[29]

Such social theories are cognate with two approaches to the understanding of human nature. Passive concepts of man are opposed to
active concepts. The former are deterministic, and reduce man to
the agent of social action, a predicate of the stereotyping social
system. The latter are grounded in a view of man as autonomous,
possessing some sort of 'substantial self'. In this second thesis
the causal explanation of action from the perspective of the world
order is reversed. Hollis claims that,'the key to explaining social

behaviour lies in the rational activity of the subject self.'[30]
For this to be possible, there has to be a self which precedes
the rationality which marks out man. Antonomous man is not only a
rational subject self, but also is self-caused and therefore is the
explanation of his own actions. In existentialism, the plea for
autonomy begins in the claim that existence precedes essence, and
that, for Sartre at least, identity is achieved from acts of
creative self-definition.

Philosophers, in their readiness to analyze concepts of action,
move some way towards an involvement in the question of whether a
substantial self can be known to pre-exist the social, given the
vexatious assumptions about modern society. In the more passive
model of man, self is easily knowable, because its explanation
derives from a causal model. This is the social self, a partici-
pant through role-playing in the theatre of society. In this
respect, norms are internalized social constraints. But from a
different perspective, norms are supposed to derive from the needs
of individuals. Durkheim's homo sociologicus stands against J.S.
Mill's homo psychologicus. If the actor in the dramaturgical
analogy 'could remove his last mask, there would be no face beneath.'
This is the moral of the passive model of man.[31] Some way between
the two apparently irreconcilable positions is Goffman's middle-
class social actor, scheming the effective management of interaction rituals.[32] This is a highly rational agent, who evinces a
self-conscious relation to normative role-playing. But he is only
an agent, not an individual self, and social norms do offer the
reasons for action. A more active model demands that role-distance

enable the self to be distinguished from the role for, although
the self needs to be social, 'the character must be able to be
distinguished from the mask.'[33]

Inevitably, a philosophy which seeks the 'logical and epistemological criteria by which persons can be identified,'[34] would be
limited if it did not take account of the claims of a sociological
theory which analyzes the implications of social structures and
their constraints on man. Equally, 'every social theory needs a
metaphysic... in which a model of man and a method of science complement each other.'[35] By analogy, problems of the self in
literature are complemented by questions of literary form as each
text is characterized by its underlying philosophical and ideological
assumptions. Fowles, Hawkes, and Simon all respond to problems of
modern identity by questioning the conventional forms of the novel
and the limitations of those forms which have been grounded in
different models of man and different interpretations of reality.

The crisis of identity, then, is intelligible at the precise inter-
section between a subject self and a social identity:

> The affliction strikes when what I am no longer accounts
> for who I am, because what I do is no longer the rational
> acting out of what I have chosen to become. 36

This crisis may well then rely on the notion that society mediates
between individuals, institutions, and situations. 'Inasmuch as
society remains the product of human activity, its living subjects
are still able to recognize themselves in it, as from across a great

distance....'[37]

In his more radical position, Adorno casts some doubt on the
type of rational action thesis which informs Hollis' argument:
'rational action is objectively just as "comprehensible" as it is
motivated.'          Given that the nature of modern society is
the root cause of the identity crisis, it ought to be the task of
sociology today, Adorno claims, 'to comprehend the incomprehensible,
the advance of human beings into the inhuman.'[38] The individual is
reified into the predicate of roles. But the role as a given fact
of societal existence is insufficient for the understanding of
human action. In functionalist sociology (Parson's The Structure of
Social Action (1949) being a seminal example), men are bound together
through social constraint which 'trains them to pure self-conservation
at the same time that it denies them conservation of their
selves.'[39] As the preceding arguments clearly demonstrate, a
thoroughgoing theory of society must not remain on the level of the
immediate observation of phenomena, but must move 'towards and understanding of their deeper social causes:  why human beings today are
still sworn to the playing of roles.'[40] Such a critique of societal
relations would want to investigate the real causes for the evident
reduction of men to agents. Marcuse's one-dimensional social man is
the result of this type of critique, whereby American society is seen
to be surreptitiously 'totalitarian' as the vested interests of the
entrepreneurial norm create the 'happy consciousness' of man; this
is the ultimate manifestation of society's control over man's consciousness, with the result of completely absorbing man into the
normative collective consciousness of mass society.[41] Mandelbaum's

malleability model gives way to Marcuse's one-dimensionality, and
the claims for rational action are undermined by society's propagandist manipulation of consciousness. This more emotive and
politically radical view of social reality utilizes the methods of
Dawe's sociology of social system, yet ideologically belongs to a
sociology of social action with its characterization of the beleaguered self.

The bounds of a sociological understanding of man can be seen in
the limitations of role-theory. For Dahrendorf, 'the category of
role accordingly falls on the borderline of sociology and psychology.'[42]
The sociologist would posit the fact of roles as an irreducible element
of the analysis of homo sociologicus; the psychologist would be more
concerned with the 'inner side' of the individual in the face of his
roles. Homo sociologicus, as we have seen, is depersonalized for the
sake of systematic and functional analysis. But, beyond such distinctions of disciplinary boundaries, a moral question remains:

> ...the vexation of society is a question of how much
> freedom of choice is left to man by the all-pervading
> constraints of society, or - to put the question more
> actively - how much he can arrogate to himself.[43]

For Dahrendorf, then, the structural study of social systems must be
linked to the psychological study of personality in order to render
the individual comprehensible. Sociology itself would never be able
to deal with the full human being, his feelings and desires, his
idiosyncracies:

> The assumptions and theories of sociology refer not to
> man but to homo sociologicus, man as the alienated aspect
> of an incumbent of positions and a player of roles.[44]

Sociology does pose questions about man and the self, but it is
predominantly concerned with offering causal explanations for man's
actions in relation to the institutionalized norms effected by the
process of socialization.  Dahrendorf's sociology is  Dawe's social
system model.  This leads him to the conclusion that to offer a fuller
explanation of man would necessarily involve a 'para-theory' grounded
in a methodological pluralism.

Role-theory, in this respect, offers only an account of an elemen-
tary form of social life, and it presupposes the absolute givenness
of the functional status of roles.  This partial explanation of
social action is rejected by the psychologist and the philosopher
who both seek to know more about the person in the role.  Functionalist sociological accounts of the human agent and the French structuralist actantial model of character in narrative fiction have, as
I have suggested, a decided kinship.  One could go even further and
emphasize the refusal to accord primacy to the Subject over the
system of functions and relations which functionalism and French
literary structuralism both share.

The intellectual climate from which such views on the self-
problematic derive is described by Culler precisely in terms of the
deconstruction of the Subject as the centre or source of meaning.
Cartesian homo significans is radically called into question.  It
fragments into component, transubjective systems.  Thus, 'the self

or subject comes to appear more as a construct:  the result of a
system of conventions.'[45]  According to Foucault, research in
psychoanalysis, linguistics, and anthroplogy, which, each in its
own way, aims to understand relational values and underlying
systems has 'decentred the subject in relation to the laws of its
desire, the forms of its language, the rules of its actions, or
the play of its mythical and imaginative discourse.'[46]  In this
respect, language speaks through man, action is predicted by
internalized norms, and desires are the deep-seated manifestation
of a total, volitionless being-for-others.  The I of the self is
therefore none other than a cipher of codes (in Barthes's sense)
given in the historicity of cultural values and social meanings.
The claim for man's unique individuality is seen to be at best a
bourgeois myth; the self is unknowable in any isolated and substantial way.  Statements of this kind are totally antithetical to
those which presuppose a need to assert self-caused action.  The
quasi-romantic idealism of a Sartrean existentialism, for instance,
presupposes the primacy of the will which remains submerged beneath
the masks of the social persona.  Man is in a permanent state of
'Mauvaise Foi' until he purposefully allows the dictates of his will
to be realized in his action in the world.  Thus, self-knowledge
and self-determined action are necessary for man to become an
individual.  The will constitutes being.  But being is always -for-
others in a positive, moral sense.  Authenticity is the avowed goal
of man's self-assertive actions.  This is only possible if one does
not adhere to the thesis of a Marcuse or an Adorno about the actual
state of the modern social life-world and its domination of human
consciousness.[47]

These two opposed modes of understanding man (the self-willed man versus the epistemologically dubious Subject) are fundamental to the differences in the worldviews of Fowles and Simon, as I shall argue in the following chapters. For John Hawkes, however, the diagnosis is Freudian. The social implications of Freud's analysis of the problematical relationship between Ego, Id, and Superego are enabling here. For man's relationship to the conventions of society is one of repression. Grounded in this fundamental assumption about the nature of social life, the Superego would be defined by _social_ expectations, but the Ego and Id remain in tensional interplay within the individual psyche. However, to understand the confrontations of Ego, Id, and Superego fully is not to isolate the psyche as a comprehensible entity in itself, but rather to account for the repressive confrontation of Psyche and Physis in social existence. A more complex explanation of the problems involved in man's relationship to his own understanding and to society may well be achieved given the awareness of the subliminal effects on consciousness of modern industrial society, as Marcuse has argued:

> The processes that create the ego and superego also shape and perpetuate specific societal institutions and relations. Such psychoanalytical concepts as sublimation, identification, and introjection have not only a psychical but also a social content: they terminate in a system of institutions, laws, agencies, things, and customs that confront the individual as objective entities. Within this antagonistic system, the mental conflict between ego and superego, between ego and id, is at one and the same time a conflict between the individual and society.[48]

Socialization as a process is analogous to (has a decided kinship with) the Superego in Freudian psychological explanation. Accord-

ing to Freud, the Superego is the internalized agent of civilization,
and, for instance disables the aggressive instinct in man, albeit
sexual in origin, by tormenting the ego with guilt.  In Freud's
words:

> ...in the formation of the Superego and the emergence of a
> conscience innate constitutional factors and influences from
> the real environment act in combination.[49]

The question then arises about the origin of desire.  When Freud is
rethought through Marcuse's analysis, then sublimation becomes a
fact of social existence, and desire becomes the unsuspected
product of vested interest manifested in advertising and the media.[50]
Freud reaches the conclusion that, given the apparent antagonism between the demands of man's instincts and the taboos of civilization,
either neurosis destroys man, or this primary mutual hostility
threatens the disintegration of 'civilized' society.  The sense of
self which derives from Freud's psychological explanation is grounded
in the conflict between the visible ego (which is not the self but may
be the persona) and the repressed unconscious (which contains the
hidden motives for behaviour).  Such repressed states of consciousness are only partially knowable through dreams and fantasies.  The
Freudian self in unknowable in any imminent form; it can be understood
through the systematic probings of psychoanalysis.  The belief in the
existence of Psyche as a scientific phenomenon has enabled many
writers to search in their narratives for the profounder, complex
identities that lurk beneath the surface of the social self.  The
work of John Hawkes is intelligible within the sphere of his mode of
explanation, and I shall discuss this in some detail below.

This compressed selection of approaches to questions about the self
and the reality of the modern world, despite the diversity of
philosophical systems from which they have derived, has uncovered
one abiding principal feature about its status today:  the self is
unknowable in any holistic manner.  Systems of knowledge break down
when confronted with the irrational and the incomprehensible.
Modern consciousness has been explained in relation to modern
institutions; role-theory explains homo sociologicus; but we know
very little about the source of motives, intentions, and the 'inner
side' of the self.  The omissions of each single theory precipitate
the essential problematics on which other theories are constructed.
One could go one step further in this search to describe the elusive
modern self and suggest, as indeed Marcuse has done, that society
does not just prescribe rightful and dutiful behaviour, but sublimi-
nally conditions man through unspoken rules and conventions, the
hidden pursuasions of mass media, advertising, institutionalized
education, and even language itself.[51]  For it has been suggested
that there is a growing accumulation of evidence that man has little
contact with experience per se.  Instead, his senses and thoughts are
channelled through an intervening set of cultural and social patterns.[52]
This results in a form of alienation, which may thus be understood as:

> A state of mind resulting from an inability to participate
> in the available patterns of experience, and an uncertainty
> as to whether the single self can generate its own patterns.[53]

This state of anxiety is prefigured in the sense of a loss of self
which the literature of the twentieth century has incresingly dramatized.  Furthermore, epistemological questions surround the loss of a

sense of the past and the search to formulate a personal history.
Following the examples of the dense, sinuous narratives of Proust
and Faulkner, Claude Simon's search for lost time is always necessarily a failure. This can be seen as a recent, pervasive example
of the entropic effect of the past on the present with, in this
instance, a commensurable loss of a sense of identity for the narrating Subject. The quest for identity is central to the narrative
fiction of Fowles, Hawkes, and Simon; and the three subsequent
chapters in this study will be concerned with locating precisely
what philosophical assumptions underpin the cognitive basis of their
works.

In order to identify the cognitive basis or the underlying belief-
system which informs a literary text, we should engage in the
characterization of its implicit ideological status. This critical
activity necessarily confronts the historicity of the text. Moreover,
in doing this, we consider issues which have been of principal concern
in the philosophy of the social sciences. The literary critic can
never pretend to offer solutions to problems which philosophers and
sociologists have not yet resolved. But this does not absolve him
from being aware of such complex and important discourse. The self-
problematic is a case in point. For the history of the novel reveals
the continuing effort on the part of the writers to reconceptualize
and reformulate in their narrative fiction the changing relations
between man and society:

> The distinction between the Subject and the World is a
> variable one that depends on the configuration of knowledge
> at a given time...54

If the production of characters in literature is governed by a set of cultural and social models, then understanding the problem of the self in literature is both conceptual and historical. Thus the realism of the nineteenth century novel, for instance, is in part intelligible through nineteenth century models of man and commensurate views of reality. For the novel today to be related historically to current thought about man and society, to the contemporary paradigms and interpretations of reality, it must be seen to differentiate itself from the interpretative models that have been largely displaced. It remains to be seen in subsequent chapters precisely to what extent Fowles, Hawkes, and Simon engage their narrative fiction with the various discourses about the problem of modern identity, and the epistemological status of the Subject. The narrative of this study leads inexorably towards questions of form, and once the cognitive basis of a text has been described, then the relationship between philosophical substructure and aesthetic and formal issues must be made more explicit. As the diverse ideas above have clearly shown, the self-problematic is perpetually disputed in contemporary thought. The division of labour effected by the methodological disputes of philosophy, sociology, and psychology at least serve to underline the complexity of an all-embracing definition of the self. The 'bricolage' of ideas about the self truly reflect the fragmented nature of modern identity.

# CHAPTER ONE

The Analysis of Identity in the
Novels and Stories of John Fowles

## (i) Man and Society in John Fowles's Worldview

The novels and stories of John Fowles have been consistently grounded
in two basic themes which complement each other:  the relationship
between art and life, and the struggle of individual protagonists
to define themselves and learn to make moral decisions for conduct,
and for courses of action in the world.  The two themes are part of
the same process which begins in introspection and self-understanding
and ends in situations of crisis where decisions are called for and
responsibility for actions demanded.  The initial process of making
sense of individual man and his relationship to the world is enabled
by articulate protagonists who use their knowledge of art and literature as modes of explanation.  The quest for self-definition is founded
on assumptions about the nature of man which are, necessarily, correlated with further assumptions about the nature of society.  The interpretation of the world in these works is grounded in a model of
reality explained in The Aristos (1968), and its intellectual analysis
is bounded by an existentialism which aims to formulate a basis for a
relative freedom in an enlightened mode of social relations between
self and other, and also to discern the possibility for authenticity in
man's relationship to himself and to others.  Fowles's narrative fiction
dramatizes 'the ability to sustain a sense of personal identity,'
which 'depends on self and not-self becoming objective to one another,
and the stability of the self may be measured by analysing its relations with the external world.'[1]  Before discussing questions of identity,
and the encounter of self and other in the novels and stories, a brief
summary of the author's theoretical statements about man and society
will offer us a clear starting-point.

The Aristos aims to discuss the problem of the freedom of the individual against the pressures of conformity which oppress him in
society. Man needs to be free to choose courses of action. For
Fowles, society is characterized by the struggle between the Few
and the Many. Deriving/from the ancient Greek philosopher, Heracli-
tus who divided mankind into a moral and intellectual élite (the
aristoi) and an unreflecting, conformist mass (hoi polloi), Fowles
wants to stress the potential for enlightenment, indeed the necessity to strive for it. Man has the onus to strive towards a state
of moral and intellectual wisdom. For the sake of clarification,
the conflict of wisdom and self-understanding against conformity
is focused on the Few and the Many differentiation. The Collector
(1963) is an allegorization of this notion, as I shall describe
below.

> Our stereotyping societies force us to feel more alone.
> They stamp masks on us and isolate our real selves.
> We live in two worlds:  the old comfortable man-centred
> world of absolutes and the harsh real world of relatives.
> The latter, the relativity reality, terrifies us; and
> isolates and dwarfs us all. [2]

If man plays the roles society demands, masks isolate his real
self. Mechanical existence in society creates the anxiety of
otherness:  'All is other to me, including most of myself.'[3]  In
this state, man confronts the myth of a separate consciousness.
Even in self-contemplation, the 'I' becomes an object to itself,
a third person (as the latest novel, Daniel Martin (1977) explicitly
demonstrates). The objective stance of self-judgement, seeing the
self as other, is enabled by the store of masks needed to impute

any one of a set of selves for any social situation. The real self
is atrophied behind the stereotyping roles of societal conformity.


Fowles's critique of modern society is qualified by a consensus
notion of existentialism, which seems to derive from a collection
of the more accessible ideas of Kierkegaard, Sartre, and Camus.
This raises a contradiction as the idea of authenticity is maintained
despite a view of the world which seems unable to support it. The
author calls on this existentialism in order to attempt to re-
establish man's sense of his own uniqueness, and his need to reassert control of his own life. The individual is invited to reject
the rigidity of conformity for the sake of a limited freedom. One
of the most common ways in which an escape from social pressures is
effected is through the 'affaire', and male protagonists in the
novels and stories persistently attempt to transcend their anxieties
through such risk-filled sexual adventures. The risk works pre-
dominately within a middle class ethos. But the solution lies not
in this 'remedy', but rather in the 'inward education.' The Magus
(1965 and 1977) clearly exemplifies this process.


The Aristos tells us that man is not educated until his self has
been analysed and understood. Because of the inauthentic life in
society, we tend to teach 'the persona not the real self':

> The persona is made up of all the incrustations, however
> formed, that hide what I really feel and what I really
> think. It is plain that we must all have some persona;
> but not that we should hide so much of our real selves
> as our societies and their educational systems now require.
> We must not teach how to conform (society does that auto-

matically) but how and when not to conform.[4]

The inner education will teach man to face these problems and choose a responsible course of action.

Man cannot truly exist until he has understood himself. Thus, being is understanding. The first phase of this process of self-analysis is the confrontation with the sense of one's own futility and ephemerality. Mask and act are pre-determined: the persona is a mask concealing emptiness. The anti-self, anti-ego is what Fowles characterizes as the 'Nemo', a feeling of non-existence, of unreality. To transcend this state of torpor, man must be critical of socially determined action and develop an independence of judgment. This relative freedom is achieved from greater intelligence and greater knowledge both of self and of life in general. Maturity is therefore defined as 'a state of knowledge of self.'[5]

Inward knowledge, self-understanding, describes the meaning of the Aristos, an ideal model of man, 'a free force in a world of tied forces.' He thinks of the best that can be achieved for any situation:

> He knows everything is relative, nothing is absolute.
> He sees one world with many situations; not one situation....
> To accept one's limited freedom, to accept one's isolation,
> to accept this responsibility, to learn one's particular
> powers, and then with them to humanize the whole: that is
> the best for this situation.[6]

In this highly moral prescription, the principal concern for man is to know himself, and to act as an enlightened liberating force in the world.

For Fowles, the Aristos is also the artist. He seeks to express
the right feelings about self, even to discover what that self
could be. Art, and especially narrative, is a heuristic device,
a mode of discovering and stating self. In a secular age, the
artist replaces the priest as the principal spokesman for the
mysteries of life:

> The modern world and modern sensibilities are increasingly
> complex; but it is not the function of the artist to com-
> plicate the complexities; if anything it should be to
> unravel them. [7]

The artist is concerned to teach through the revelatory and spell-
binding nature of storytelling. In this respect the Many are the
audience under the spell of the conjuror, the magus, the wise
magician. The Aristos knows that his true destiny 'is to become a
magician himself.' Being an artist is discovering the self and
then expressing it. Fowles's narrative fiction exhibits artist-
figures who teach through narrative, and articulate characters who
interpret events through their knowledge of art and literature.

The existentialist imperative in Fowles's work is emphasised in
his characters' liberating quest for authenticity: modern man is
seen to attempt to establish a personal identity in a world noted
for its hostility to the self. Thus questions of self-definition,
individuality, freedom, choice, and responsibility for decisions
are thematically central. The conflict of the Few and the Many is
allegorized in The Collector through the relationship between Clegg
and Miranda. The reaffiliation between art and life founds the
mode of characterization, whereby each of the two protagonists

'stands for' given attitudes.  They are socially bounded figures
who represent given 'class' distinctions.  The contrast of
opinions and attitudes is authenticated on the level of articulate-
ness.  Clegg's language enforces his feelings of inferiority, and
his social conditioning.  He is the epitome of the Many:  stupid,
ignorant, and easily molded:

> She wasn't la-di-da, like many, but it was there all the
> same.  You could see it when she got sarcastic and impa-
> tient with me because I couldn't explain myself or I did
> things wrong.  Stop thinking about class, she'd say.
> ... when she was really angry she could get right up on
> her high horse and come it over me...[8]

Miranda contrasts markedly with Clegg, and the insertion of her
diary in the text of his narrative allows us to see the way she
characterizes herself.

> I love honesty and freedom and giving.  I love making,
> I love doing.  I love being to the full, I love everything
> which is not sitting and watching and copying and dead at
> least.[9]

Her reactions to Clegg's lepidoptery and photography are that of
the fine artist.  She is literally and figuratively imprisoned
and stifled by his mind.  But he is self-opinionated:

> ... if more people were like me, in my opinion,
> the world would be better.[10]

He relates to other people, especially women, by photographing
them, freezing their reality, so to speak, and collecting their
images.  Nature, in the form of butterflies, is also collected;

and this is extended to his 'collecting' Miranda herself, encasing, photographing, and eventually causing her death. Miranda reinforces and interprets Clegg's representative status. She asks, 'Why should we tolerate their beastly Calibanity? Why should every vital and creative and good person be martyred by the great universal stodge around? In this situation I'm a representative.'[11] She sees herself as subject to the whims of the Many: she wishes they would allow the Few to grow and then in turn to teach, but instead, 'they persecute us, they crowd us out... they blindfold themselves and stuff up their ears.'[12] Her attitude may be violently elitist, but within the context of the novel it appears to be wholly necessary. Imprisoned and thus denied growth, her freedom like that of the butterfly to the lepidopterist is denied. Clegg is seen to be the real prisoner, entrapped by his stultifying mentality. He is 'a harbinger of a new class that has neither taste nor feeling.'[13] This new class, the Many, are encapsulated in the figure of Clegg. The message from this, Fowles's first published novel, is a simple one:

> ... we must create a society in which the Many will allow
> the Few to live authentically, and to teach and help the
> Many themselves to begin to do so as well. In societies
> dominated by the Many, the Few are in danger of being
> suffocated.[14]

Clearly, this novel dramatizes the central aspects of Fowles's views of Man and Society which are outlined in The Aristos.

Moreover, as I suggested above, this situation of conflict is contained in the different attitudes to art's relationship to life which the two characters embody. Miranda, having learnt

from her mentor, George Paston, knows that great art is the expression of the very essence of life, 'a window to the centre
of the self.'[15]   She has been accused of collecting other fashion-
able artist's paintings on which to base her work.  She has to
learn to open herself to the expression of passion, and the
freedom of self-analysis.  At this point she is 'captured' by
Clegg, whose 'art' is everything she has been taught to avoid.
A collector-photographer, Clegg is 'a closed being unable to
feel, neurotically self-conscious yet terrified of self-definition
or self-expression.'[15]   Miranda acts as spokesman for this theme,
when she despairingly exclaims:

> Do you know that every great thing in the history of art
> and every beautiful thing in life is actually what you
> call nasty or has been caused by feelings that you would
> call nasty?  By passion, by love, by hatred, by truth...
> Why do you take all the life out of life?  Why do you
> kill all the beauty?[16]

Photography instigates a death of the represented object.  She
sees this process as symptomatic of Clegg's inability to face the
emotive side of life.  He is only able to see the surface of life.
His art of collecting and photography masks his solipsism.  A
perverse artist, he remakes the world in the image of his desire:
he collects and photographs his victim, voyeuristically watches her.
Contact with the other is no more within his scope than expressing
deep feelings.  Miranda characterizes him as both anti-art and anti-
life.  She attempts to explain her situation to herself through
literary archetypes, and sees herself as subjected to Caliban's
most evil art.  It is that art against which she must struggle,

but which eventually destroys her. The reality of the other is completely undermined, but so is the expression of any but an imputed, callow, socially bounded self. Liberation from the privacy of his solipsism is denied because he will not allow for the alien truth of another mind.

The allegoric potential in The Collector effects a reduction of psychological complexity in the two principal characters in order to enable them to be clearly representative of given ideas. In The Magus[17], however, Fowles subtly internalizes the Few/Many dichotomy within the central protagonist, Nicholas: it is his journey of self-discovery that concerns us throughout the long and involved narrative. An artist figure, Conchis, guides the protagonist through this process, offers him the story of his own life as exemplar for self-revelation. The mirror that art can create of life heuristically functions as a mode of self-questioning. Nicholas, himself a failed poet, articulates his own past experience, and comes to terms with the strange events by aestheticizing essentially moral experiences. The lesson is that life makes sense by imitating art, and man makes sense of life by using his knowledge of art as a mode of explanation, as Conchis's drama without audience or stage demonstrates. The principal lessons are existential and moral. For the Magus, Conchis, attempts through artifice ' to jar Nicholas out of a limited egocentric conception of reality'[18] and into a world of larger, hazard-given and more meaningful realities. In Conchis's world, art stimulates introspection, and story both entertains and instructs. Nicholas is taught to accept life's hazards, to interpret the world, and finally to use the 'godgame' devised by Conchis as a model of action and of encounter with the other.  The Magus's story is archetypal, and Nicholas attends the 'salle d'attente', awaiting his release through ordeal into self-understanding.  In order to become 'elect,' he must confront his inauthenticity, his selfishness, and learn to appreciate the separate existence of others and the possibility of genuine rela-tionships.  Masque is exploited by the Magus to underline the fictionality of role-playing, both in drama and on the stage of society.  Existentialism and a more sociological critique of roles and action are thus combined in Fowles's moral perspective. Nicholas is supposed to learn that the 'true self' is not the mask, and the imputed role is not authentic action.  The moment of authenticity comes when he is/faced with a responsibility-laden choice, and he has to learn from Conchis's example that freedom,

> ... was something that passed beyond morality but sprang out of the very essence of things - that comprehended all, the freedom to do all, and stood against only one thing - the prohibition not to do all.[19]

There is always a conflict between a reasoning grounded in a public morality (the pressures of opinion), and the recourse to one's own freedom of choice, which for the sake of maintaining a personal freedom offers you the right to deny.  Conchis's decision during the war not to kill causes the death of eighty hostages; Nicholas likewise uses his right not to inflict pain on Lily.  He is made to realise the situation of terror that such genuine decisions in-flict on the self.  Aware finally of his moral inaction, Nicholas actively searches for Alison, albeit initially for the wrong reasons.

In the foreword to the revised edition of The Magus, the author
explains that beneath the sinuous narrative there is a notebook
of exploration. By projecting a very different world from the
one that is, the author puts Nicholas, a middle-class Everyman,
through a 'heuristic mill', in order to understand himself and the
world better. The lessons to be learnt by both the protagonist and
the reader are that

> ... true freedom lies between each two, never in one alone,
> and therefore it can never be absolute freedom. All freedom,
> even the most relative, may be a fiction.[20]

The heuristic process instigated by Conchis has to combat the
rational scepticism which instils Nicholas with bitterness and
cynicism in his attitude to his ordeal. The interpretation of
the world as a stage and man as a role-player is eventually entan-
gled with the intrusive sense of artifice and fictionality, to the
extent that Nicholas', and the reader's scepticism is undermined
by the loss of certainty about the masques. Nicholas as narrator
assaults the mysteries with an obsessive realism which belies
those instructive mysteries and enhances his rational scepticism.
The realization that all is artifice, that action is acting, that
identity is unreal because it is mask, leads Nicholas to confront
the case that authentic existence in the world is only viable if
'we learn to see through the roles we give ourselves in ordinary
life.'[21] Nicholas has both the selfishness and the narrow-
mindedness of his age; he is meant to achieve the wisdom of a
magus. He sees that he has always turned life into a fiction,
always viewed himself in the 'third person'. It is left to

Conchis's surrogate, Mrs. de Seitas, to explain that the 'godgame'
begins from the premise that 'in reality all is fiction, yet no
single fiction is necessary.' 'The basic principle of life is
hazard.'[22] And man needs to be prepared to meet each contingent
situation in its own terms and to act decisively. The apparent
contradiction between the diagnosis of modern society as mask-
orientated, and the onus on man to transcend the fictionality of
roles is thus belied by Fowles's belief in an autonomous model
of man. This is enforced by his existentialism.

Miranda tried to teach Clegg, in The Collector, but failed.
Conchis teaches Nicholas in The Magus, and achieves a measure of
success. In The French Lieutenant's Woman (1969), Sarah creates a
damaging fiction for herself, is outcast by society, and is able
to offer Charles an alternative rationale for life which would
enable him to transcend the bounds of a stifling society. The
world of 1867 is a mirror for the problems of contemporary society
in terms of morality (public and private), sexuality, art, and
intellectual history, and all focused on the consistent, principal
concern of Fowles's work: the relationship of self to other. The
repression which Victorian society effects on man is symbolized in
Charles's problematical encounter with the enigmatic Sarah. The
isolated self is seen to doubt and question the nature of existence
and this is re-inforced by the many references to the poetry of
Arnold, Clough, Hardy, and Tennyson which reflect the anxieties
of an age, its uncertainties and its social demands on the individual. Man, and especially Charles, has been taught by Darwin
that the species survives by adaption, and by Marx that man trans-

cends his alienation by making history through purposeful action.
As the previous novel dramatised, life is as artificial as the
theatre, and man must learn critically to suspend his disbelief in
the world as well as in art.  The metaphor becomes pervasive,

> ... touching not only the question of whether the theatre
> of society, in which we act our parts, is substance or
> shadow, but whether the stage is one we can ever leave. [23]

Sarah offers Charles the chance to break with hypocrisy and attain
authenticity.  His search for fossils is symptomatic of a far
greater fossilization under the aegis of social convention.  He has
to learn that the determinism which entraps the social agent must
be usurped by the free-thinking man, that such a situation demands
the involvement of the whole being:

> ...the risk!... self-directed anxiety...  He kept saying
> to himself.  I must act.  And a kind of anger at his
> weakness swept over him - a wild determination to make some
> gesture that would show he was more than an ammonite stran-
> ded in a draught, that he would strike out against the dark
> clouds that enveloped him. [24]

His socially-bounded duty conflicts with his new-found sense of
purpose.  To emerge as an enlightened individual, transcendent of
the restrictions of his age, he has to take the Kierkegaardian
leap in the dark, the risk, and be rejected by the society that
molded him.  This he does.  Charles is made to realize that the
fundamental principle for human action is the pursuit of humane
and authentic lives.  He has to realize

... that life, however advantageously Sarah may in some
ways seem to fit the role of Sphinx, is not a symbol,
is not one riddle and one failure to guess it, is not to
inhabit one face alone or to be given up after one losing
throw of the dice; but is to be, however inadequately...
endured. And out again, upon the unplumb'd, salt,
estranging sea.[25]

Existentially conscious man sees life as the yet-to-be-discovered,

not the given, and identity as the purpose of discovery not the

mask offered by society. Dawe's social action model of sociology

is taken one step further by Fowles in his demands for authenticity.

(ii) The Question of the Self in the Novels and Stories of

John Fowles

The metaphor of theatre encapsulates the artificial basis of social

relations. The ending of The Magus is a ritual confrontation of I

and thou enacted dramatically, imitating Conchis's theatre of no

audience. Such an abiding image of ritualistic encounter informs

Fowles's view of normative relations in the world. Characters in

his works have to reach a point of realization whereby they can act

in such a way as to

... preserve the sense of being a subjective, deliberative and
free individual, and simultaneously admit the reality of
another person beyond oneself.[26]

Such action is both creative for the self, and mediative with the

world. But it is still deliberative and ritualistic. The limits
of action are bound up with the limits of self. If being is defined
as being-in-the-world, and - for-others, then the self truly realizes and knows itself in the world. Prior to such action, man, in
these novels, has to realize the need for introspection and self-
analysis. The novels and stories are replete with such enquiry.

Principal characters in the works of John Fowles formulate the type
of person they wish to be in their imagination, and this is contrasted to the person they appear to be in their relations with others.
In this sense, such characters are motivated in their self-analysis
by dissatisfaction. For Charles, in The French Lieutenant's Woman,
discontent is born out of the critical awareness that Sarah enables
him to learn. Nicholas, in The Magus is acutely conscious of his
inauthentic existence in England. He wants to be a very unbourgeois,
authentic person, expurgate the ghost of his father, so to speak,
write poetry, and have sexual relationships with the women he meets
without any emotional involvement. The experiences he undergoes in
the novel expose his failings in every aspect of his ambitions. He
is made to realize his total inauthenticity, and his emotional
shallowness is highlighted by the implicit contrasts between himself
and the women he encounters. In the revised edition (1977),
Nicholas clearly understands the situation, and offers the reader
an explicit summary of Conchis's intentions:

> I was being taught some obscure metaphysical lesson about
> the place of man in existence, about the limitations of
> the egocentric view.[27]

He is overwhelmed with a sense of being taken apart, disconnected
from his previous self, and then of waiting to be put back together
again.  At this point, Fowles allows his protagonist to offer a
definition of the constituents of self as 'the linked structures
of ideas and conscious feeling.'[28]  Nicholas has always exhibited
an interest in knowing his real self, and his only access to such
knowledge is through his relations to others.  He is described as
typically selfish for his age, for the human race has become less
important than the self.[29]  Despite this awareness on the part of
the protagonist, his quest for Lily, and then for Alison, serves to
confirm his unchanged nature.  His egocentricity confirms the thesis
that every man is an island, and that because modern man's apparent need
for masks and role-
/playing (exploited fully in this novel), Nicholas feels as far
from his true self as the masks he wears.[30]  All is artifice,
self-consciously, in this world, where all the characters are
actors; none of them is what he really is.[31]  Nicholas's own
identity crisis is worsened by his habit of turning life into
fiction, and of viewing himself as a 'third person'.  Literally,
as he appears to narrate the story of himself, and figuratively,
he creates a fictional self for others and for himself, partly
to produce the image of himself which may be to his best advantage,
and partly to create the distance necessary for rendering personal
experience intelligible:

> So we talked about Nicholas:  his family, his ambitions,
> his failings.  The third person is apt, because I presented
> a sort of fictional self to them, a victim of circumstances,
> a mixture of attractive raffishness and essential inner
> decency.[32]

The obtrusive sense of fictionality in the narrator's efforts
to articulate his identity, coupled with Conchis's series of
masques, causes a loss of certainty in both the reality behind
the artifice of masques and the fictional self.

As the intruding twentieth century voice comments in The French
Lieutenant's Woman:

> You do not even think of your past as quite real; you
> dress it up, you gild it or blacken it, censor it,
> tinker with it... fictionalize it, in a word... your
> book, your romanced autobiography. We are all in
> flight from the real reality. This is a basic defini-
> tion of Homo sapiens.[33]

Learning to see through these self-imputed, or determined, roles
in ordinary life  becomes the key issue.  Clegg, in The Collector,
can  never transcend his class-bounded self; Charles Smithson,
in The French Lieutenant's Woman undergoes vigorous self-purgatory
in order to reach a state of qualified enlightenment.  Nicholas
returns from his ordeal in Greece in a highly critical state of
mind about contemporary society.  In Rome, he contrasts the art
and architecture with the Italians themselves (after the simple,
Greek peasant).  They,'like their Roman ancestors, wore a great
mask of luxury, a cosmetic of the overindulged senses, between
the light, the truth, and their real selves.'[34]  The nakedness of
Greece, and his feeling that the naked truth about his self has
been exposed, have caused this state of mind.

As I have shown in the introduction, the idea of a real self
hidden beneath the one that is presented to other people in social

relations and in the personal encounters of I and Thou has been
central to crucial debates in sociological theory and philosophy.
The novels of John Fowles have engaged in this debate. The
stories collected in The Ebony Tower (1974) have shown a more
explicit concern with problems of self, role-playing and authenticity. One of the girls living with the artist, Breasely, in
the title story, explains her feeling of loneliness to David, the
bemused visitor: she wants people to see who she really is; and,
he exclaims, 'that's rather difficult. If you're hidden away.'[35]
The honesty and fidelity syndromes of chivalric love are implicitly contrasted to the strange hazardousness of modern existence,
and to the impossibility of such feelings for modern 'artificial
man'[36]. The safety in middle-class values, as well as received
ideas and trends in art, is undermined by the very eccentricity
of Breasley's life-style. Such a disturbing 'assault' on the
protagonist's life is also reinforced in the story Poor Koko.
The situation in these stories revolves around the socially-
boundedness of characters. The Enigma is Fowles's most explicit
discussion so far of social role-playing, and the overdetermined
self, both as character in the novel and in the social world.

Simply writing a story about an M.P. who has disappeared, despite
its topicality, seems at first uninspiring. But John Marcus
Fielding enigmatically disappears, and the story, The Enigma, is
an account of various attempts to make sense of his disappearance.
From the outset, a character is described as a substantial persona,
a person of status and of a clearly discernible public image and
social function. This plausibility on the level of identity enhances the quality of the enigma which surrounds the apparent

irrationality of his action. A detective searches for clues and
explanations grounded in all the usual avenues of inquiry. But
the mystery prevails. The M.P. seems to have been determined to
give no clue about his eventual destination, nor about the cause
of his action. The character of John Marcus Fielding is authenticated on every level as a person of status and substance, and in
the story he is, so to speak, present in the mode of his absence.
Indeed, it is the fact of his absence which motivates the interest
in him. The necessity to know him as a person, through his social
position, and his interests, are traditional sources of a character-
building realism in literature. But also they are commensurable
with the knowledge through which we aim to understand the person
in society. Such a mode of rational explanation informs both
character in literature and the notion of self.

Fowles, through this story, offers a more explicit account of the
constraints of social role-playing, while also commenting implicitly on the distinctly determined role of character in literature.
Lest we have not grasped the point, it rests with another enlightened
female character to offer an unconventional explanation which transcends the limitations of the detective's evidence. She explains
how, given the analogy of a novel, the main character has broken
the rules, and has absconded, walked out of the plot:

> There was an author in his life. In a way. Not a man.
> A system, a view of things? Something that had written
> him. Had really made him just a character in a book.[37]

He led a life like a character in fiction who has everything planned for him, mapped out. In this sense he is as fossilized as Charles was in <u>The French Lieutenant's Woman</u>. His conformity makes him no more than a 'cog in a phony machine'. The only way to transcend his state of total non-entity, sameness, unreality, is to do something inexplicable, and then he will have written himself out of all the predestined fictions and into his own, self-created fiction. 'Nothing lasts like a mystery'. His disappearance must remain unsolved, otherwise any explanation would be tantamount to his being written back into a story (the man who had a nervous breakdown, for instance).

Society determines its 'characters' just as a story places its characters in roles and relationships which are pre-determined. The disappeared M.P. is comprehensible on both these levels. Charles Smithson also walks out of a socially and historically determined world. Without these purposeful actions, the self would remain hidden and unknowable behind the public image deman- ded by social life-worlds. In <u>The Enigma</u> the middle-classes are portrayed as leading a life of pretence, of never showing what they really feel or think. When the detective asks Fielding's son questions about his father, the reply is significant:

It's like asking me about an actor I've only seen on stage.[38]

Fielding's wife is described as 'welded to her role in life and her social status, eminently poised and eminently unimaginative.'[39]

Because of his unexplained disappearance, people would now assume
that a someone else, very different from the man everyone knew,
existed behind the social facade. The real self and the public
self may well be different, but once that real self has been discovered and differentiated from the artificial one, it too may
well be only a fiction. The stories and the novels of John Fowles
are all concerned with the problem of the reality of the self, its
creation through narrative, and its existence in the world of
others. The question which the works continually pose is: are
there any authentic selves in such a pluralistic and anxiety-
filled experience? Criticism of the author's worldview could be
levelled precisely at this point: how can 'artificial' man ever
really attain authenticity if society is always the stage for
false values and unreal relations. Fowles's latest novel, Daniel
Martin (1977), continues the discussion, focusing on the nature of
post-war English (and American) society.

(iii) Daniel Martin : The Analysis of Identity and the English
Middle-class Ego.

> I'm very aware in ordinary life of the problem of estab-
> lishing relationships with other people, and I think that
> the English are particularly prone to turning other people
> into objects. (John Fowles).[40]

Daniel Martin, the successful Hollywood script-writer creates the
scenarios for other people, in his professional capacity. This
enhances his ability to write the history of himself and those
people he has met in life. He becomes the principal example of

a process felt generally to be at the core of the very mechanism
of societal relations: he reifies himself and others. As
narrator of his own life, he wants to escape the first person, and
become his own third. [41] In writing about himself, he, the skilful
scriptwriter and maker of scenarios, creates a fictional persona.
His whole life has been spent creating personae for other people,
and on his return from America he is able to understand the way in
which English society itself endorses the reification of the other
as a mode of interaction. From the vantage point of his enforced
absence, Daniel Martin analyses the 'Englishness' of his middle-
class society. The golden rule is never to show what you really feel
or think. 'Perfidious Albion' is characterized by duplicity. The
narrator offers us as an example a situation in a railway carriage
compartment where his fellow-passengers are symptomatic of

> ...that chosen isolation, that hatred of the other, as if
> we were all embarrassed at having to share our means of
> travel... a terror of revealing... so characteristic of my
> own past... this fear of exposure, this onanistic fondling
> of privacy (pp 150-151).

A double life of public image and hidden private feelings was
analysed as the hypocrisy of the Victorian age in The French
Lieutenant's Woman, and it is fundamental to contemporary English
society in The Enigma. Daniel Martin feels that he is among
people, 'whose values had remained bizarrely petrified (p.211)'.
Like John Marcus Fielding in The Enigma, he has the impression
of being locked inside a middle-class novel (259), where past
convention and public status are the only substance of his persona, and where censorship and concealment are the abiding

features of English life.  The flight from frankness which Daniel

notes  is reflected in the language.  And this may well be a

positive quality when compared to the American ethos of Hollywood

against which English life is polarized.  The 'enormous semantic

subtleties of middle-class English intonation'  are contrasted to

'the poverty of nuance' in the American equivalent (83).  The

indirect, euphemistic use of language plays on the richness of

ironies and innuendos, but is also symptomatic of an avoidance

of the direct and naked expression of 'truth'.  The Americans may

be the 'outward cynics', but 'the true quietists' live in Britain

(84).  A life based on hidden realities and polite deception is

seen, in this novel, to be the cause of unsuccessful relationships

and destroyed marriages:  it is the silences that destroy.  The

reification of the other, and the refusal of self-exposure, frank-

ness, indicates the fundamental selfishness of such a society.

The post-war 'Oxford' generation is characterized as essentially

egocentric, concerned narcissistically with self to the total

exclusion of otherness.  Daniel Martin himself is preoccupied

with his apparent inability to transcend the bounds of his own

selfishness.  This novel is a record of his mature attempts to

understand himself.  But also it is a portrait of an age, and a

view of man:  through his narrative he has tried to put 'flesh'

on words, to articulate 'a world of value-systems, prejudices,

repressions, false notions of faith and freedom (698).'  In such

a world where political establishments were 'a conspiracy of the

humourless against laughter, a tyranny of stupidity over intelli-

gence'; where man was the product of history, but in contradis-

tinction to 'his true inner, personal, nature (524)', the narrator prefers to diagnose the malaise in existential terms:  'a universal failure of personal authenticity, faith in one's own inner feelings (525).'  Man must learn to feel.  And this is the existential thesis which persists throughout Fowles's stories and novels, that one has to discover one's true feelings.  Protagonists embark on an 'education sentimentale', because   man's depersonalized life in society, and especially the English middle class ethos of duplicity and the public image syndrome, need to be transcended.

If the onus is on man, then the diagnosis, the examination of the situation, places the microscope firmly on society.  The drama-turgical analogy of the world as a stage and man as a role-player, an actor in the theatre of society, has become increasingly more pervasive in Fowles's work.  Significantly, Daniel Martin is surrogate author, script-writer, and playwright.  Scenarios and created roles are his province, and he frequently resorts to the analogy to explain societal and personal relations.  The encounters between I and Thou are always organized, and ritualized.  Convention has written the script for models of behaviour, and the Marcusian diagnosis (described in the introduction above, and endorsed by Fowles implicitly)  underlines the role of belief-systems and the processes of mystification which create the realities on which life may be based.  American society presents a clear example of the effect of media and popular entertainment, initially propagated by the Hollywood syndrome:  'Idiotic cheap models of how successful people should dress, speak, furnish their houses (265).'  Society is like a stage-set without a playwright.  The quest for the authentic self is belied by the pre-eminence of the mask.  Self is

the sum of roles performed, and, therefore, self as being-in-the-
world is reduced to a one-dimensional inauthentic persona. The
self is fragmented into a set of 'fictional' identities written by
the script of society. The Protean self evoked to enable self-
assertion in the previous works seems to give way in this novel
under the pressures of the social world.

Given the inauthentic nature of existence in the polite world of
middle-class society, the narrator's analysis of identity constantly refers to the various selves, past and present, both of
himself and others. The 'sadistically stereotyping system (90)'
and its ritual codes underlines the ultimate problem: 'knowing
what one's true nature is (178).' The basis of such existence
founds the aetiology of the increasing retreat into privacy and
selfishness. Daniel's generation 'broke up into tribes and classes,
finally into private selves (179).' Man became obsessed with self,
and with personal identity. This concern is fundamental to
Daniel's narrative. For in his quest to constitute a comprehensible identity for himself, he realizes the fragmentation that
the past has effected on being. How indeed can the narrator hold
together a unified sense of being, when the self is dispersed into
multiple selves? Such recalcitrance problematizes his characterization of identity. He is reduced to being 'a psychic investiga-
tor who began his inquiry by requesting a service of exorcism that,
if it worked, would leave him no ghost to inquire about (453).'
The failure of his bid for the reality behind the mask explains
the enigmatic opening line of the novel. For even Daniel's
humanism, his 'emotional attempt to see life totally, in its
essence and in its phenomena (560),' is atrophied by the impossi-

bility of 'seeing whole'. The multiple sequences of scenarios that make up the past, and the sets of personae which substitute for real selves, deny 'whole sight'. The total perception, and the unification of being,is an impossible ideal.

The final, and only, solution is the retreat into privacy. Daniel persistently resorts to the evocation of place as a mode of fixing identity in a spatial image. The sense of self, of being there, is evoked firstly through the loss of place from childhood and secondly through the eventual return to a private domain in the English countryside:

> The theme of a lost natural paradise, a search for some enchanted domain is after all one that seems to haunt all his fiction... In /Daniel Martin/ the theme returns. There is Thorncombe, the 'Orchard of the blessed', where jaded disillusioned film scriptwriter, Daniel Martin dreams of writing his novel.[42]

The narrator has always evinced a need for such self-containedness, which is 'a symptom of his inability to relate to anything but a place (40).' Compton is another 'country enclave', partly neces-sary as a matter of self-preservation from a world which destroys self, and partly as a real need which came from the depths of his unconscious (364). The return to the original territory of his boyhood memories is a final recognition of his solipsistic inability to reach other minds: the narcissism of his early Oxford days per-sists into middle age. Finally, he endorses a Beckettian truth, that 'the loneliness of each, /is/ the bedrock of the human condi-tion (260).' Some hope, however is achieved at the end of this,

the latest John Fowles novel, when Daniel Martin plans to settle
in his private domain with his estranged wife's sister, herself a
lover from his past.  The quest for authenticity in Fowles's work,
so optimistically, if naively, asserted, now seems to accede to
the other side of his dualistic, and seemingly irreconcilable view
of the contemporary world.  The protagonist's sentimental education
is only possible once private territory has been established, for
the nature of the world militates against any 'authentic' self.

# CHAPTER TWO

The Image of Man and the Problematic of the
Self in the Novels and Stories of John Hawkes

(i) <u>The image of man and the world in Hawkes's early works</u>

The fundamentally hostile world depicted in the early works
of John Hawkes has been described by the author in terms of
'the whole Panorama of dislocation and desolation in human
experience.'[1] <u>Charivari</u> (1949), <u>The Cannibal</u> (1949),
<u>The Beetle Leg</u> (1951), <u>The Owl</u> (1954), and <u>The Goose on the
Grave</u> (1954), are each grounded in such a view of the world.
These works are decidedly post-war, finding ways of evoking
a war-torn landscape, and of peopling it with victims: the
maimed, the crippled, the violated, and the tortured. Such
warscapes recur in <u>The Lime Twig</u> (1961) and <u>Second Skin</u> (1964),
but here they function more evidently as symbolic manifestations of individual states of mind, where questions about the
solitary will, the self, and subconscious yearnings implicate
the reader through the use of first-person narrator-protago-
nists who attempt to resort to artful rhetoric in order to
persuade the reader, and themselves, that they are capable
of asserting their 'identity' and of giving order to an
otherwise destructive and hostile world.

<u>The Cannibal</u> (1949) creates the image of an absurd and chaotic
world which epitomizes Hawkes's landscapes of war. Significantly, the setting is a Germany typified by the teutonic
fervour on the brink of war in 1914, and its outlet later in
the fascism of National Socialism. The juxtaposition of the
two periods (1914 and 1945) reinforces the satiric intent,
and this is primarily embodied in the contrast between the

Sportswelt Brauhaus before the Great War, then an austere
place with black-jacketed waiters serving beer to straight-
backed officers and their tall, nordic girlfriends, and its
ruin through war itself. It is the effect of this destructive
world on the people which receives most attention, and they
are characterized as symbiotic with the landscape itself.
The inmates of the Asylum, the thieves, beggars, and the
prisoners that wandered unchecked in the Spitzen-on-the-Dein
of 1945, serve to duplicate the decomposed, deracinated,
and vastly ruined physical surroundings. Society itself
has collapsed, and the land is barren and uncultivated.
The satire on the effects of war on human aspirations is
carried one step further, when the fascist revolution planned
by Zizendorf is doomed to failure, not only because we know
he narrates after the fact and is in exile waiting to return
and try again, but also because those who are going to
organize his new society are the insane, the crippled, and
the perverted.

In this brutal world of war and destruction man is either
victim or victimizer. The latter are figures of authority,
strong-willed characters who epitomize the single-mindedness
and the violent intolerance of the spirit of Fascism.
Zizendorf, the potential dictator, and Il Gufo, the hangman
of Sasso Fetore in The Owl, are Hawkes's clearest examples of
this. Such strong-willed figures dominate the early novels
and stories, and the prominent examples are, perversely,

parodies of the writer making a world after his own image.
Cap Leech, in <u>The Beetle Leg</u> (1951), is also a man of power,
the power 'to put them all to sleep, to look at their women
if he wished, to mark their children.' [2] It is he who
'brought something of clear vision and bitter pills to the
fields of broken axles,' [3] and who finally usurps the central
position of authority, hitherto firmly occupied by the sheriff,
himself a man who holds the reins on people. But leadership
and control in this novel produce both a restrictive vision
of the world and also an obsessive prevention of normal
relationships, whereby the people are as arid and barren as
the noxious, infertile land.

The possibilities available in the theme of victimization are
explicitly realized in the two shorter novels, <u>The Owl</u> (1954)
and <u>The Goose on the Grave</u> (1954). Il Gufo, the 'owl' and
hangman of Sasso Fetore is portrayed as the archetypal
tyrant, a symbol of power and ruthless order, perched high
above the medieval Italian community, with his 'prey' (the
prisoner) awaiting execution. Adeppi, the orphaned boy in
<u>The Goose on the Grave</u>, travels through modern, war-torn Italy,
in a highly picaresque fashion, in search of a protector after
his mother is inexplicably torn away from him by three jack-
booted priests. Both victimizer and victim are in one sense
images of the artist, the first imposing his own design and
rigid order on the world, the second, an innocent singer fail-
ing to achieve any impression on the overwhelming sterility of
a world which is itself a victim of war, evident in the consequent

collapse of society, religion and moral values. Adeppi
encounters various villains, and his naive innocence is
frequently violated. In both these stories history and
tradition are synonymous, and the characters tend to adhere
to states of mind and forms of action dictated by past
convention. Myths of order and excellence (especially
Fascism) result in a further extension of the victimization
theme: the present is characterized by decay and sterility
because it is a victim of the neurotic constriction of the
past. Any renaissance will be abortive; the artist will
always be impotent, and a war-ravaged people apparently too
weak-willed for decisive action. In the desperate search for
order amidst such chaos, they turn to the unchanging form of
convention, which manifests itself in myths, rituals, ceremony,
and obedience. The present is no more than a mythologized
version of the past ritualistically, and perpetually, re-enacted.
Within this situation a dominant, strong-willed figure is able
to exploit the need for order, and manipulate the power of myth
for his own ends. He is able to bring about the 'advent of a
certain reality.' [4]

The predictions of sterility and barreness in the horoscope at
the beginning of The Beetle Leg (1951) are partially explained
in the novel through the similarity between the lives of the
people and the landscape that surrounds them. Death, destruction,
entropic erosion are the dominant features of the astrological
predictions in a novel that shows the destructive (but necessary)
effect of an overall preoccupation with the past. The past is
a source of myth which manifests itself in this novel in the

form of a misguided nostalgia. 'The Great Slide' may well have
been the only serious (and tragic) event in living memory,but
in the barren lives of the people in this mid-West desert town,
the event is magnified to a mythic status. In this respect,
the past produces myths of consolation in such a desolate and
hostile world.

The ideology of Fascism, born out of the teutonic past guides
the actions of its believers in The Cannibal, and the result is
seen in rape, murder, and mutilation. The ritualistic relationship of the people to the hangman in The Owl is dictated by the
'covenant' which allows one young man to be executed as a
sacrifice, thus denying the possibility of procreation (he, being
the only available potential husband). The sheriff in The Beetle
Leg is preventive of normal sexual relations as he searches for
couples 'too easy found doing things a man can't talk about.' [5]
This novel is characterized by repression, hints of sexual
perversion, and the overwhelming potential for violence on the
part of the average citizen and the forces of law and order.
Significantly, the work depicts a landscape of sexual barrenness
as well. Dolce, the arch-victimizer in The Goose on the Grave,
evinces a menacing power whereby the whole story is characterized
by overtones of a perverted relationship between sexuality
(usually homosexuality) and religion. The Christian ideology
represented by the church and its 'missionaries', the priests,
is portrayed as a force of evil. These worlds are places of

spiritual decay, violence, death, and sterility. Ruthless
leaders, men of authority, designated either by past convention or by having usurped power by the strength of their will,
cannibalistically 'devour' their victims, either figuratively,
or literally as in The Cannibal. Such spiritual and political
decadence are features of works which encapsulate the mood of
a world effected by two world wars. In the end, the victimizer
is equally a victim through his dependence on his narrow,
sadistic relationship to the Other. His restrictive view of
the world is undermined through the structural dislocations
in The Cannibal, for instance, where the aftermath of one war
is placed prior to the idealistic fervour at the start of an
earlier war, and where the proud teutonic officers become the
insane, cannibalistic 'aristocrats' that stalk their prey
later. In other novels mentioned above the authority, order,
and control of leading characters are equally undermined by
the sterility and desolation of their worlds, prefigured in
both the people they dominate and the landscape itself. These
works demonstrate the beginnings of one of John Hawkes's major
concerns:

> ... to objectify the terrifying similarity between
> the unconscious desires of the solitary man and
> the disruptive needs of the visible world.[6]

The entropic vision of a world in decay, chaotic landscapes
of violence, destruction, and desolation, have a 'terrifying'
similarity to the figures of power who cause violence, death,
and mutilation. Hawkes is able to investigate this manifestation of violence through internalizing the problem, delving

deep into the 'pyschic sores', the wish fulfilling dreams
of characters, and then allowing the psychological truths
to manifest themselves in the 'visible world' with all its
destructive results.

Before discussing the thematic centres of Hawkes's early
works in particular, brief mention must be made of the use
of 'landscape'. In Charivari (1949), there is the description
of a 'town of water' which reveals the beginnings of Hawkes's
own 'insistencies'. As the author claims:

> ...the wind and rain become animated and start to
> take over the passage, the writer dwells...on
> images and details of decay and corruption...the
> association of the 'barely remembered woman', who
> is idealized for her 'faint flush of youth', with
> a vast violent world of death, sexlessness, and
> misogyny, is in fact the thematic centre of all
> that I've written.[7]

The darkening storms, the cataclysmic chaos, the battering
rain, and its unavoidable terror are features of Edwin Honig's
poem Island Storm [8], which for Hawkes contains the deathly,
disruptive aspects of his 'landscapes'. This symbolic use of
landscape reaches its most far-reaching structural exploitation
in Second Skin (1964) as the barren, wind-swept, and desolate
Atlantic Island contrasts with the tranquil, tropical 'Spice
Island'. The landscape which objectifies the narrator's
'brutal acts' is this cold barren Atlantic Island and it recalls
the imagery and motifs of the 'town of water', in Charivari
and Island Storm. These landscapes underline the author's
'special sympathy for decay, deterioration, destruction (and
for the maimed and victimized).' [9] Landscape creates a world
through motif and inference, and thus functions as an evocation
of themes. It enhances that terrifying similarity between

destruction and desolation in the visible world and the needs
of the solitary will. The barrenness and hostility of the
miasmal landscape in The Beetle Leg is symptomatic of the
people who dwell there. The desolation and destruction of the
land in The Cannibal is seen again in the maimed, the crippled,
the violated, and the murdered of the town. Life is as corrupt
as the landscape itself in these novels and stories. Landscape
replaces society because Hawkes is interested in implying through
more 'poetic' means [10] abstract levels of meaning which could
serve as correlatives for psychological truths (unconscious
desires and disruptive needs). In Second Skin (1964), Hawkes
first introduced an alternative landscape which led to the more
'pastoral' idyllic descriptions of The Blood Oranges (1971).
But the function remained the same: landscape implies the state
of man and the world, and symbolizes the hidden terror and violence which stems from the inner 'dream' world of the unconscious.

These violent worlds of the earlier works enable the demolition
of man's image of himself as a rational creature. [11] The victims
in these works are the young and the helpless; the victimizers,
the powerful and the strong-willed, authoritative 'adults'.
Adeppi in The Goose on the Grave and Selvaggia in The Cannibal
are examples of child-victims. But ineffectual, weak adults
are also victimized; Henry Van and Emily in Charivari are early
forerunners of many of the characters in The Lime Twig (1961).
This novel, as John Kuehl points out, is full of

> ...specific victimized children and childlike adults who
> variously experience adult domination, neglect, mental
> and physical cruelty, war, and sexual perversion. [12]

But in the works prior to 1960, characters were less defined,
less personalized than in those subsequent novels. For the

early works exhibit two dimensional, representative types;
not individuals but more often symbols of forces (of evil,
for instance) or ideas.  But any allegoric potential in
these works is belied by the language itself, the absence
of any semblance of parataxis, the use of a poetic,
evocative imagery, and a highly dislocative structure.
Rather, groups of characters form patterns of meaning,
essential oppositions (victims and victimizers for
instance), which blend with the use of landscape.  There
are recognizable patterns of physical handicap: 'mutilation,
deformity, disease and deterioration.'[13]  Impotent males
contrast with promiscuous females (and this occurs throughout
Hawkes's works).  But the conflict between representative
groups in the early works gives way to the internalized
conflicts prefigured in the investigation of psychic states
of 'individuated' characters after 1960.  The novels of John
Hawkes offer 'a compelling image of twentieth century man
who, bruised by reality, can find solace only in his imagination.'[14]  The images of man and 'reality' are established
in the pre-1960 works, but the solution of imaginative
alternatives dominates the post-1960 novels.

In Hawkes's early literary fiction, mythology, that 'aggregate
in which ideals can be kept so securely,'[15] is seen to be a
unifying element in the realm of narrative perspective and
'world-view'.  In such a way, order can be imposed on the
world and meaning made readily available.  These systems of
comprehension firmly establish man as the source of order
and meaning in the world.  Yet this mode of self-assertion is

also seen to be restrictive. The strong-willed characters who
shape the world after their own image are also seen to imprison
man within the restrictions of that design. A mythology
blindly adhered to is seen in Hawkes's novels and stories as a
denial of growth and a guarantee of permanent stagnation.
Examples range from Il Gufo's 'covenant' in The Owl, and the
Mulge Lampson myth in The Beetle Leg, to the incessant recurrence
of nationalistic fervour despite the lessons of history in The
Cannibal. As Tanner rightly claims:

> The desire or compulsion to project the shape of one's
> unique consciousness against the imprisoning shapes of
> the external world.16

is part of a desire to create one's own system of meaning. Ruthless manipulators, from Zizendorf in The Cannibal to the gangland
leader, Larry, in The Lime Twig, imprison others in their own
'system'. Such omnipotence gives way to the self-deluding
impotence of the first-person narrators from Second Skin onwards.
The patterns    these characters impose, both the manipulators of
the early works and the narrators of the later ones, are seen to
be wrong patterns. The strong-willed characters maintain their
impositions, and intentionally destroy; the weak-willed narrators
unintentionally destroy through the self-delusional nature of
their pattern-making, and through their destructive sympathy.

(ii) Thematic centres: sexuality, violence and repression

The extremes of violence and sexual perversion are explainable
with reference to the following three statements by the author,

which then need to be examined in the light of his works:

(i)    I think of the act of writing as an act of
rebellion... I enjoy a sense of violation,
a criminal resistance to safety, to the
security provided by laws or systems. [17]

(ii)   ...the function of the true innovator is...
constantly to test in the sharpest way
possible the range of our human sympathies
and constantly to destroy mere surface
morality. [18]

(iii) ... my fiction is generally an evocation of the
nightmare or terroristic universe in which
sexuality is destroyed by law, by dictum, by
human perversity, by contraption, and it is
this destruction of human sexuality which I
have attempted to portray and confront in order
to be true to human fear and to human ruthless-
ness, but also in part to evoke its opposite,
the moment of freedom from constriction,
constraint, death. [19]

The most overt dramatization of the repressive effect of the
family is in the social satire of Hawkes's first short novel,
Charivari (1949), where the parents (Henry is the parson's son,
and Emily the general's daughter) dominate the children
(themselves middle-aged) who have accepted their infantile
submissive roles, and who are subjected to the ridicule of
the mocking wedding-ceremony indicated by the story's title.
But in their dreams and fantasies they appear to be
violently resisting. The movement between violent and erotic
fantasy and the world of social convention is never distinct,
and the reader is given a privileged and disturbing insight
into their repressed thoughts. Emily and Henry are characterized
by their fear of parenthood. There are intimations of an abortion
for Emily, and Henry's feelings of insecurity and his isolation
from others makes for a desperate bond between himself and

Emily. Yet their childlikeness is probably the only link
between them. We are told that they sleep in separate
rooms, and the space between them is patrolled by a massive
dog. Their 'match' drives Henry into a 'sleeping activity',
and when in company they both 'seemed irresistably drawn
into the negative contemplation of each other'. [20] Intimations about Henry's sexual impotence are scattered
throughout the novel. For not only are Emily and Henry
incapable of any mature adult relationship, but also Henry
appears uninterested in the 'Green Lady', the arch-temptress
at the party who is intending to seduce him. Even in the
seaside boarding house, women are surprised that he is, 'so
completely uninterested'. [21] Emily herself has a violent
fear of sexual contact of any kind, exemplified in the
medical examination scene where she envisages a violent
physical assault. [22] The novel is characterized by a
general fear of life, enhanced by insinuations of sterility,
impotence, and apparent sexual apathy. The proposed
marriage of Emily and Henry is seen to be totally bizarre,
undermining any potential for procreation, or even any form
of relationship other than one of childish dependence.
They are ridiculous figures in an absurd drama, where the
real force of conflict is contained within their unconscious
thoughts. It is the predisposition for psychological revelation that allows the reader the necessary measure of awareness to understand that what appears to be reality, that is,
the social conventions within which the characters relate
(the family unit), is only the dull, ritualistic surface of

life, an enactment for the sake of convention. The profounder reality is contained within the unconscious thoughts
of Henry and Emily. The potential for violence is seen to
be engendered by the pressures of domineering parents, and
the constrictions of traditional conventions. The aetiology
of repression, therefore, is constituted by the relationship
between the solitary will and the destructive constrictions
of conventional life. The interplay of inner psychic needs
and the hostility of a destructive world features more
extensively in subsequent novels.

Hawkes's Freudian analysis of the relationship between man
and the world introduces a mode of explanation of aberrant
sexuality and gratuitous violence in these works. Man is
portrayed as a prisoner of the past, either through his
reliance on myths of order and excellence, or through the
dominance of convention often to the extent of ritual. In
this respect, the past is a neurotic constriction, and
'neurosis is an essential consequence of civilization or
culture'. [23] Freud analyzed this problem in Civilization
and its Discontents (1930), where his main theme was 'the
irremediable antagonism between the demands of instinct and
the restrictions of civilization'. [24] Hawkes first attempted
to expose the violence of the repressed unconscious in
Charivari, and later in The Lime Twig (1961) he dramatized
the disruptive interplay between the hidden urges of impoverished lives and the havoc of wish-fulfilled dreams actualized
during a night of 'lawlessness'. The question at the centre

of Hawkes' dramatization of repression has been aptly posed by
Marcuse:

> In Freudian terms, is the conflict between pleasure
> principle and reality principle irreconcilable to
> such a degree that it necessitates the repressive
> transformation of man's instinctual structure? 25

In what follows, I shall briefly describe problems of sexuality,
violence and unconscious desire in The Lime Twig, initially, and
then go on to outline aspects of sexuality in Hawkes's work,
generally aiming to reach the point whereby the problematical
relationship between sexuality and psychosis in the most recent
novels may be explained. The slogan for this abiding preoccupation in Hawkes's work is to be found in Charivari:

> And have you heard, or do you think we are likely to
> hear what very private shames and resentments and
> misgivings these people are harbouring? May we be
> cruel enough? 26

The sustained realism of William Hencher's 'prologue' in The
Lime Twig (1961) creates a world of urban squalor and loneliness in the dreary life of war-torn London. It is in this
situation of the lonely lodger that the lives of Hencher and
the Banks are characterized as impoverished. Hencher demonstrates
the need to escape into fantasy which Margaret and Michael later
endorse. For just as Michael's 'own worst dream, and best, was
of a horse which was itself the flesh of all violent dreams,' 27
so his wife, Margaret dreams of 'swimming in the petrol tank
of a lorry, or watching three rubber dolls smartly burning'. 28
The dreams harbour the repressed wishes caused by a banal existence, just as they did for Emily and Henry in Charivari. Margaret's
routine of a shopping outing once a fortnight is a symptom of her
simplicity and ordinariness. Michael interprets his

relationship to her in terms of sexual impoverishment as
he stands next to their bed, 'the bed of ordinary down...
with the course of dreams mapped on the coverlet.' [29] She
is 'ordinary' and 'timid', and he is left to embrace 'two
hanging and scratchy dresses' [30] in the clothes-closet.
The inner psychic needs of these characters are rendered
plausible by this dichotomy between impoverished, frustrated, and banal daily lives, on the one hand, and, the
dreams and fantasies of the night, on the other. Michael's
involvement through Hencher with the horse-stealing
intrigue, releases, on this level of plot, those powerful
and destructive forces caused by the collision between 'the
unconscious desires of the solitary man and the disruptive
needs of the visible world'. [31] The visible world in this
novel is the self-styled, ruthless gangland of Larry, where
normative moral standards are ineffectual, and where Michael
is able to fulfil his wildest sexual fantasies in one
orgiastic night, only to realize in the end just how much
he is a victim of Larry's machinations. Margaret's brutal
assault by Thick and raping by Larry, gratuitous as the
violence may seem, enacts many of her strange fantasies.
Both characters are 'limed' through the terrifying similarity
between wish fulfilments and the violent world of crime.
Michael's redemptive act in the end, as he dies preventing
the horse from winning the race,is ineffectual in a world
which creates its own laws. The traditional forces of law
and order are both violent and ineffectual. The problem of
response in this novel is facilitated by the realism of the
early sections, the delineation of banal lives, and the

recuperative relationship between fantasy and reality.

If society, the family,or civilization in general is responsible for the neurosis of repression and its outlet in
violence and sexual fantasy, an analysis fundamental to
both Freud and Hawkes, then the pervasive image of the
chastity belt in The Blood Oranges (1971) shifts the
emphasis to Christianity and its puritanical overtones.
Cyril, the narrator and central protagonist of this novel,
has attempted and failed to establish a polygamous relationship with his wife and another couple.  The failure is
grounded in the conflict between Cyril's 'candor', his
theories of sexual extension, and Hugh's reticence and
onanistic sexuality.  The discovery of the chastity belt
in the depths of a medieval fortress, and its subsequent use
by Hugh on his wife, is interpreted by Cyril as symbolic of
past constriction and sexual repression.  The journey into
the depths of the old, abandoned fortress is described as
a symbolic journey towards the revelation of Hugh's unconscious.
The 'monstrous momento of Hugh's true attitude towards all
our well-intended loves' [32] is a barbaric reminder of the
restrictive 'chains' of convention, an 'artful relic of
fear and jealousy,' [33] a pervasive emblem of man-made
contraptions which embody obsessional fears of infidelity,
and which stand for the 'imprisonment' in age-old, conventional marriage vows.  This 'medieval atrocity' is a
central image, not only for this novel, but for all
Hawkes's works.  It emphasizes the author's concern with
the destruction of human sexuality by man-made laws,
customs, and beliefs.

In <u>The Beetle Leg</u>, the damming up of the river, and the consequent sterility of the land, is symptomatic of the denial
of life forces in the people themselves.  The Sheriff,
representative of law and order, prevents normal sexuality;
yet the novel is replete with intimations of sexual perversion.  Deviant sexual behaviour pervades the earlier works,
where marriages are seen to disintegrate, societies dissolve
through the destruction of war, and children to be victimized,
assaulted, mutilated and murdered.  Figures of authority
(aristocrats,  priests, nuns, policemen, sheriffs, and
doctors) perpetrate these violations.  In the works prior
to 1960, 'infantile wishes and sexual anxieties abound.' [34]
They manifest themselves in violence and grotesque humour.
This world has a kind of psychoanalytical validity, as <u>The
Lime Twig</u> and subsequent novels more explicitly demonstrate.
The reader  'is carried beyond outer actuality to inner
reality, an inner reality whose instability is symbolized
by Hawkes's landscapes and settings.' [35]  The existence
of various forms of aberrant sexuality enable causal relationships to be implied between public aggression, psychological disorder, and sexual repression.  In the post 1960
works, characters appear to experience their fantasies,
as <u>The Lime Twig</u> clearly shows.  The interplay of sexuality
and the self-problematic becomes a central concern in the
more recent novels, whereby the problem of other minds,
solipsism, and even psychosis are related to sexuality, and
particularly to onanism.  These first-person narratives will

be seen to bear out Hawkes's claim that, 'the true sources of fiction ... lie buried in some inaccessible depth of the psyche.' [36]

In a recent article on Death, Sleep and the Traveller (1975), one critic has rightly asserted that,

> Repeatedly, /Hawkes/ has dramatized the conflict between man's instinctual needs and the repressive customs and conventions of our civilization, showing it to be a battle of life and death.  In each of Hawkes's earlier works, as in the present one, his characters either live out their private and sexually aggressive impulses by using conventional public institutions as a pretext for preying on their fellow citizens or, falling prey to victimizers of one kind or another, retreat into fantasy or death. [37]

Hawkes's work demonstrates the Freudian thesis 'that sexual problems are the most frequent causes of sadistic or masochistic behaviour, that almost every act of violence begins with a justifiable need that had to be repressed ...' [38]

## (iii) The Problematic of the Self

> ...as if sleep were a decay fishing her beneath the visible surfaces... as if her life lay through her in ungainly luminous deteriorations - the troubling structure of the born somnambule, who lives in two worlds - meet of child and desperado (Djuna Barnes, Nightwood).

For Zizendorf in The Cannibal it is 'the struggle, the piling of bricks' [39] that is important.  His narrative is a persistent reminder that he is asserting his will in dictatorial fashion. This need for self-assertion is further underlined by a lesser character, Ernst, who 'tried to run his own smallness into something large.' [40]  But he is doomed to failure because only the strongest willed can withstand the force of events in 1914.  He must realise, 'that Krupp, perhaps a barbarian, is more the peg

where history hangs than a father who once spoke of honour.' 41
If the actions of men in pursuit of their ends is a definition
of history, then in Hawkes's 'world' only those men who are able
to dictate events in a totalizing manner will be able to pursue
those ends. Zizendorf is a member of that select breed of
manipulators who lead, and cannibalistically devour, those
they subjugate. But even he fails. Such strong-willed
characters, Zizendorf, Il Gufo, Dolce, the Sheriff, Cap
Leech, and Larry, are all ruthless victimizers who are
apparently able to enforce their presence through the strength
of their will. But they are also satirized for their narrow-
ness of vision, their lack of self-awareness. Some of these
victimizers in the early works are prominent examples of damning
portraits of the writer as dictator and as propagandist. Their
authority over people is symptomatic of the exclusive 'vision'
which their narrative point of view engenders. Il Gufo's and
Zizendorf's unusually complete omniscience is consistent with
their ruthless coercion in a very political sense.

Character in the pre-1960 works is more symbolic, typifying
ideas or themes, less individuated. Even the principal figures,
often telling their own story, are not clearly 'portrayed',
but exploit their stereo-typicality. The examples of dictators,
leaders, lawmen and gangsters have already been noted. In
The Lime Twig (1961) however, some characters become more
complex, less symbolic, and evince a marked moral and psychic
self-awareness. Hencher, Margaret, and Michael Banks expose

their innermost fears and desires, their unconscious needs,
and as victims of one sort or another they attempt to assert
their will, to transcend their impoverished lives, albeit
through the enactment of fantasy in the 'visible world'.
Michael's final attempt at purposeful action is in some sense
a more successful gesture than Ernst's efforts, in The Cannibal,
' to run his own smallness into something large'. Michael's
sacrificial death is described as a gesture of self assertion,
where he is 'small, yet beyond elimination, whose single
presence purported a toppling of the day, a violation of that
scene at Aldington, wreckage to horses and little crouching
men'. [42]

Throughout his work, Hawkes has been concerned with the
assertion and subjugation of the will, and the form of his
novels and stories are intelligible through this thematic
preoccupation. In Part Two of this study, I shall consider
the question of form, and especially Hawkes's crucial notion
of structure grounded in verbal and psychological coherence.
As Professor Rovit claims:

> Hawkes finds ready to hand a potential of form in
> an art based on existential perceptions. The
> individual "there's" of his fictions interlink
> thematically and expand into emotional coherence
> in terms of the underlying patterns existent in
> each individual embrace; and the consistency of
> human beings to will their own positions in the
> eternal dance insures the total coherence of the
> disconnected assaults. [43]

The need to will one's own position becomes more perplexing in
the post-1960 novels, where form serves to expose the efforts
of narrator protagonists to assert, analyze, or create a self

from a basically hostile and 'damaged' existence.

The iron will-power and orderly vision of the early dictator-narrators and protoganists gives way to the self-deluding artful rhetoric of the unreliable narrators of Second Skin (1964), The Blood Oranges (1971), Death, Sleep and the Traveller (1974), and Travesty (1976). These novels are penetrating studies in psychology, whereby inconstencies in narrative structure allow an implied author to offer a critique of the narrator. In Second Skin, for instance, Skipper tells his story in the way most advantageous to the view of himself he wishes to convey. He can both overindulge in his apparent love of detail, and yet spare certain crucial details, and it is this latter 'perogative' that creates suspicion in the reader. Just how reliable is Skipper? If his psychology dictates what can be revealed and what must be suppressed, then we might well be justified in suspecting that the circumstances he describes, and in which he participated, and through which he has often been victimized, might well have been different from the picture he creates. Tanner rightly states:

> ... one could see the whole account as an
> egostistical attempt to impose on the reader
> a self-justificatory and delusional version
> of events which might well have afforded a
> different reading. [44]

One can never divorce the question of narrative perspective from the self-problematic in Hawkes's works, because stories often serve to reveal the problematic itself through the very nature of their telling. Psychology and form are

problematically interrelated, and especially in those novels
where narrative is grounded in a mode of self-revelation.
Skipper, in _Second Skin_, is very keen to stress at the outset
of his 'serpentine tale' that he is lover of all the people
and experience that seem to have conspired to harm him
physically or mentally.  He claims to love the bright needle-
point of the tatooist's art , but we soon see him scream in
pain at the 'exquisite torture' of 'every puncture of the needle'
which is as 'fast as the stinging of artificial bees'. [45]
Recalling the 'small naval boat' in endearing terms is equally
misleading, for later he remembers being physically assaulted
in a life-boat on the U.S.S. Starfish during the war by the
mythically demonic Tremlow, a figure who appears constantly
to facilitate the explanation of another 'brutal act'.
Finally, when he declares that  'it will be clear... that
I am a man of courage as well,' we must qualify the claim
with a prior revelation which may well be nearer the truth:


> But most of all, $\sqrt{I}$ am$\sqrt{}$ lover of my harmless
> and most sanguine self. 46


This untruthfulness to himself manifest in these statements
alone, is a symptom of his unreliability as 'chronicler' of
the past.  But it must always be emphasized in this connection
that it is precisely this mode of self-deception which
functions as a protective layer, a second skin, enabling
Skipper's survival in such a hostile, death-ridden world.  I
shall return in more detail to the structural effects of Skipper's
unreliability and self-preservation in _Part Two_ below.


Skipper is morally and psychological, hypersensitive to the
extent of being neurotically preoccupied with his self and
his relationship to others. He senses the presence of

his 'destructive sympathy' which may have driven his
father, wife, and then his daughter to their deaths.
Yet he is very much concerned with rewriting, recreating,
and healing his damaged self. He refers to the tailor's
dummy (a reminder of the way others see him) as 'that
hapless effigy of my disfigured self,' [47] but, as the first
chapter clearly underlines, he is very concerned with
establishing a clear identity for himself. By 'naming
names', Skipper not only establishes his version of
himself and those around him, but he also attempts to
elevate his status to that of a hero of classical, mythic
proportions, with all the commensurable allusions to Greek
tragedy. Significantly, however, the names appear
arbitrary, and do not coincide with the 'actual' course
of events, nor with his involvement in them, which amounts
to ineffectual 'bungling'.

The idea of second skin, its various connotations, its
figurative status, emphasizes the abiding preoccupation
with the question of identity. There are two dominant
references of second skin to clothing. The first part
of the 'Drag Race on the Beach' section is concerned with
the boat excursion on the Peter Poor, and the need for
protection against the rough sea and bad weather is
emphasized. But the oilskins that skipper calls his
'second skin' serve not only to protect but also to
hamper his movement. In the 'Soldiers in the Dark'
episode there is detailed description of the absconding
soldiers' uniforms, and the discarding of them as a
symbolic gesture of destroying one form of identity.

Clothes, therefore, both give an identity to man and also serve
to restrict him, both in terms of imposed identity, and in a
purely physical sense. The soldiers undress, suggesting a
desire to **recover** original nakedness, to rid themselves of
a rigidly imposed identity. For Skipper this is symbolic of
his attempts to tell his 'naked history', [48] which implies both
the notions of innocence and exposure, and the idea of stripping
off an imposed identity and recovering the 'true' one. Through
the vantage of his rhetoric, Skipper deviously strips away the
layers of time to reveal the traumas of that 'actual' past.
Skipper's second self, created from the tranquility of the
Spice Island, contrasts markedly with the first self of his
damaged past life. The reader has to come to terms, as much
as Skipper himself has to, with his 'schizophrenic flesh'. [49]
As one of life's failures, he creates for himself a second chance
to hold out against the 'seeds of death' and find 'love at last'.

Skipper is both artist and creative solipsist. He has moved in
the novel from a guilt-ridden self, an imposition precipitated
by his inability to exist with others, through a process of
denuding, both literally and figuratively, towards a discovery
of his 'authentic self'. But we must realize that the two
selves, the one on the Gentle Island, the other on the Spice
Island, are both in themselves personae: as he uses language
to create who he is, his final 'triumphant' self is 'as fictive
as his early guilt-laden self'. [50]

John Hawkes's three most recent novels are best summed up in
the phrase, 'the pure space of psychic activity,' [51] where
the author focuses more sharply than ever on the psychological
problems of a single narrating consciousness. The self-

problematic in these novels is more **explicitly** formulated.
Cyril, in The Blood Oranges (1971),tells us of his efforts to
break down the repressive taboos fundamental to monogamy, and
the novel is a record of his failure to relate in a polygamous
manner to the Other, prefigured in the attempts to establish
sexual relations between his wife and himself, and another
couple. The implications for the self and its realization
through Others are crucial for this chapter. Cyril's idyllic
paradise is not peopled with those who suit his design, as
Skipper's Spice Island apparently is. Illyria is not secured
from the threat of those who wish to oppose its creator. This
is a world of profound conflict which eventually results in its
own destruction. The novel is narrated after the fact, as it
were, and Cyril,refusing to admit despair, spends the 'present
time',in which he is narrating, attempting to restore his
paradise world with Catherine, and also desperately trying to
absolve himself of any blame for Hugh's suicide which caused
the final dissolution of that 'harmonious' set of relationships.

To understand the nature of the conflict between Hugh and Cyril
is to appreciate the damaging effect of the narrator's, Cyril's,
solipsism both on those he involves in his scheme and on his
present situation at the time of narrating. His 'theory' of
ideal love is instrumental in this failure. In Second Skin,
Skipper's love manifests itself altruistically in a small and
thriving community on the tropical island. Cyril's love in
The Blood Oranges,however, is expressed in his theory of
'sex-singing' which egotistically engulfs the passions of other
people, destroys their private selves, and consequently destroys

itself by undermining the essential basis of its communal
structure. It is a theory of love grounded in eroticism, sexual
multiplicity and the denial of conventional marriage. In
this, it is the nadir of fertility, a mode of sexuality which
can only be justified for its own sake; quite the reverse of
Skipper's descriptions of the fertile cycle of regeneration
which the end of Second Skin looks forward to. For Cyril,
sex is apparently aestheticized, and much of his narrative
is preoccupied with explaining and defending his theory of
'sex-singing' despite its actual fatal and destructive
results. His declarations are characterized by smugness, a
factor which is enchanced by his overindulgence in sensuous
language, poetic imagery, and mythic symbolism. Like
Skipper before him, Cyril is a very articulate and skilful
manipulator of rhetoric. But as the narrative unfolds, the
reader progressively becomes aware of the problems created
by the narrator's belief in the absolute rightness of his
viewpoint: what he might call sexual aestheticism others, of
a more conventional frame of mind (Hugh himself), would label
adultery.

I shall discuss the structure of the novel in the following
section of this study. But suffice it to emphasize at this
point that, as in previous novels, the past and the present
comment on each other and partially liberate the reader from
the confines of the single viewpoint. Cyril's claims for
success, and his obvious failures,enable a critical perspective on the narrator's psychology to come into operation,and
a stress on his unreliability. He narrates from a situation

which is quite at odds with his paradise of love: his
'tapestry' is in ruins; Catherine is convalescing from
an apparent break-down; he lives in a derelict Villa with
only an ignorant,'sexless ' native girl who can understand
nothing of his 'lengthy erotic declaration.' In talking
about the past he is seducing Catherine with words; but
he must overcome the barrier of incredulity that she offers.
His incessant talking is thus rendered plausible by his
need to convince and to cure Catherine, and to repair his
damaged tapestry:

> My ritual, my weekly ritual of hope and fidelity,
> and in the process I suppose I reveal vestiges of
> the former lover, a former man of good taste. [52]

Therefore his period of 'uselessness' is transcended by
using his 'very nearly aesthetic memory'. But this may well
be delusional. For his monologue covers up an abyss of
loneliness which conditions his incessant, but artful,
babble:

> ...the silence ... fell between Catherine and me
> like a festering marsh whenever I stopped talking. [53]

The landscape echoes the overbearing emptiness of Cyril's
life in the 'silent villa'. [54] It is primitive and desolate;
his life lonely and isolated. His obsessive need to prove
the workability of his theories and to assert hope for the
future are now seen to be intelligible through his neurotic
desire to overstep the bounds of his solipsism. His

omniscience is constantly undermined by the proliferations of
questions: 'were they listening? were they interested?' He
has to admit that he would never know.[55] He can never really
know the contents of other minds; but he is primarily obsessed
with convincing others of the pre-eminence and validity of his
own thoughts. Paradoxically, he needs other people for the
practice of his theory of sexual extension, yet, at the same time,
he must deny their separate existence. Not only does Cyril need
to convince others (including the reader) of his omniscience
(although he seems to doubt it himself at times) and of the rightness of his theories, but also he attempts, desperately, to verify
for himself the separateness of other minds:

> Could it be that one of my speechless creatures... had
> torn itself loose from the tapestry that only I could see?[56]

Characteristically, he realizes pompously that he really does not
need others to provide the answers to his questions.

> Once more... Psyche was on my side and that given time
> and thought I could always count on myself for answers.[57]

This quality of arrogant self-assertion founds the very reasons for
his destructive conflict with Hugh's 'medievalism'. We must be
critical of Cyril's version, for it is in his best interest to favour
his own ideas and totally denigrate those of his 'adversary'. The
narrator's account of the discovery of the chastity belt is a highpoint in this conflict. Its symbolic status as the representative
of institutionalized constriction and repression was discussed above.
On this level, Cyril does appear to offer a healthy alternative to
the puritanical overtones of Hugh's monogamy. But the ironic

undermining of Cyril's ideas by events themselves portray him
as no heroic champion of free love, despite his assertions to
the contrary. The contrasts extend to various levels, but
both alternatives are criticized. Art for Cyril is a means
for creating fantasy : 'sex-singing' is his most aesthetic
expression. Hugh, however, is another kind of artist who
invades Cyril's imaginative territory (Illyria) with his
direct, frozen copy of reality prefigured in his photography.
Attitudes to art and to sexuality are figuratively commensurate,
one with the other. For Cyril, freedom of the imagination
(tapestry, sensuous language and poetic imagery and fantasy)
is analagous with sexual freedom: his idyll of love is
encapsulated in his Illyria of sexual multiplicity. For Hugh,
reality is kept at a distance, controlled. In watching the
photographer-artist at work, the narrator significantly comments
that, 'he seemed to be listening to the girl's silent life
rather than staring at the visible shape of it.'[58] Hugh's
obsession with pornographic photography is a symptom of his
masturbatory tendencies. He is described as reticent, while
Cyril talks of his 'aching candor'. Cyril's attempts at sexual
openness finally destroy Hugh.

This multiplicity of apparent contradictions is contained in
the pervasive image of the novel's title. The orange is sweet
yet streaked with the colour of blood. The paradox functions
at all levels in the novel: death and love in 'paradise';
desire and agony; onanism and sexual polygamy; Cyril's comic
rituals of courtship and love, and the bitterness of the
destructive conflicts they cause: a paradoxical relationship
between tragedy and comedy. Significantly, Cyril talks of the

presence of 'several modes of incongruity,'[59] and perhaps
his pompous language and arrogant theorizing are most
incongruently related to their product and to his obsessional
self-delusion, as he perpetually seeks signs around him that
could be interpreted as messages of hope.

Finally, his efforts are undermined by the doubts cast on
the subject-matter of his 'tapestry': 'Am I embracing air?
Could that be all' he desperately asks himself. The self-
problematic is appropriately contained in the following
words:

> Is that what it feels like to discover with absolute
> certainty that you yourself have simple disappeared
> from the filmy field? When love withdraws her breath
> from your body, and as with the tip of a long green
> tail flicks the very spot where you stood or thought
> you stood in the upper right or lower left-hand
> corner of the endless tapestry, is that what it is
> like? Embracing air? 60

For this novel, like Second Skin before it, is about the
writer's idiosyncratic use of language and imagery to fashion
a world out of his solitary consciousness. This dramatizes
what Hawkes himself has defined as the true purposes of the
novel for the writer (and these narrators are images of that
writer): to create 'the shape of his meaningful psychic paradox'.[61]
The paradoxical interplay between Cyril's omniscience, and his
arrogant self-assertions, on the one hand, and his anxieties and
doubts, on the other, testify to the disabling parody of the
writer's position in search of form, and the problematical
quest for the self.

As _Second Skin_ and _The Blood Oranges_ clearly demonstrate,
the use of first-person narrators who base _their_ work on
calculated self-exposure enumerate a clearly defined self-
problematic grounded in psychology. The two subsequent
novels continue the manipulation of narrative form as a
means of revealing the psychological traumas of a pervasive
narrating consciousness. Thematically, _Death, Sleep and the_
_Traveller_ (1975) is about death, guilt, and the problem
of meaninglessness. Having his source in those unreliable
narrators in Hawkes's previous novels, Allert also uses
language and narrative to create a calculated view of
himself and his apparent crises. Intentionality is partially
concealed and partly revealed by the narrative structure.
For, just as Skipper in _Second Skin_ found it difficult to
recognize his destructive sympathy, so Allert in this novel
refuses to accept his guilt for murdering his former mistress.
Allert's unreliability, his obsessive repression of the
'truth', is offset by the psycho-analytical validity of his
wife's interpretation of his dreams. Hawkes has always
exhibited a marked interest in psychological revelation, but
in this novel it becomes more explicit.

The journey may well be less intelligible as an actual cruise,
and more as a descent into the unconscious, a search for a
meaningful self. Allert discovers meaninglessness on the
'journey':

> Now I realize that I had hoped for more, had
> expected more, and yet in the midst of such
> silence and immobility I also realize that
> my disappointment is nothing compared with
> the journey I have taken and the barren
> actuality I have at last discovered. [62]

Allert's problem is acute: not only is he unable to
admit guilt, but he ritualistically chants the chorus of
his frightened, exposed, and damaged self as a mode of
repressing that guilt:

Who is safe, who is safe, who is safe? [63]

Finally, he points to the central problem of the novel,
and one which is central to Hawkes's work:

> We spend most of our lives attempting in small
> ways to know someone else. And we hope that
> someone else will care to peak into our
> darkest corners, without shock, or condem-
> nation. We even hope to catch a glimpse of
> ourselves, and in this furtive pursuit we
> hope for courage. [64]

The desperate need for others is fundamental to the self-
problematic. The relationship between self and other minds
is instrumental in the transcendence of solipsism. But for
Allert, the problem appears more complex than just a concern
with the 'various unfamiliar shadows that comprise wife,
girl friend, or friend.' Significantly, he asks, ' who
can confront his own psychic sores in the clear glass?' [65]
In admitting his guilt, Allert would demonstrate the courage
to face those 'psychic sores', but he ends the novel on an
almost hysterical note at the departure of his wife and the
realization of the vacuum of loneliness that she leaves behind,
affirming, at least to himself, that he is 'not guilty.' [66]

The world of dream dominates Allert's narrative. In the
constant self-analysis, and in the analysis by Peter (friend
and psychiatrist), and his wife Ursula, he seems partially

convinced that he ought to commit himself for psychiatric
treatment. He decides to forego this alternative, and
instead to'simply think and dream.' [67] But Allert may
well be already committed into psychiatric care.[68] He seems
to use dreams to 'travel' into the depths of his psyche, but
persistently attempts to verify a reality that will give him
proof of his existence in the world rather than solely in the
unreality of dream. Abandoned to 'death, sleep, and the
anguish of the lonely traveller,'[69] Allert appears, in
Ursula's words, 'a psychic invalid.' [70] As he cannot differentiate between reality and dreams, he is unable to transcend
his solipsism. In answer to his wife's accusations that he has
no feelings, and that he is uninterested in her, he underlines
his most perplexing problem:

> It is simply that I want to please, want to exist,
> want others to exist with me, but find it difficult
> to believe in the set of characters on the stage.' [71]

The unreality of other people for Allert founds his self-
problematic. Problems of epistemology and phenomenology are
not merely academic questions for him, or for us in trying
to understand him. Rather they are part of the problem of
Allert's difficulty in accepting meaninglessness, and of
his desperate bid to define and assert an identity which
transcends his solipsism.

Like all Hawkes's narrators Allert is a parody of the writer
'an impresario, the director of a magical actor on a secret
stage.' [72] That actor is, of course, himself. As he realizes:

'I myself am my only access to what I want to know.' [73] He

can delude himself, but he can never be sure about that know-

ledge. His dreams take him on a journey to the beginnings of

his self, and he discovers the origin of his insecurity and

masturbatory, voyeuristic, deviant sexuality. Like Hugh in

The Blood Oranges, he is obsessed with pornographic photo-

graphs; and this, coupled with his onanism, is symptomatic of

his total divorce from others, and his narcissistic obsession

with himself. His dreams offer a mode of psychological explana-

tion for his narrative. They are significantly characterized

by a journey backward in time, and in some instances he even

visualizes a return to the womb. He feels he has always

been a victim, 'overexposed', and he yearns to return to his

'newly discovered place of utter privacy.' [74] When he finds

himself inside such a 'structure', he surveys the desolation

of his own beginning. [75] He has discovered meaninglessness in

the 'barren actuality' of his solipsism. Paradoxically, a

heightened sense of himself through fetishistic, deviant

sexuality also reinforces his solipsism. Finally, his

perplexing identity crisis leads him to admit an 'inability

to believe in the reality of the human self...' [76] The

confusion of dream and reality, past and present, make Allert

a very troublesome story-teller: he not only creates narrative

from the contents of his traumatic dreams, but he also creates

a fictive persona for himself. But in all his weakness, he

does embody the strength that comes from 'knowing that there

is nothing else in the world except what he creates and the

figures he discovers in his creation.' [77] Allert's

'archaic cure', the intense sleep of the coma whereby the

patient travels deep into himself, and in a kind of sexual

agony is 'sinking into the depths of psychic darkness, drowning

in the sea of the self, submerging into the long slow chaos
of the dreamer on the edge of extinction', [78] which Peter,
the psychiatrist explains, may well suffice as a psychological description of the narrative through which Allert
attempts to come to terms with his self-problematic.

Death, Sleep and the Traveller is written in the form of a
dramatic monologue addressed to a judge-auditor. This
produces confessional overtones. But Allert appears to
expose himself through a 'faulty' rationalization. Travesty
(1976) is also in the form of a monologue, but in this case
the monologue masquerades as a dialogue, as the self-opiniated
narrator appears to address his 'confessions' to Henri,
sitting next to him in the speeding car. His calculated
confession serves to accuse his listener of his own 'psychic
slippage', of his 'shattered self-confidence', as life seems
to have damaged him, like previous narrators in Hawkes's
novels. The title is instructive of the book's derivation,
just as the epigraphs are. The quotation from Camus' La Chute
(1956), and the exploitation of a similar form, is born out by
the novel on all levels. Hawkes's narrator travesties the
monologue of Camus' Jean-Baptiste Clamence. But the narrator
of Travesty indulges in 'psychic fishing'[79] revealing his
onanistic sexuality, and his destructive relationships with
others. His reprehensible narcissism is characterized through
his oppressive politeness and domineering tone. But he is
decidedly unreliable: his belief in paradox as a form of
harmony allows him to aestheticize his troublesome contradictions. He believes in the 'utter harmony of design and debris';

the relationship between 'planned symmetry' and incongruity;
mystery attracts him, but also specific fact; he talks
about the 'happy ritual of disruption and reconciliation',[80]
which has characterized his marriage. His claims for omniscience and his propensity towards total coherence are
undermined by the doubts which erupt into the text. The
question,'who knows?' contrasts markedly with the narrator's
claim: 'I know what you are thinking?'[81] Sex for this
narrator is 'the dialogue of the skin', but, as his monologue
clearly demonstrates, he is incapable of dialogue, and his
sexuality is totally onanistic. Finally, the narrator's
'theory of likeness'[82] enables us to suspect that his illusion
of dialogue is a symptom of his pretence of transcending his
solipsistic self through communication. The intimations of
schizophrenia are confirmed in his obsession with paradox
(the two conflicting selves) within the narrative of his
'private apocalypse.'[83] As the narrator declares to his
apparent interlocutor, 'it is I who chose you to be present
with me tonight.'[84] Finally, _Travesty_ is Hawkes's most
sustained reduction of narrative to the vagaries of the
single narrating consciousness. In this manner, the author
clearly dramatizes problems of the self at the level of a
vexatious interplay between solipsism and the creation of
narrative form. The continual enactment of a Freudian critique
of consciousness witnesses the displacement of the obsolete,
'old stable ego' with a very unstable, often psychotic Id.
It is precisely this recourse to psychological explanation
that enables strange narrative texts to be rendered
intelligible.

# CHAPTER THREE

Man, Time, and the Epistemic Status of
the Subject in the Works of Claude Simon

(i) The Image of Man

> ...comme ces types dans les films comiques, entraînés
> par un tapis roulant, et qui gesticulent d'une façon
> grotesque ou tentent de courir en sens inverse avec
> de moulinets de bras, et terrifiés, et qui ne réussissent
> qu'à se ficher par terre et être emportés encore plus
> vite (Le Vent, p.100)

In the novels of Claude Simon, the action of men always necessarily

produces derisory results because History is the evidence of

eternally recurrent patterns of behaviour, despite an impersonal

and ceaselessly destruction flow of Time:

> ... et peut-être étaient-ce toujours les mêmes (les
> mêmes camions, les mêmes gladiateurs) tournant et
> retournant autour des pâtés de maisons, comme dans
> ces opéras où les figurants à peine sortis de scène
> se dépêchent de galoper derrière le décor pour rentrer [1]
> par le côté opposé, retraverser la scène en courant ...

The theatricality of this image and the incisiveness of its

cynicism characterizes the Simonian narrative which attempts to

deal with real historical event and purposive action in the world.

The most pervasive symbol of futile action can be found in La

Route des Flandres (1960): the French cavalry officer de Reixach's

death is described in terms of the fall of a crumbling equestrian

statue, as he, sword raised in apparent anachronistic defiance is

killed. In Le Palace (1962), a novel recalling certain days in the

Spanish Civil War in Barcelona, the notion of the cycles of repetitive

behaviour in relation to the impersonal flux of History is ironically

enforced by the alternative definition of revolution which heads the

text:

mouvement d'un mobile qui, parcourant une courbe
fermée, repasse successivement par les mêmes points.[2]

Action is reduced to derisory, mechanical, and repetitious

gesticulation. Again, the image is highly theatrical:

> Comme ces ensembles de marionnettes, d'automates figés
> au milieu d'un geste, d'un sourire, et qui tout à coup,
> au déclenchement de la mécanique, se mettent tous en
> même temps à se mouvoir et à babiller tandis que s'élève
> un air de boîte à musique et que s'allument les rampes
> d'éclairage ... ou du moins (de même que pour les
> marionnettes, les automates condamnés à répéter sans
> fin les mêmes mouvements ou reparcourir le même itinéraire
> sans espoir de changement ni d'évasion) cette agitation,
> cette gesticulation ...[3]

History is not affected by man's actions in Simon's works. It

is an impersonal, imperceptible, and impacable force which destroys

any form of idealism, as Le Palace clearly demonstrates. Simon

states his view of History in the epigram from Pasternak

which heads his novel, L'Herbe (1958):

> Personne ne fait l'histoire, on ne la voit pas, pas
> plus qu'on ne voit l'herbe pousser.

There is sufficient ambiguity is such words for an alternative

reading to be possible, as one critic has recently shown.[4] I shall

have recourse to this alternative interpretation in the following

section of this study. Suffice it to suggest at this juncture that

for Simon not only does man not make History, but also the process

of History is not in itself perceptible. Time is only visible

in its destructive effects on man and his world. Under the massive

overwhelming shadow of the cosmic force of passing Time man appears,

'face à face avec sa fragilité, son insignifiance et sa
solitude.'[5] The attempts by man to enhance his significance,
and to give meaning to the world, though the means of idealism and
heroism, are derided in these novels: any endeavour to impose
personal necessity on implacable contingency is condemned as
aberrant illusion. The former student, whose fragmented recollections of the Spanish Civil War fill the pages of Le Palace, finally
confronts this painful realization about his illusions. Marie,
the ageing spinster in L'Herbe, leaves the evidence of her temporal
existence for the inquisitive Louise to read: Marie's account
books, the minute details of every expenditure and every profit
meticulously recorded line by line throughout the years, are
implicitly contrasted in their apparent pettiness with the incontrovertible and overwhelming evidence of Time's destructive
progression in the dying, decrepit old woman herself:

> ...les menus événements (et même pas événements: faits,
> incidents, - et même pas incidents: le quotidien, le
> tout-venant - et même pas menu: minuscule, insignifiant)
> ressurgissant hors du temps, de l'aboli, à la façon de
> jalons plantés ça et là dans la grise immensité sans
> commencement ni fin, leur insignifiance, leur petitesse
> même, hors de toute proportion avec le cadre où ils
> s'inscrivaient, leur conférant une sorte de grandeur
> insolite ... et les immemoriales histoires de barrières
> enfoncées, de bornes renversées, les immemoriales
> contraintes.[6]

Louise, turning these pages, witnesses not the spectacular events
of a tragic life but the very fabric of a banal day by day
existence. Such apparent insignicance is the best that man can,
and should, hope for. Alongside the images of decreptitude and

inevitable death encapsulated in the omnipresence of Marie is the
notion of negativity. She is described as a 'fragile amas d'os et
de chairs déssechées',[7] and as the symbol of death, the negation of
life, her life has amounted to nothing significant. Her gesture of
sacrifice for the education of her younger brother leads to the
total negation of her self, remaining celibate, virginal and
negating, therefore, the one principal life force: love. Her
negation of the forces of life is markedly contrasted with the
vital pulsation, the fecund luxuriance of the earth, the grass
itself of the novel's title, and also with the plenitude of the
surrounding autumnal landscape. The implications for this abrupt
contrast of Plenitude and Negativity will be discussed as a
structural phenomenon in the following section of this study.[8]

L'Herbe is the work which contains the most extensive references to
the inevitable shadow of death that hangs over the actions of men.
The image of death is contained in the physical decline of the
human body in time, the 'écrasante prison de chair'[9]. Man is a
prisoner of transcience and Marie's decrepit body is our constant
reminder. The smell of rotting fruit and vegetation are a symbolic
reinforcement of autumn, the season of death, a leitmotif which
Simon often exploits in his novels;[10] and this smell is always
related to the stench of rotting corpses. Le Palace contains a
pervasive image of rotting corpses in the sewers of Barcelona.
Finitude, transience, and the destructive workings of Time,
severely undermine any meaningful gesture towards purposeful action.
In this respect Simon offers us a totally bleak view of man and his
place in the universe. Such humanistic pessimism is intelligible
in contrast to the massive plenitude of nature and the dominance
of elemental forces over diminutive man.

Simon's novels are replete with gestures towards significant
action which are never allowed to transcend the theatrical, the
stereotyped. References abound throughout Simon's works to all
forms of theatre: tragedy, vaudeville, opera, music hall, circus,
cinema, carnival; but also to the more solemn, institutionalized
forms of masquerade where man is once again playing a role: weddings
and funerals. The most extensive example of the latter is the mock-
heroic 'Funérailles de Patrocle' chapter in Le Palace. Character
is frequently reduced to stereotypes: the surprised lovers feature
in both Le Vent (1957) and La Route des Flandres; and, in the latter,
de Reixach mimes the 'heroic' action of his ancestor in the face of
death, sword drawn in anachronistic defiance. Unreality and
anachronism are the dominant effects of the use of theatricalism
and stereotypes.[11] For such ceremony exaggerates gestures and
portrays a grotesque image of man who is reduced to a role-player
in a masque, a marionnette, and finally a mere shadow.[12] Man is
stripped of his individuality and often made to play a supporting
role as the mere symbol of an idea (De Reixach stands for futility;
Corinne is the symbol of Woman-as-sex-object in La Route des Flandres).
The types of action are limited to the staging of violent struggles,
death, or sexual coupling of various sorts. The frenetic and
furious action of love-making is always exaggerated[13] and obsessive in the
couples' apparent attempts to transcend the bounds of their solipsism and banality?
Often described as part of an old film where the movements of people
are jerky, fast and unreal, love-making becomes the derisory parody
of itself. Simon makes his point emphatically: all such desparate
action is merely an illusion, a camouflage for life's inexorable
movement towards death. Such spectacular theatricalism is strangely
and absurdly removed from banal quotidian existence, and this particularly pervasive mode of role-playing is ironized because, at best,

it is the mere illusion of action. Character is reduced to stereotype; and man reduced to mask. Experience is seen to reactualise
itself from generation to generation, especially the experience of
love-making. Man is void of any autonomy, as he is condemned to
reiterate, fatalistically, the hollow, futile actions of his
predecessors. The former student in Le Palace recognizes, finally,
that people change nothing substantial; there are few 'molecular
displacements', but as the American in that text frequently asserts,
'c'est ce que c'est': for, just like the Italian before him, so the
former revolutionary student mellows in time and resigns himself
to accept things as they are. The past invades the present, and
the result is one of deep irony as the futility of action is evident
later in the streets of Barcelona.

(ii)  Thematic Parameters

> La parodie dérisoire de gestes d'amour dans une
> pantomine furieuse - ou plutôt frénétique - et
> saccadée ... (Histoire)

> ... l'infranchissable épaisseur du temps (L'Herbe p.233)

The thematic consistency in Simon's work has been noted by many
commentators, and the image of man described above enables one
critic to conclude that, according to these novels:

> ... our actions are determined from outside ... our
> reason or wills are puny instruments when they are
> compared with the juggernaut of blind chance.[14]

Action is destroyed by Time and by Death.  The inevitability of
Man's growth and decline towards his total extinction and disintegration is contained in the successive phases of life
described in the formula, 'l'enfance, l'adolescence,et à la fin
l'inévitable décrépitude.'[15]  Man and the world are always in
process, irredeemably subject to transience.  Any attempt by man
to impose a fixity a stability on this ceaseless 'va-et-vient' will
always be fictitious.  This realization is not just intelligible
on a physical level, nor just in terms of action.  The attempt to
reconstruct the past is always a distortion, a fiction, as man
once again attempts to give order and meaning to his life.
Descriptions of the past are inadequate substitutes for the flux
of experience, and Simon's imagery encapsulates the problem:

> ... et plus tard il lui semblera les voir, immobilisés ou
> conservés comme sur une photographie, dans cette sorte de
> matière figée et grisâtre qu'est le temps passé, cette
> espèce de gélatine qui garde indéfiniment choses et gens
> comme dans de l'alcool, légèrement déformés sans doute ... [16]

Time is impossible to retain, and,in Le Vent, Montès suffers
nausea and terror as he senses the 'déchirante nostalgie du temps
s'écoulant, impossible à retenir, comme le sable, l'eau entre des
doigts d'enfants, s'enfuyant ...'[17]  Time in which man acts and
moves is itself 'impossible à mesurer'[18] although we are reminded of
Time's progress, its 'lent passage ..., lente et pendulaire
oscillation ...',[19] perceptible in the regularity of seasons, types of
fruits and the kind of purchases recorded in Marie's account books in
L'Herbe.  Time is also visible in its effects both on people - the
decrepit old woman remembered at the beginning of Histoire (1967);  the
dying Marie in L'Herbe  - and also on the world of nature (the stench
of rotting fruit, especially in L'Herbe) and the world of objects:
the dust and debris of Time is described in the opening of Leçon de

Choses (1975), where the fragments of a partially destroyed room
are covered '... de la même poussière blanchâtre.'[20] If Time is
only knowable in static, 'frozen' images, '... figés immoblisés
pour toujours,'[21] then it must be acknowledged that these images
are themselves at the mercy of Time's destructiveness. Not only
are photographs yellow with age, but also those statuesque figures
into which the lovers are transformed by the narrator in La
Bataille de Pharsale (1969) are characterized by their partial
disintegration ('le marbre érodé'[22]). The erosive force of Time
is seen to effect the very desperate attempts of memory to recall
the events, people and the aetiology of the past in relation to
the present. This process of imposing meaning, of interpreting
the past, is always seen to be at best an inadequate substitute.
In this respect, Georges' desperate self-interrogation which forms
the substance of the sinuous narrative of La Route des Flandres is
always doomed to failure, albeit because of the impossibility of
his ambitious quest. The text of his remembered fragments is always,
necessarily 'inachevé'. Memory is inadequate, and the thinking
Subject fills in the gaps with invented approximations. For, as
that novel so forcefully concludes, the failure of such a project
is apt witness to Time's entropic work:

> ... le monde arrêté figé s'effritant se dépiautant
> s'écroulant peu à peu par morceaux comme une bâtisse
> abandonnée, inutilisable, livrée à l'incohérent,
> nonchalant, impersonnel et destructeur travail du
> temps.[24]

It is in La Route des Flandres that a fully-fledged psychological
account of themes and formal idiosyncracies is first available.
The entropy of memory is rendered intelligible by reading the
narrative as evidence of the vagaries, the obsessions of a

narrating consciousness. The predominance of eroticism is
comprehensible in these terms.

The sex-act in Simon's works, and especially in <u>La Route des
Flandres</u>, is always explosive, violent, and totally engulfing.[25]
It is often described in terms of the defeat of Time and the
transcendence of self into other;  it is also the momentary death
of the isolated, solitary self.  The image of orgasm is
figuratively present in the following epigram from Malcolm de
Chazal which heads part three of the novel:

> La volupté, c'est l'étreinte d'un corps de mort par
> deux êtres vivants.  Le "cadavre" dans ce cas, c'est
> le temps assassiné pour un temps et rendu consubstantiel
> au toucher.[26]

The sexual climax    achieved by Georges and Corinne transforms
them into 'deux morts ... comme si nous avions un instant été
vidés tout entiers ... s'arrachant s'extirpant de nous de moi de
ma solitude se libérant ... sans fin nous inondant l'un l'autre sans fin n'y
avait pas de fin comme s'il ne devait plus jamais y avoir fin ... [27]
But this liberation from the solitude of self and from finitude
is but a fleeting illusion - 'mais ce n'était pas vrai:  un instant
seulement'[28] - a fraction of second in the guise of an eternity.
The violent act is often described in Simon's novels as the 'brusque
anéantissement', the 'foudroyant arrachement',[29] the 'courte mort',
the little death.  The transience of man and the world, the
ceasless 'va-et-vient' of process, the regressive role of time,
are transcended in the all-engulfing love-making described in
these novels.  Georges' obsessive descriptions of the female genitals
are also comprehensible through the determinism of a pervasive

psychology which may well be explained by his need to obtain total
knowledge of the past, of the possible promiscuous behaviour of
Corinne before and during the war, and by his hopes of achieving
this knowledge some years after the events through Corinne herself.
But the gaps in his memory and the doubts cast on the very sources
of his 'information' condemn this operation to inevitable failure.
The night spent with Corinne solves nothing and he is left with the
solitude of this meandering thoughts and inadequate speculations.
The desperation of his quest for 'truth' is reflected in his
obsessive concern with the physical reality of Corinne's body,
partly as a substitute for the unavailability of her thoughts.
The unknowability of other minds is only fleeting transcended
in the moment of abrupt self-annihilation, the 'courte mort'
of sexual climax.

By organizing the anomalous text as evidence of the vagaries of a
personalized narrative consciousness, the critic is able to
comprehend in a novel like La Route des Flandres the prodigious
and unyielding presence of solitude. Simon's novels up to and
including Histoire (1967) are all characterized by such a
pervasive sense of solitude, a factor which enables an explanation
of the massive accumulation of words, synonyms, approximate
expressions, and similes which attempt to describe what amounts
to the ineffable, in terms of a bid by the narrating Subject to
exceed the bounds of his own isolated thoughts. The interminable
'parole exigeante'[30] of Georges' narrative in La Route des Flandres
fills the silence of his long night in the hotel bedroom as he lies
next to Corinne. The pervasive image of a child whistling in the
dark to mitigate the fear of loneliness is the precise analogy of

Georges and his 'voix solitaire s'obstinant'[31], continuously
filling the void of a dead past, because for him also, 'rien
n'est pire que le silence'.[32] Psychological explanation recuperates
an unconventional narrative text by accounting for it in terms of
the Subject's obsessions and apparent aberrations.  This leads us to the
point where we can begin to understand the idea of the self in Simon's work.

(iii)  The Problematic of the Self

> ... ce n'est pas souvent que l'on arrive à sortir
> de soi (La Corde Raide p.20)

In La Route des Flandres, the reader is allowed certain privileged
moments of insight into a more normative, realist, level of
plausible explanation of the narrative.  Georges is described with
'une femme à côté de lui',[33] in the dark and silent night, sleep-
lessly attempting to recall the faded and confused memories of
'des années mortes'.[34] The past invades the present and the reader
is offered a mode of recuperation of a manifestly 'strange' and
difficult text at the level of psychological realism.  Georges'
narrative is seen then as a quest for lost time, a search to discover and constitute a self.  The digressions, the fragmentariness,
the doubts, the obsessive repetitions are all intelligible as part
of the narrating Subject's anxiety to re-discover the past and to
find the self in that past.  The dense and sinuous form of such a
narrative was first clearly demonstrated in Le Vent (1957).

In this novel the narrator is more clearly personalized, and levels of
plausibility are more readily available to the reader.  The narrator
is seen to attempt to construct a logical, sequential story around

the events concerning Montès, a strange, innocent character who
has come to a windswept south-western French town, apparently to
claim the estate of his dead father.  But  the attempts at
narrative continuity are broken, 'because of a perpetual
vacillation in the mind of the narrator.'[35]  Traditional sources
for retelling the events are available in local gossip, hearsay,
and eye-witness accounts.  A major supply of information comes
from  the Notary, but he is particularly unreliable, because of
his limited view of people.[36]  In fact, the unreliability of the
available sources of information for the collating narrator allows
him in the end to produce no more than a approximate logic grounded
in a 'connaissance fragmentaire, incomplète.'[37]  The endeavour to
gain knowledge of Montès is always frustrated and the resultant
'portrait' inevitably fragmentary.  A potential realist-project, a
logical, sequential narrative grounded in the knowability of other
minds by an omniscient narrator, breaks down at its most fundamental
level:  knowledge of other minds is seen to be impossible.  On the
very first page of the novel, the fictional result of such a quest
is clearly indicated in the  words 'raconter', 'inventer' and
'essayer de déduire ou d'expliquer'.


The quest for the knowledge of other minds in Simon's novels may
well be his most radical and fundamental critique of the basis on
which conventional Realism is grounded.  To tell the story of what
happened to someone in the past, to outline their thoughts, motives
and the causes and effects of their relationships to other people
relies on the a priori belief (or at least the suspension of
disbelief), in the knowledge of other minds.  The narrator in
Le Vent, together with Louise in L'Herbe and Georges in La Route

des Flandres, each attempt to construct a conventional story
about the events concerning someone in the past, and the strangely
dislocative narratives which result from these attempts are
evidence of their failure.

The failure which Georges's narrative constantly acknowledges is
also a manifestation of his atrophied struggle to transcend his
solipsism.  What Simon characterized in an earlier text as
'le bruit de sa voix dans le silence de sa solitude',[38] is an
appropriate comment on the situation of the narrating Subject,
understood as a personalized psychological entity.  The question
often arises: how is it possible to constitute an identity in
narrative form, through words, which exist  prior to the writing
activity, when all knowledge of the past by the perceiving Subject
can never be more than a fictional construct, an illusionary and
approximate recreation? As each event dies with the moment, so
the self is never completely knowable, as it is always an absence,
never a stable presence available to the reflecting consciousness:

> Moi qui ne suis jamais le même pendant dix minutes à
> la file, moi qui ne suis pas le même pendant la durée
> d'un millième de seconde, puisque je ne suis pas moi'[39]

If the principal modes of knowledge of the self are personal
memory and other minds and self-consciousness,[40] then Simon's
novels provide  ample evidence of the unknowability of the self in
any more than a fragmentary, and possibly a fictional, form.

La Route des Flandres, Le Palace, and Histoire are dominated by the

near frantic endeavours of an isolated thinking Subject to reach
back into the past and to relieve the oppressive burden of this
isolation in the present. Such a motivation for narrative is made
plausible most persuasively in <u>Histoire</u> where the narrator appears
to have been recently estranged from his wife, who may or may not
have committed suicide, and where, consequently, a process of
self-censorship seems to operate at moments when she erupts into
his memory. The desperate, anxious interrogation of the past in
this protracted instance is thus explained as an immense compensation for an overwhelming sadness. The narrator is hypersensitive
to the 'silence s'écrasant dans l'éternelle obscurité.'[41] The
flow of words often reaches a frenzied pitch in his need for the
consolation and presence of the Other as a confirmation of self:

> Mais moi aussi moi aussi tu le sais moi aussi
> est-ce que tu ne le sais pas moi aussi moi aussi...[42]

The torrent of words must never cease because of the fear of
silence and solitude. The act of narrating is a desperate reaching
back to fill this emptiness in the present with the eventful
activities of the partly imagined life of his mother and her
fiancé prior to their marriage. The post-cards found in an old
trunk are the apparent source of such recreation. But words are
seen to be inadequate in such a representational role:

> ...disant ou essayant de dire et plus que dire
> persuader mais comment peut-on? [43]

In the 'foudroyant discontinuité' of memory and imagined incident,
the narrative sequence follows a logic of its own through the
digressive association of words, the perpetual 'va-et-vient' of
repetition, and this results in the apparent effacing of the self.
As the epigram from Rilke which heads Histoire suggests, the
attempts to organize, to give meaningful order to the chaos and
enormity of the past, will only in the end serve to dissolve the
organizer in its confusion. The best that the narrator can hope
for is the imagined 'pre-uterine' self envisaged in the last lines
of this text. Significantly, that self is also in doubt.

We are now in a position to indicate the wider implications of the
self-problematic in Simon's work. If the narrative is organized
as evidence of a narrating Subject, and that Subject is therefore
seen to be engaged in attempting to construct a normative narrative
logic, then at the centre of these texts is the image of the
writer himself working in total isolation with only the bounds of
his own consciousness as source for his 'story'. A recent analysis
of Le Palace by Loubère will serve to endorse the claims for this
type of reading of Simon's novels. In Le Palace, the urgent
exploration through language by the former student of the events
in Barcelona during the revolutionary days in the Spanish Civil
War is partly motivated by the disturbing search for otherness which
the novelist needs, especially on the level of characterization.
It is also an exploration of the possibilities of writing History,
retelling the events of the past and their effect on the former
student's self. On a very basic level, the narrator wishes to
discover the link between himself and the others in his past, and
then to integrate the total experience into the coherent order of

of a conventional story, with characters clearly defined, events
described, and causes related to effects. Coherent sense may
then be given to the chaos of History. He tries, therefore, to
distinguish in his interrogation a world of objects which bear
the mark of gradual change (focused principally on the Grand Hotel
of the novel's title); characters who have retold experiences of
their past to him; an actual historical event; another more
elusive character who may have made prophetic statements about the
meaninglessness of purposive action; and finally a past self which is
clearly separable and estranged from his 'present' self. All these
aspects of otherness, the disparate elements of the past, must be
fused into the one narrating consciousness in order to make coherent
sense. But historical action and historiography are vastly removed
from each other. Close involvement with an event may well, and
often does, produce a fragmented and confused version of what
happened. The reconstruction some years after the event can only
produce further distortion. The most pervasive example in Le Palace
is the story by 'l'homme-fusil' about a murder in a Parisian cafe
where the actual event is described in minute detail, causing an
elongation of time - the act itself only taking 'une fraction de
seconde'. The complexity of the event is reduced by this particular
storyteller to a schematic, but roughly sketched out, pencil drawing
where the exactness of detail and the necessary simplifications of
the scheme constantly appear to struggle against each other in what
must be the mirror image of the novelist's paradoxical, and
impossible, enterprise. For this is the difficulty facing any
'storyteller' (both the writer of History and the novelist): to
represent a world other than, and pre-existent to, the consciousness
of the writer, is seen to be an impossible project. The perpetual

and imperceptible change (flux) of the world (a constant theme
in Simon's work) will ensure that our possible knowledge of
the world now, coupled with our blurred and faulty recollection
of the world then, will always render the past unknowable, except
in its speculative and confused reconstruction.


The questions raised in Le Palace, in more explicit terms than
in the preceeding novels, indicate a problematic of the self:
'How can a single consciousness reconcile its subjectivity with
that of others?  How can it be one with itself?'[44]  The conclusions
in this novel are lessons already perceived in Simon's work, and
ones which must be fundamental to the significance of his
interrogation of novelistic form.  For as Loubère concludes:


> The student, who continually attempts to discover his
> place with regard to others and in the world, fails in
> his quest because his consciousness, while perpetually
> turning inward upon itself, never reaches the still
> point of total solipsism.  It is neither engaged in the
> true dialectics of Self and Other, nor blessed with the
> "absolute density which would free it from time"[45]


The novelists anxiety is clearly outlined:  'can he play the
roles of Ego and Alter without annihilating Self?'[46]  Here Simon
is undermining the whole aesthetic foundation of the conventional
Realist novel.  Can the novelist pretend to describe the Other
from the outside reducing man to a schematized version?  Or,
conversely, can he claim knowledge of other minds in an intimately
intersubjective realism.  Georges's anxious cries of 'comment
savoir?  Comment savoir?' indicate the epistemological difficulties
which will undermine this quest for truth.  Can these potentially

autobiographical narratives finally reconstitute any truth
other than their ultimate failure to satisfy the demands of a
realist aesthetic? Can the principal medium of representation,
the self, be a source of order and knowledge? Le Palace may well
be interpreted as the final comment by Simon about the impossibility
of retaining the traditional structures of the realist novel on
philosophical grounds. Subsequent novels move further away from
the use of personalized narrative Subjects as possible sources for
identifying textual idiosyncracies.

(iv) The Epistemological Status of Narrative Texts

> Si le roman du xix$^e$ siècle était un roman de savoir, le
> roman moderne est essentiellement un roman de non-savoir[47]

In the novels considered above, if there was to be any substantially
constituted self, then it would be understood as the sum of its
past. But, the argument continues, that past is never knowable,
only fictional, therefore the self is unknowable. The Other is
equally unknowable, if only because it seems impossible for the
narrating Subject to ever distinguish otherness from self. Selves,
in the form of a gesture towards normative characterization, are
never clearly set apart from the apparently confused thoughts of
the narrator. The former student in Le Palace demonstrates the
claim that we have no knowledge of other people beyond our
recollection of our observations. In this respect, other people
are part of ourselves. This realization frustrates the former
student's quest:

> ... l'Américain, l'Italien et l'étudiant - ou plutôt
> ces trois parties, ces trois fragments de lui-même
> qui étaient un Américain, un homme-fusil et un jeune
> étourneau. . .[48]

Those works of Claude Simon which I have considered in this
chapter evince a profound epistemological doubt.  From the
ultimately disappointed endeavour of the narrator in Le Vent to
collate the evidence about Montès from all the unreliable sources
available, to the reliance, in La Route des Flandres, on the
single consciousness as a source of knowledge, the result has
always confirmed the thesis that any such attempts to go beyond
the approximate and the speculative to the positive assertions
and gnomic statements of the conventional Realist novel must
always fail.  Memory is often described figuratively as a badly
synchronized, old film, because as these novels imply:

> ... le propre de la réalité est de nous paraître
> irréelle, incohérente, du fait qu'elle se présente
> comme un perpétuel défi à la logique.[49]

The epistemological problem is evident through a psychological
interpretation of form.  The anxieties of retelling the past are
dramatized in the text by the perpetual questioning of the results
of such dispersed and fragmented reconstitution;  by the often
reiterated 'comment savoir?  Comment était-ce?'[50]  Also one could
mention the vexatious eruptions into the text of 'exactement', which
is always undermined by the proliferation of 'peut-être', and the
'as if' of simile with its never ending digressions;  and, finally by
the whole text continually, and perversely, indicating its own
artificiality.  The frantic demands for omniscience, total
subjective knowledge of other minds, and

a totality of viewpoints, is for Georges in La Route des Flandres
the need  to be 'derrière la haie le regardant s'avancer'[51] as
the German machine-gunner plans the death of De Reixach:


> ... l'oeil immobile et attentif de son assassin patient
> l'index sur la détente voyant pour ainsi dire l'envers
> de ce que je pouvais voir ou moi l'envers et lui l'endroit
> c'est-à-dire qu'à nous deux moi le suivant et l'autre le
> regardant s'avancer nous possédions la totalité de l'énigme
> (l'assasin sachant ce qui allait lui arriver et moi sachant
> ce qui lui était arrivé, c'est-à-dire après et avant ...)
> ... comme ce qui allait se passer dans cette espèce de néant
> (comme on dit qu'au centre d'un typhon il existe une zone
> parfaitement calme) de la connaissance, de point zéro:  il
> lui aurait fallu une glace à plusieurs face ...[52]


The perpetual undermining of the stable narrative is intelligible
on the epistemological level as a general questioning of realist
narrative structure and normative characterization, grounded in
the Cartesian model of man as thinking Subject and giver of sense
and order to the world.  The lessons of Le Vent and L'Herbe
demonstrate that Simon's initial concerns are:


> ... the possibility of truth in place of mere verisimilitude
> in narrating, the ambiguousness of consciousness and memory,
> the questionable reliability of evidence from oneself and
> others, and the workings of time.[53]


From these earlier novels there is already an explicit rejection
of the traditional, carefully constructed story, 'dependent on
psychological "truth" and traditional links between cause and
effect.'[54] La Route des Flandres, Le Palace and Histoire
internalize the problem of form more rigorously, as narrative
attempts, and necessarily fails, to give order to the general
fragmentation of Being.  The baroque structure of these novels

is made intelligible through its echoing of the 'transience
of being', and this will be discussed in the following section
of this study.

The formal manifestations of extreme epistemological 'dispersion'
undermine the 'old stable ego' of character. The 'merveilleuse
illusion' of a coherent character in our conventional sense has
always relied on an equally coherent model of man in which to
ground it. But if man is visible in Simon's work, he is only a
reduced, theatrical stereotype, viewed from the outside, never
really knowable. Action is reduced to recollection, which itself
is fragmented and cast in doubt. The traditional Subject of realist
literature,the coherent and knowable character, is denied centrality
in the work of Simon. As Simon would claim, man, the self, and
other minds are all epistemologically unproblematic concepts in
the conventional novel of realism, because they all enable the
incontrovertible representation of reality. The novels discussed
above are profound interrogations of the properties of such a
convention, and finally these novels move towards an effacement
of the person as a totally knowable entity predominantly through
undermining the epistemic status of the narrating Subject. Once
this epistemological problematic has been clearly formulated,
then Simon's works (after Histoire) are no longer wholly intelligible
through a subjective relativism. The reader is denied recourse
to psychological explanation. The Simonian narrator undergoes
progressive transformation from the personalized grammar school
teacher of Le Vent, through the 'confusions' of the 'il' and 'je'
points of view in La Route des Flandres, to the unnamed voice of
loneliness in Histoire. Narrative perspective is reduced to the
'O' ('observateur'?) of La Bataille de Pharsale (1969) and to the

eye through which we observe works of representational art in
<u>Les Corps Conducteurs</u> (1971). By this stage the Simon novel has
been finally 'stripped of its original trappings ... and the
"weave laid bare"...; it has been liberated from a fixed
epistemology.'[55] Once Simon has demonstrated the inadequacies
of the Subject-centred narrative with its coherent characters[56]
and its impossible causality, then he is able to concentrate his
efforts on language as a source of structure and as a representation of its own generative powers (the beginnings of which are
seen in the erotic play on words as narrative linkages in
<u>La Route des Flandres</u>, for instance; I shall return to this
below.) By analyzing the problem of structure in the following
section of this study, it will be seen precisely how the
epistemological 'dispersion' which characterizes Simon's texts
works in detail. This will require a more formalistic mode of
analysis.

## Conclusion

Fowles's attempts to understand the self stem initially from his
specific assumptions about the nature of post-war society, and
about the place of man in it. The antagonistic relationship
between the Few and the Many, which The Aristos outlined, is
dramatized on the level of social class distinctions and their
cultural and intellectual implications, in The Collector. The
fundamental 'calibanity' of man is supposed to be transcended,
as selfish middle-class protagonists are taught to perceive the
possibility for authenticity in the stereotyping system of society.
The highpoint of self-understanding is always prefigured in the
status and role of the responsible artist himself. He it is who
perceives life behind the social mask, genuine feeling behind the
polite facade. But with The Magus, Fowles demonstrates the
complexity of the identity crisis, as he embodies thoughts about
the problematic status of the self. Characters journey towards
states of self-knowledge, and on the way, they encounter that
vexatious situation often analyzed by modern sociology: whether
a substantial, knowable self exists prior to the social personae
which constitute a man's identity. Even given that the wiser
protagonist realizes that the true self is not the mask, can that
self be truly knowable? Art and literature may help us to understand the world, and even to encourage introspection, but can they
really belie the anxiety of establishing authentic identity?
Fictionality has been an abiding concern in Fowles's work and
this extends to a critique of both literature and society. For
when the masks are peeled away, and a self laid bare, that identity
may well still be only another fiction. But for Fowles, the

existential humanist, man must strive towards self-knowledge in
order always to stand against the stereotyping nature of the
social system. Daniel Martin offers a solution to the problems
as the beleaguered protagonist retreats finally into a private
domain, thus acknowledging the essential loneliness of man in his
quest for the self.

John Hawkes founds his mode of characterization in an image of
man as the victim of a desolate and destructive world. More
especially in the earlier works, the apparent collapse of a
rational social order and its normative morality is seen to be
the direct effect of war. But this bleak worldview, symbolically
encapsulated in the images of decayed landscapes, is the back-
cloth for the confrontation between the violent unconscious desires
of solitary beings and the destructive potential inherent in the
larger spheres of the 'visible world'. Man's relationship to the
constrictions of social conventions is given a Freudian diagnosis:
the old, rational, stable ego is seen to collapse under the
pressures caused by the repressive forces from the hostile Other
and from society itself. Once these assumptions about society
and the further assumptions about the nature of man are established,
then Hawkes's later works focus the problems more sharply on a
single consciousness. Here, narrators, exploiting the rhetoric
of narrative as a mode of self-revelation, attempt to repair their
damaged identity, often within the confines of their own imaginations.
These 'psychic invalids' confront their own meaninglessness. The
more recent works substantiate the claim that every man is an
island, so to speak, 'inaccessible, drifting apart, thirsting to
be explored.'[1] Man's fundamental limitations are prefigured in
the bounds of his solipsism. As these narrators are portraits of

the writer, they also bear out Hawkes's claim that the true
sources of 'fiction' lie buried in some inaccessible depth of
the psyche.  Herein lies a fundamental paradox:  narratives
which are grounded in psychological self-revelation emphasize
both the bounds of the single consciousness searching for self-
definition, and also the impossibility of ever transcending
those bounds.  Hawkes's protagonists encapsulate those acute
modern anxieties: the unknowability of the self, and the need to
accept the separateness and inaccessibility of other minds.  In
such psychoanalytical studies, and especially in the first-person
narratives, Hawkes had discerned a basis for form, albeit
perpetually and intentionally tentative, and the reader has been
offered a persistent mode of recuperation through the interplay of
psychology and form.


The view of man and society, in the works of Claude Simon considered
above, is characterized by its humanistic pessimism.  Action
produces derisory results;  man is a diminutive role-player who
can have no lasting effect on History.  Idealism and heroism are
cynically undermined;  the lessons of History are continually
ignored as a new generation repeats the futile gestures of its
predecessors.  Man is fragile, alone, insignificant, and subject
to transience.  Time dominates his every action; its effect abounds
in the surrounding world.  Time is the harbinger of ceaseless
destruction, and of man's imperceptible movement towards decrepitude
and death.  The sex-act always momentarily allows the illusion of
stasis, the postponement of flux.  It also offers the isolated
consciousness the myth of communion with Others, before returning
to a state of lonely isolation.  In his bid to withold a fragmenting
identity, man looks to the past, but discovers that time erodes

memory. All that remains is distorted and fragmentary. But, for Claude Simon, this entropy of knowledge rehearses a philosophical critique of the conventional bases of literary realism. The self is as unknowable as the past from which narrators attempt to reconstitute it. Other minds are inaccessible if only because other and self, I and not-I, are apparently indistiguishable for the narrating consciousness. The dislocations of narrative form, its hypothetical status, reflect this problematic of the self. The question implicitly posed by these texts is, what can narrative legitimately (philosophically) and meaningfully constitute? If man as a giver of sense and order is epistemologically undermined, then how can an explicit thinking Subject be the reliable source of an intelligible narrative text? If coherent characters need to be grounded in coherent, stable models of man, then the conventional parameters through which we understand the concept of character and its basis in our knowledge of persons is being questioned in these works. Once the epistemological problem has been evoked, Simon's more recent novels are apparently able to offer different sources of narration. This will be discussed in the following section of this study.

As the works by Fowles, Hawkes and Simon discussed above clearly demonstrate, sources of narrative are comprehensible in terms of assumptions about the world and about the nature of man. If, as I have argued, our understanding of literature in part relies on our knowledge of the world and our available models of persons, then these three writers go some way towards embodying such crisis-laden discourse into the very form of the novel. The crisis of identity which has progressively fragmented the old stable ego of

character in the twentieth century, is articulated variously in these
works.    The ideas which have concerned the philosophy of social
science and psychology, and which I outlined briefly in the introduction above, also preoccupy Fowles, Hawkes and Simon.    The concept
of the self has become problematical, and the three writers respond
within given systems of thought which differentiate their works.
Although questions of the self, other minds, and the knowledge of the
world are common to all three writers, they differ radically in the
conclusions reached, the systems of thought found most persuasive,
and the overall implications for the aesthetics of the novel.    Fowles's
qualified optimism about man's ability to attain an ideal model of
himself, to relate to others, and to act meaningfully in society is
largely conditioned by his existentialist mode of understanding.    The
fundamental realism of his novels is not unrelated to the traditions
of thought in which he works.    His notion of the self, and his belief
in a degree of character in the novel, is in effect enabled by his
realist aesthetics.    The realist tradition in the English novel and
its liberal humanism reaches a highpoint of sophistication and self-
consciousness in the work of John Fowles.    Hawkes and Simon both
confront questions of irrationality, and produce a more pessimistic
and disquieting view of the world.    Equally, their works stem from
different national traditions, and the cognitive aspects of these
texts relate to different modes of explanation.    This will be elaborated
in subsequent chapters.    Hawkes's critique of conventions of writing
tests the bounds of realism, while remaining within its scope.
Simon, more obviously, adheres to that tradition which refuses the
primacy of the Subject as a source of knowledge and order.    His
concern with the relationship between epistemology and rhetoric
derives from a tradition which may well stem from Mallarmé and
Proust, and find its contemporary proponents in French structuralism
and French experimental literary fiction.

If, as Lowenthal has claimed, 'it is the task of the sociologist of literature to relate the experience of the writers' imaginary characters and situations to the historical climate from which they derive,'[2] then it must also be clearly acknowledged that, although the cognitive foundations of characters and worldview relate these writers to their contemporary world, they may well, and often do, engage in conflicting systems of thought which presuppose antithetical assumptions about precisely what the novel may be today:

> The intellectual foundation of every human society is a generally accepted model of reality. One of the major intellectual difficulties of human existence is, I think, due to the fact that this model of reality is in every single case a mere interpretation of the world, and yet exerts as long as it seems the valid interpretation the subtly compelling claim to being accepted as the only true picture of the universe, indeed as truth itself. This difficulty, manifesting itself in the deeper strata of doubt, by which, at all times, certain intellectually sensitive men have been affected, develops easily into a mental epidemic in epochs in which a certain model of reality crumbles and collapses. It seems that we have lived in such an epoch for a long time.[3]

PART TWO : <u>Narrative Structure and the possibility of</u>
<u>formalistic analysis</u>

Thus, the need for a more comprehensive historical-
structural angle of reference becomes apparent.
To reinstate the contexts in their reciprocal relations
with the achieved art work is to ask the larger question
of function;  it is finally to correlate the function of
technique to the social and individual quality of consciousness.  The resulting concepts of structure are as
dynamic and as wide as the functioning correlations of
literature and society that they reflect and promote.
Again, the concept of structure is as meaningful as the
contextual sphere of relationships in which the structure
potentially functions.

Robert Weimann

## INTRODUCTION

### (i)  The 'logique du récit' thesis

If the cognitive content of a narrative derives its particular
intelligibility from the structure of that work, then the critic's
task is to formulate a descriptive analysis of that structure in
order to specify the conditions through which meaning is indeed
realized.   The critic could either transform the narrative into a
more schematized version which would explain its internal relationships and the functions of its constitutive parts, or he could
analyze structure as a function of reading, the manner by which the
reader perceives narrative and 'structurates' it.   I shall discuss
this second process below.   The schematic analysis has been central
to what I shall call the 'logique du récit' thesis (leaving the
expression in French to give it a specific status and to differentiate it from my central argument about the logic of narrative —
the reading of character, structure and self-consciousness in the
post-Modernist novel).   Such a methodology is clearly exemplified
in the French structural analysis of narrative.[1]

It is the intention of this introduction to offer a critical account
of some prominent methodological issues in the formal analysis of
structure in narrative fiction.   The two most salient and apparently
contradictory methodologies are those which derive from French
structuralism and from Anglo-American literary criticism.   The
'logique du récit' thesis stands against 'point of view' analysis.
The comparative analysis of these two approaches will enable us to
indicate the possibilities for formalistic analysis of the novel.
The three subsequent chapters in this section of the study will
investigate precisely to what extent such formalistic methodologies

enable the works of Fowles, Hawkes, and Simon to be understood.
Are texts intelligible purely through a description of a set of
functional properties and internal relations?  Or, does the reader
rely necessarily on the transcendence of the text, its sets of
relationships with the world?  The wider implications of my
conclusions will be seen to be related to the bounds of any given
novel's intrinsic aesthetic and ideological presuppositions.

A 'structural attitude' to the novel would be based on the assumption
that  'a prose fiction text is a certain kind of (abstract) object
whose nature can be specified in terms of its elements and their
interrelationships.'[2]   In general, the structural analysis focuses
on the text as a given object.  Understanding the formal constraints
on narrative order is crucial for the intelligibility of a work.  In
this respect, the avowed aim of the French structural analysis of
narrative is to evolve a metacritical account of the conditions of
meaning.  An abstract, schematized version of structural relations
would thus enable the reader to understand not only how parts of
narrative relate to the totality of the compositional phenomenon,
but precisely how meaning is made available.  When describing the
structure of a narrative text, the implicit mode of intelligibility
contains in itself a particular theory of narrative.  The structural
analysis seeks out a 'logique du récit' which informs the sequentiality of the work.  Intention is partially concealed in the relationships of the parts to the end, and this may be perceived and made
sense of teleologically.  The reader's apprehension of coherence is
apparently constrained by a rational scepticism which, according to
Kermode, demands a satisfying 'concordance of beginning, middle and
end which is the essence of our explanatory fictions,'[3] a practice

commensurable with the day to day explanation of the world, whereby
fictions are concordant modes of accounting.  This daily practice
of explanation is analogous to the process of narrative where time
and contingency are perceived in their organization into logical
structures.  As Kermode explains, 'this is the time of the novelist,
a transformation of mere successiveness,' into significant moments
of crisis.[4]  Thus, the process of formulating structure is cotemp-
oraneous with the imposition of meaning on time and contingency.

If coherence is attained through the analysis of structure, then
even in more complex narratives meaning is delimited by the narrative
order, and by the order formulated by the reader.  As Barthes rightly
claims, the reader, guided by the formal constraints of meaning, does
not make sense in any way he chooses.[5]  Because of logical, sequential
constraints imposed by the shape of the book, its typography, on the
reading of its contents from beginning to end, all written narratives
have a look of completion about them, 'they have afixation on the
eidetic imagery of beginning, middle, and end, potency and cause.'[6]
The question then arises:  to what extent is the description and
analysis of the intelligibility of a work a description of a
narrative logic?  In order to go some way towards formulating an
answer, I shall initially turn to the work of Barthes and the French
structural analysis of narrative which directly concerns this question.

Given the primary assumption that narrative consists of a structure
of meanings, the structuralist activity is grounded in an explicit
investigation of the organizational categories and universal properties of the narrative text, itself defined as an intentional system
of signs.  If that text is a system of relationships where units of
meaning contribute to the intelligibility of other units and of the

narratives a certain ambiguity is often built into the text based
on the apparently intentional confusion between temporal sequence
and logical outcome.   The reader, under the coercions of his rational
scepticism, dechronologizes the narrative continuum and effects an
explanation within the realm of a particular logic.   The task is
to reach the point where the apparent chronology is given a structural
description, no matter how dislocative it may be.   Narrative logic
and the implicit intention of the text is therefore fundamental to
the intelligibility of structure.   The French structural analysis
wishes to offer a methodology which could outline precisely how
these conditions of meaning function.

The second level of description is that of action.   I have discussed
the limitations of the actantial theory of character in part One
above.   This need not be reiterated here.   Spheres of action are
seen to function as constitutive units of structure.   While this
enables a certain methodological consistency, it could never account
for more complex motives of behaviour, nor the more complex psychology
in sophisticated novels.   The third level of description, however,
remains within the bounds of the pragmatic analysis of visible
phenomena, and it also encompasses the other levels.   Narration is
the process of exchange enacted by giver and recipient which founds
the communicative cycle.   At this level the language model is an
effective analogy, especially when the text is organized as a speech
act.

The structural analysis aims to go only as far as the level of
narration permits.   To construct a typology on this basis is to
segment the text into its component units, and then to re-integrate
them through an available structural logic fundamental to its mode

of articulation. Two principal components facilitate this type
of analysis: _Histoire_, or story, and _Discours_, or narration itself.
The story-element evokes a possible 'world' which may refer directly
to the reader's own social world (particularly in mimetic narrative),
and that story is related by a narrator to the reader. At this
second level, it is not so much the reported events which matter
but rather the manner by which that knowledge is made available.
What classical rhetoric termed _inventio_ and _dispositio_, the French
structuralists understood as only separable for the purposes of
analysis. _Histoire_ and _Discours_ are interconnecting parts of the
compositional phenomenon. Barthes encapsulates this process of
structural enquiry with the example of the _catalyst_ where often
narrative sequences are reducible to _kernels_ (noyaux) from which a
logical hierarchy of sequence may be deduced. The total narrative
syntagme is reducible to component units which function in the
progression of narrative, and thus the reader is apparently able to
recuperate the intentional logic of the text.[11]

Structure, then, is defined through the _a priori_ assumption that
narrative functions logically, grounded in a hierarchical system
of kernels, for instance, whereby all the parts are accountable
through their relationship to the end. Functional units cohere
through, and the intention of the narration is understood by, the
prominance of the _catalyst_. The aspect of time is indicative of
the very complexity of narrative acknowledged in the process of
integration which enables the effective production of meaning. In
this way, the questions of succession and discontinuity, of predictions,
and repetitions are all crucial elements of textual coherence. As
Barthes himself suggests, like any architectural construction the

final object can consist of an infinity of simple elements related
to a complex whole, or a more fragmented structure consisting of an
incessant play of potentials.

At its most effective and elusive, narrative is seen to be an
enigmatic process of gradual revelation.   Its hold on the reader
is therefore commensurable with the relationship of Histoire to
Discours.   Barthes's S/Z develops this notion.   He concludes his
introduction to the 'analyse structurale du récit' by suggesting
another use for the language model.   For our knowledge of language
may tell us that narrative is apparently co-temporaneous with monologue
while it seems that the process of creation is posterior to dialogue.
If narrative is to be understood in terms of the activity of reading,
and this in turn related to literature as a given institution, then
the structural analysis needs to be relocated in History.   S/Z
appears to transcend the formalistic, synchronic bounds of the 'analyse
structurale'.   In his analysis of Sarrasine, Barthes produces a more
thoroughgoing methodology, relating the text to its underlying
cultural and literary paradigms.   His codal model acknowledges the
historicity of narrative.

The principal claim of the structural analysis of narrative is that
narrative structure is perceivable and intelligible by describing
and making sense of the 'logique du récit'.   Such an intrinsic form
of literary criticism has one fundamental flaw.   According to
Weimann:  the notion of structure is divorced from 'genesis', in a
wider transcendent context, and from 'effect'.   The aesthetic mode
and the underlying weltanschauung should never be divorced.   The
historical world of both reader and author are crucial.   Weimann's
thesis stands as a critique of such formalist literary criticism:

> the structure of literature is correlated with
> its function in society and this correlation
> deserves to be studied in terms of both 'genesis'
> and 'impact'.[12]

The word 'structure' for Weimann, denotes, 'the art work's verbal

and conceptual modes of organization.'[13]   It is on the basis of

the need for the historical interpretation of literature that

Weimann rejects the structural analysis.   For him the analogy with

Structural Functionalism in American sociology is pervasive.

Weimann's critique of structuralism, and its reduction of the

relationship between signifié and signifiant to functional qualities,

is justified.   But one must reject his wholesale tirade against the

work of Barthes.   For, despite the formalism, and the ahistorical,

pragmatic nature of the structural analysis, Barthes's S/Z (1970)

is precisely a relocation of narrative structure in the historicity

of social Praxis.   Creation for Barthes, as well as for Weimann,

is indeed an historical category.   Weimann's critique, encapsulated

in the following words, I would claim, remains as an adequate

description of S/Z itself.   For  the antihumanism of a structuralist

ideology (noted in Part One of this study in connection with the

Subject), for Weimann, opposes a theory,

> in which the dialectical relationship of literature
> and society and the interaction of creation and
> reception provide the basis for literature becoming
> history.[14]

Weimann seems to ignore the fundamental differences between the

structuralism of the introduction to the 'analyse structurale du

récit' (1966), and the more pervasive semiological methodology of

S/Z (1970).   Ironically, it is Weimann who acknowledges the influence

of Saussure on such a methodology, whereby, the nature of the sign
is defined 'more comprehensively by turning it into an object of
epistemological analysis.'[15]   He omits any reference to Barthes's
considerable achievement in S/Z.   I shall now briefly discuss
this work in order to assess precisely how far Barthes has extended
the foreclosing limits of formalistic literary criticism to incor-
porate the more historicist approach.

Understanding the conditions of meaning in any text may not only
lead to a hypothetical typology (the 'logique du récit', for instance),
but may also serve to discover what Gérard Genette has called the
strange, artificial, and problematical aspect of narrative.[16]   In
S/Z, Barthes has attempted a type of exposition on the text of Balzac's
story, Sarrasine, which begins with the separation of two levels of
narrative discourse.   The surface level of the narrative denotes
a certain structure of events and actions which are then only fully
coherent when the level of connotation is made explicit by the critic.
That is to say that Barthes aims to expose the ideological content
which is normally hidden beneath the conotative surface and which
gives the structure an historical coherence.

S/Z has been described as a 'sustained yet pulverized meditation on
reading.'[17]   At the outset, Barthes draws attention to the distinction
he wishes to make between two types of reading, the one founded in
the 'classical' text through which the reader becomes a more passive
consumer of the text, itself a finished product, the other founded
in the 'modern' text which relies on the reader to produce the text,
itself intentionally 'unfinished', indeterminate.   He coins the
terms, 'lisible' for the former and 'scriptible' for the latter (I
shall not attempt to translate these terms in order to maintain a

certain definitional clarity).  In the 'modern' limit-text the
model of _production_ is critically antithetical to the more traditional model of _representation_ (Mimesis).   Barthes is not offering
a prescription for modern writing as such, for no text could be
entirely 'scriptible' without being incoherent, given our models of
coherence;  rather, he aims to suggest an extreme, radical position
through which the historical differentiation of a 'modern' text
may be indicated in opposition to the traditional notion of
representation.   This theory of literature marks a certain stage of
critical awareness of precisely those procedures through which meaning
is produced in the practice of writing itself.   It remains to be
seen, subsequently, to what extent the works of Fowles, Hawkes, and
Simon, oscillate between the conventions of 'lisibilité', and the
radical refusal effected by the 'scriptible'.

The 'texte scriptible' signals the plurality of its possible
meanings through its apparent concern with the fundamental essence
of the process of writing.   Consequently, the reader is supposed
to (re-)write the text as he engages in the process of 'structuration'
whereby possible units of meaning are produced, but the finished
structure is never achieved.   Thus the text is perpetually in a
state of regeneration, never in any sense finished, always in need
of completion.   Barthes categorically states, as his starting-
point, the case that the notions of plurality and 'structuration'
are fundamental propositions in the distinction between the 'lisible'
and the 'scriptible'.   His argument hinges on the infinity of
meanings inherent in such a text and indicated in the seemingly
arbitrary choice from amongst the innumerable codes (systems of
meaning) available in the text.   As the activity of 'structuration'

is a bid to attain meaning related to the intention of the text,
for such a text to be indeed 'scriptible', it cannot by definition
have a positive narrative structure, nor a perceptible logic of
narrative.    To place this rational constraint on a text would be
tantamount to reducing its strangeness, naturalizing and hence
falsifying it.    Barthes goes on to demonstrate that not only does
Sarrasine contain a highly teleological narrative structure, but
his methodology, as a semiotic critic, is itself delimited by the
constraints of a certain logic of relevance indicated by the choice
of codes which enable a formal analysis of the Balzac story:
hermeneutic, semic, proairetic, or actional, cultural or referential
and symbolic codes form a kind of network across which the whole
text passes while coherence is sought for.    Thus, the **code** is
defined by Barthes as  'une perspective de citations, un mirage de
structure.'[18]    The codes which Barthes is constrained to select
all serve to illustrate the modes of representation in the Balzac
text.    We are assured of a logic of narrative, and meaning, through
the expression of certain truths which guarantee its comprehensibility.
Sarrasine is characterized as predominantly a 'texte lisible',
symptomatic of a specific historical and cultural moment.

In the 'texte lisible' of Balzac a certain well-defined ideological
framework delimits the attempts to structurate on the part of the
modern reader.    This mode of writing describes characters and actions
within a firmly established world of social knowledge that the
pedagogic narrative voice clearly delineates.    The outcome of Barthes's
method in S/Z produces the image of the text as the social history
of a given moment in capitalist society.    The story is naturalized
by this reading, but Barthes goes further by emphasizing the differences in the 'texte lisible' of Sarrasine from the world of the modern
reader.    These are evident in:

the immense pedagogic confidence, the faith in
intelligibility, the pre-individualistic conception
of character, the conviction that rhetoric may
become the instrument of truth; in short, the
differences of his (Balzac's) approach to the
problems of meaning and order.[19]

Barthes's analysis demonstrates, then, the limited plurality of
Sarrasine by recognizing the differences between the system of primary
signs expressed in the surface structure (the level of denotation),
and the concealed sub-text where the ideological foundation of the
work is contained (the level of connotation). Traditionally,
denotation is grounded in the a priori claims for truth, objectivity,
and reason, and is afforded the prestige of the linguistic surface
and the apparent logic inherent in the structural relations of
component parts in a sentence understood at its most fundamental
level. Often, the ideology is indicated by the difference contained
in the transformation effected from connotation to denotation, from
hidden implication to expression. However, one must distinguish
between the plurality which is apparent in all literary texts, albeit
delimited and subtextual in the 'lisible', and the very notion of
the 'scriptible' which refers to an ideal model of a radical, self-
conscious mode of writing grounded in a fundamental critique,and
subversion, of the traditional assumptions of the 'lisible'. The
idea of a 'texte scriptible' problematizes our conventions of reading
as well as those of writing.

Barthes's first declaration in S/Z concerns the rejection of the
earlier work of the structural analysis. He no longer sees the
necessity to search for the universal model of structure in any one
text. Rather, the new task is to demystify the denotative surface
of the 'texte lisible', in this instance, by analyzing the ways in
which the reader 'structurates' and thus produces such a text.
Reading is thus defined as an active process through which the

compositional phenomenon is finally realized in its limited plurality
by the reader.  Barthes, therefore, wants to characterize the
ideological status of the text of Sarrasine, and this he does
through his codal model.  The 'logique du récit' thesis is transcended by going below the denotative surface of functions and unity to
perceive the layers of meaning at the level of connotation.  This
deep-structural information is available through the network of codes
which Barthes devises, and such a dissemination of meaning leads one
to conclude that connotation itself appears to be the self-evident
key to narrative logic (to be distinguished from the 'logique du
récit') in relation to meaning and purpose (the intention of the text).
This more thoroughgoing demystification is wholly consistent with
Barthes's work elsewhere (Mythologies (1957); Système de la Mode
(1967); L'Empire des Signes (1970) for example) on aspects of the
modern bourgeois world.

Connotation derives from the articulation of an encoded 'voice'
characterized by a given historical relevance.  It functions on
the principle of double-meaning in its structural relationship
with denotation, rendering the narrational act of communication
problematical.  Literature is thus understood as the discourse of
the intentional.  The intention is contained in the text itself,
in its implied codes.  For Barthes, the 'classical' 'texte lisible'
is assured a certain innocence because the surface structure poses
itself incontrovertibly as truth.  As S/Z clearly exemplifies, the
intelligibility of such a work relies on the critic's analysis of the
connections between deep and surface structure, between the linguistic
signs and their hidden inferences.  The issue will always be
complicated for the modern reader who confronts the historicity of a
work, if only because he is a cipher of codes, a carrier of social,

historical, and literary knowledge which he brings to bear on the text.

Barthes defines his task in S/Z:  to go beyond the structural analysis
of narrative, and not to attempt a typology of narrative universals
nor the final categorization of the macro-structure of the text.
He aims to fracture the single text into its multiplicity of micro-
structures and, moreover, demystify the apparent naturalness of the
linguistic surface and its claims for objective truth.   Sarrasine
is divided into a series of short contiguous fragments, or lexies,
each indicating their own plurality.   But these fragments of reading-
units are interrelated through general, overriding codes of meaning,
and this implies a logical narrational process.   One cannot overlook
the abiding influence on S/Z of the earlier work on the structural
analysis with its emphasis on the description of a 'logique du récit'
as the clue to the structure, and Barthes's consequent attempts to
transcend the formalistic limitations of his earlier 'logique du
récit' thesis.

A powerful example of a fundamentally logical process directed to
the end is the use of the enigma which Barthes perceives in Balzac's
story.   The enigma imposes its own structure by raising the primary
questions, who is Sarrasine? who is the old man?   The answer is
suspended in various stages in order to increase the reader's
inquisitiveness.   The narrative reaches a point of revelation at the
end with all the questions resolved.   Barthes, therefore, demonstrates
precisely how the Balzac work is founded on the logical movement from
enigma through to the revelation of truth.   Such a narrative strategy
enables control of the reader's participation in his search for
knowledge.   It will be seen subsequently that the notion of enigma
is central to John Fowles's narratives, and is a target for degrees

of subversion in the more epistemologically critical works of
Simon and Hawkes.

Another type of logic is that based on the sequences stemming from
Barthes's proairetic code, the code of actions and behaviour which
lean on the authority of the moral.   All five codes in $S/Z$ form
that network of references which characterize the text historically.
For in Balzac's work, these codes have a gnomic function:  they
refer to general social and cultural truths which in themselves
expose the intentional logic of the text.   The generalizations of
such cultural stereotypes found the cultural 'vraisemblance' of the
work.   The codes have, therefore, a specific discoursal function:
they condition the reader's perception of values, and characterize
the narrator's preoccupations.   More especially in the Balzac work,
the narrator may be given the status of a speaker, uttering socio-
psychological wisdom, expressing universal values, and clearly
establishing a certain readership.   This narrator does not just
relate the story, but he also displays his own authority.   In fact,
he 'authorizes' his world-view in a manner befitting the nineteenth
century, middle-class, realist novelist.   It is precisely this
'voice' which founds a whole set of different assumptions, both
rhetorical and epistemological, which the novel today must acknowledge
for the historical reasons which Barthes's analysis firmly endorses.
His ideal model of the subversion of conventional realism, the 'texte
scriptible', creates the possibility for a scale of self-conscious
criticism in the novel which could oscillate between the two poles
of writing.

The logic of narrative based on the timely revelations in Sarrasine,

coupled with the constraining factor of an epistemological certainty
on the plurality of meanings, define the nature of unquestioned
authority in the 'lisible'. The coercions of a logico-temporal
order, the constrictions of traditional verisimilitude, and the
'natural attitude' (to represent a certain set of actions in a
given social background), all serve to found the ideology of the
'lisible' of which Barthes's mode of analysis is itself precisely
a critique. His description of the enigma underlines a fundamental
structural movement from disorder to order, from doubt to certainty,
through the wisdom and aegis of an omniscient narrative 'voice'.
The world is finally held in its completed, authorized, descriptive
state. The origin of narrative, then, is that of desire, and it
represents the contract between reader and narrator: the desire to
know and the desire to tell, a function easily accomplished once the
semantic transformation from connotation to denotation arrives at
'natural truth' and is therefore able to assert a zero degree of self-
conscious production. For, as Barthes's S/Z persistently demonstrates,
the 'texte lisible' does not postulate the problematic status of
metonymy in language, but our 'modern' reading does, in the distinction
between connotation and denotation. Subsequently, I shall discuss
questions of structure and interpretation in the works of Fowles,
Hawkes, and Simon, to ascertain precisely how far they may be
comprehensible within the bounds of such an argument. In more
normative terms, conventional realism will be seen to stand against
attempts at its subversion, from within the analysis of the narrative
basis of the novel. The idea of a logic of narrative and the reader's
search for satisfying causal explanations is apparently endemic to
conditions of meaning. A notion introduced in the early study of
the structural analysis, and problematized in S/Z through the

separation of denoted meaning and ideological base, is finally seen
to be exploited effectively in writing that aspires to the ideal
of the 'scriptible'.   The self-conscious manipulation of such modes
of intelligibility in the post-war novel, and especially in the nouveau
roman, bears witness to the persistence of 'modern' texts in the
twentieth century, where denotation and connotation merge in a
self-ironical realization of what Stephen Heath has called the very
'practice of writing'.[20]   I shall deal more fully with self-
consciousness and the relationship to literary conventions in the
post-Modernist novel in Part Three below.

The enabling notions of structuration and connotation (the ideological content of a text), conveniently overcome the constrictions
of a formalist literary criticism and its implied formalist poetics.
The two works of Barthes which I have considered in some detail clearly
assist the emergence away from the initial limitations of literary
structuralism for the analysis of the novel, towards the reintroduction
of History into the intelligibility of the text.   This is not to
say that structuralism must be rejected.   For the analysis of
narrative units, coupled with the method of S/Z, enable a thoroughgoing formal understanding of precisely how narrative functions:

> The task of formalization is, of course, essential not
> only in relation to Barthes' codal model, but generally
> for all interested in questions of abstract structure
> and the derivation of the narrative text.[21]

In S/Z, the codes mostly concern the level of Histoire as they
enable an understanding of the structure of content in a less
formalized analysis than that of the earlier structuralist work.
Yet, as Fowler rightly argues, the 'referential code' seems to concern
the level of Discours, or expression.[22]   The cultural truths of

Sarrasine, therefore, are conveyed by the communicating mode of narration itself. For this the reader relies on the narrator. Prejudices which are filtered through the functional narrator, typifying precisely an historically given culture, may well be considered in relation to the concept of 'point of view' which has dominated Anglo-American narrative theory, and especially in its analysis of the novel. Questions concerning narrative authority, and the rhetorical connections between an implied author, a narrator, and the implied reader, are traditionally discussed under the rubric of 'point of view' in literary criticism. S/Z encourages reflection on the constructive role of the reader in the codal model of connotated meaning, but tends to have a conception of the narrator as a non-personalized function of cultural revelation, and of the reader himself as a cipher of codes. The tradition of 'point of view' analysis is Anglo-American literary criticism has both a formalized (technical) and a personalized conception of these relationships. This fundamental difference between the two methodologies has clear doctrinal reasons. For French structuralism, as I have argued above, has relocated the idea of a transcendent Subject in the notion of the sign, the code, and the differential relation, whereas 'point of view' analysis maintains its credibility through a continued belief in the transcendent Subject and the direct referentiality of the text to the world. The profound differences between the work of Fowles and Hawkes, on the one hand, and the later work of Claude Simon on the other are instructive on this point, as the subsequent three chapters will show.

## (ii) 'Point of View' analysis

Henry James had a very precise notion of what he called 'point
of view', giving the text its particular mode of authority.   He
expressed the need for a mirroring consciousness through which the
novel could be dramatized in the absence of an intrusive author.   In
this precise sense, point of view provided a strategy which enabled
degrees of authorial extinction by having the story told in the
third person but apparently by a central character.   Furthermore,
a means of unified presentation of narrative was thus provided which
was fundamental to an ideal of organic form, wholeness, germane to
both the Jamesian text and the mode of literary criticism which
emerged from it.   The question of who speaks in a text is crucial
here.   For  the disparity between the values of a narrator-protagonist
and the subtle intrusions of an implied author created the possibility
for irony.   The reader, actively participating in collusion with an
implied author, is able to question the reliability of a narrator
whose version of events, so to speak, may well be at odds with the
evidence implicit in the disjunction between professed motive and
behavioural manifestations.   Sometimes the irony in this type of
writing is difficult to locate, occasionally it is more ostentatiously
displayed, but it always seems to be definable as a critical mode of
discourse which may undermine certain types of narrative authority.
Irony always relies for its optimal effectiveness on the creation of
perspectives which offer cues to the reader.

Despite the influence of the Jamesian tradition on Anglo-American
literary criticism,[23] narrative authority is more than just a question
of 'point of view' (as James conceived it, and of course, many writers
before him).   It can be viewed more broadly in terms of the development of narrative forms, and the changing emphasis on the status of

authority, truth, objectivity, and eventually irony itself.   For it
must not be overlooked that, as Barthes has demonstrated in S/Z, the
demands made on the reader may well correspond to the inherent
historicity of the text.   In Balzac's Sarrasine, for instance, the
referential and cultural code appears to personalize a particular
a priori readership.   This story implies a community of readers
with a shared worldview.

Barthes shows how Balzac's story is narrated in such an arrogant,
confident manner, and Culler has shown how Flaubert undermined the
mode of irony by the play on uncertainties whereby he collapsed the
pompous, moralizing function of irony in 'classical' literature.
With the withdrawal of irony as an authoritative strategy, or a
mode of assurance, Flaubert instigated a subsequent proliferation
of degrees of ironic narration which has finally caused the critic
to admit that he no longer knows precisely what irony is.   Wayne
Booth calls for the restriction of literary meanings to 'stable
ironies' which would enable coherent interpretation, and therefore
would avoid the worst form of uncertainty for him, which is
'irresponsible irony', whereby irony takes itself ironically!
In Booth's words:

> the serious loss comes when readers, barraged with
> critical talk hailing the discovery of ambiguities as
> a major achievement, learn  to live with blurred senses
> and dulled attention, and deprive themselves of the
> delights of precise and subtle communication that
> skilful stable ironists provide.[24]

This kind of anti-Modernist moralizing does not in any way help us
to account for those more ambiguous, less easily definable ironic
narratives which still exist in history and cannot just be wished
away!   As Barthes has said in S/Z, the first indication of 'modern'
irony is the abdication of certainty.   The loss of the certainty

invested in the 'old stable ego' of character is yet another
indication of this emergence of the 'modern', as I have discussed
in Part One above.

As the problem of perspective has clearly demonstrated, the twentieth
century has progressively witnessed an undermining of certainty, and
the discourse of absolutes exemplified in Sarrasine differentiates
itself clearly from the more tentative relativism of the 'modern'.
Despite the avowed disappearance of the author in the work of Flaubert,
Henry James, and Joyce, narrative has been rendered problematic by
being situated in the ironic gap between limited understanding and the
quest for knowledge and truth.   Ambiguity undermines the pretentions
to reduce the text to a final and primary meaning.   To understand
this abdication of the truth-establishing authority of omniscience
is to acknowledge the increasing proliferation and sophistication of
point of view strategies which embody this problematic.   For
ambiguity, irony, and a general fragmentation in modern art reflect
the collapse of the philosophical substructure of literary realism
and its crucial belief in the authority of the omniscient, authorial
voice.   A more thoroughgoing structuring of the epistemological
critique of any claim for objectivity and authority in narrative fiction,
and in historiography, is fundamental to 'modern' writing, especially
in Barthes's precise formulation of the latter.   Moreover, a profound
understanding of the interplay between writing, the world, memory and
interpretation, indicates the role of bias and exclusion in narrative
(literary or historical).

Two aspects thus serve to complicate the issue of point of view:
firstly, that awareness on the part of the modern reader of the
subtext of writing defined in S/Z as the encoded ideology; and
secondly, the self-conscious realization of modes of authority

in narrative which may be subverted by the modern text as it
perpetually underlines its own process of coming to be, and its own
status as fiction.   Such texts vary from those more normative ones
which play on the ironic gap between narrator and implied author for
their intelligibility (the works of Fowles and Hawkes may be compared
on this level)  to the more radical claims of the Tel Quel group
in France, and the 'literature' with which it is associated, whose
critique is profoundly epistemological.   Claude Simon's narrative
fiction is comprehensible within this ethos.   A literary criticism
that aims to understand the conditions of meaning of the 'modern'
text through its marked difference with the 'classical', traditional
work, to use Barthes's broad distinctions, must therefore account
for these complexities of narrative authority within a critique of
point of view grounded in both cultural and historical assumptions
fundamental to the changing emphases of narrative forms and the
presuppositions of the criticism which derives from them.   In this
respect, Henry James is to be seen as a transitional figure who
bridges the traditions of late nineteenth century literary fiction
and its theoretical ethos whose tendencies he carried to their limits,
and the emergence of the modern, whereby he pointed the way to
innovations in novelistic technique and critical concepts of which the
notion of point of view is a prime instance.

Wayne Booth's The Rhetoric of Fiction (1961) has been largely
responsible for revising the Jamesian tradition.   He argues for the
abolition of the distinction between showing and telling, claiming
that the process of narration is based on dramatic showing, and
discoursive telling.   The French structural analysis of narrative
finds common ground with the post-Jamesian tradition in asserting
the fundamental constitution of these two principal narrative elements.

Their functional interplay founds the process of narrative, and the possibility of its abstract analysis. The relationship of the story to its telling, the content to its narration, is precisely that fundamental distinction between _Histoire_ and _Discours_. Booth's notion of a rhetoric of fiction is a critique of the conditions of meaning of narrative based on the analysis of its modes of effectiveness, the degrees of its rhetorical persuasion. Therefore, it differentiates itself from the French structural analysis by 'personalizing' the relationship between the activity of reading and the production of meaning: Booth emphasizes the manner by which particular qualities of a narrator, characterized as a psychological entity, relate to specific rhetorical effects. The distance between the perspectives of an unreliable, even reprehensible, narrator, and the subtle critique of him by an implied author, implicates the reader in the process of judgment. This distance is often difficult to locate in cases where there is a noticeable tension between sympathy and judgment. Camus' _La Chute_ (1956) and Nabokov's _Lolita_ (1955) are examples from recent literature, and Defoe's _Moll Flanders_ (1722) is an early forerunner. Thus rhetoric, in Booth's sense, is the control of sympathy and detachment, and its modes of persuasion are often the subject of a type of traditional irony whereby collusion between an implied author and the reader serve to undermine a single and apparently dominant central consciousness which may well try to enforce a self-justificatory perspective through the seductive skills of rhetoric. John Hawkes's first-person narrators are perplexing examples of this situation.

Fundamental to the changing emphases of the novel-form has been the variety of strategies to overcome the problem of telling a particular tale in a certain way to a given audience. As Genette has argued,

from classical times through the work of Cervantes, Fielding, through
the various forms of fictive biography and autobiography, first-
person protagonist narratives, epistolary novels, and those based
on the interior monologue and, later, the stream of consciousness, the
principal concern has been the problematical relationship between
Discours and Histoire, or in more traditional post—Jamesian terms,
between narrator, story, and reader.[25]   Modes of authority, and
attitudes to authority, are comprehensible through varying ideological
and philosophical preoccupations.   The question of point of view may
best enable a clear understanding of form and its content.   For
point of view is, finally, not just a technique but also a way of
thinking, the evidence of a whole weltanschauung.   Narrative
technique and perspective relate the formal aspects of a text to
History.   From perspective we characterize the problem through
interpretations of the world, and more actively through epistemology.
The historical connections between theories of knowledge and attitudes
to writing underline the status of authority in a text.   In this
respect, point of view should be seen, since the late nineteenth
century, as problematical, if only because the epistemological doubts
cast on consciousness, the ego, or the self, which I discussed in
Part One of this study, are part of the wider context of the twentieth
century crisis of perspectivism in the arts generally.   Formalistic
analysis of structure at its most dogmatic refuses the historicity
of both form and its cognitive basis.   Barthes's S/Z goes some way
towards the correction of this foreclosure.   The connections between
more stable societies and more stable, less perplexing, subversive
forms of literature has been well noted.[26]   Given the claims about
the world and about man in Part One above, it is no surprise to
discover equally varying degrees of formal disruptions of conventional
literary paradigms.

Narrative structure is intelligible precisely because the text is
read in a certain way. It is not an isolated object of analysis,
but rather only comes into being, so to speak, through the reader.
This process largely depends on the cultural-historical code-norms
of a given reader. To allow for reader-participation in the creation
of meaning, the text needs indeterminate areas, and Barthes's notion of
the enigma is an abiding example. To a certain extent, aspects of this
process are normative in that they are universal properties of all
narratives. But deviation from these normative canons of intelligibility arise when the text foregrounds inherent problems of sets
of relationships either in the formal structure of component parts
(temporal dislocations which undermine the sequential logic of
narrative, for instance), or in the more external connections between
reader and text (the level of discourse). Such 'modern' narratives
defamiliarize normative conventions of writing with varying degrees
of intentional subversion. Fowles effects a play on aspects of
realism, but remains within the bounds of that tradition. Hawkes
foregrounds the perplexing interplay between rhetoric and psychology.
Claude Simon's texts reject the epistemological primacy of the Subject
as a priori to a fundamental critique of realist assumptions for the
novel. The analysis of narrative structure must in the end acknowledge the basic process of mediation which may tell us something of
the historicity of structure itself. Mediation concerns the complex
interplay of reader and text, but also past forms and present writing.
For, as Weimann rightly claims, 'the creation and interpretation of
structure are affected by the changing dialectic of tradition and
originality that is characteristic of the writing as well as of the
reading of literature.'[27] If the structure of narrative is perceivable and intelligible by making sense of narrative logic, then
analyzing the interconnections of narrative units must only be one,

more formalized, process, which should then be supplemented with
further attempts to understand the complex mediation process.    The
'logique du récit', therefore, needs expanding to include a more
complex analysis of the totally mediated narrative phenomenon.    The
relationship between structure and the ideological character of a
work is fundamental to my formulation of a logic of narrative.    The
limits of such theoretical discourse, the possibilities for abstract
formalization of the underlying properties of narrative in the novel,
may well be bound up with assumptions which found the very texts
under scrutiny.    The following three chapters aim to engage the
works of Fowles, Hawkes, and Simon with those aspects of the debate
about the analysis of structure and interpretation which seem
appropriate for an elucidation of the underlying formal assumptions
on which their works are indeed grounded.

CHAPTER FOUR

Structure and Interpretation in the

Narrative Fiction of John Fowles

The analysis of narrative structure in the works of John Fowles coheres around three thematically central aspects, which function in this chapter as interpretive models. I offer a more formalized reading of his works in terms of narrative logic grounded in the notions of the Quest, the symbolic relationship between Adam and Eve (and the centrality of the Jungian Anima in that relationship), and the function of Enigma and Revelation in the seductive manipulation of storytelling. Finally, the interpretation of these narratives is seen to be further complicated by the use of literary models by the protagonists themselves to understand the world. On this level these works are largely self-interpretive, and tend to pre-empt the hermeneutic work of the critic, or at least to problematize the search for meaning itself. I discuss this crucial aspect of Fowles's narratives under the rubric of Modes of Understanding.

(i) <u>The Quest</u>

The narratives of John Fowles cohere through the idea of a
quest. Characters are seen to journey towards self-discovery,
figuratively and literally. Principally the male protagonists
undergo a process of self-examination, and attempt to find
something out about themselves. This informs the narrative
structure. Beneath narrative there exists a notebook of
exploration .[1] Nicholas in <u>The Magus</u> literally takes flight
from the 'real world' and enters the more 'fictional' world
of the magus's psychodrama, initially for the wrong reasons;
he is made to experience a bewildering heuristic process
whereby the journey becomes one of time, through Conchis's
storytelling. Lines from the poetry of Eliot and Pound
indicate the intention of the elaborate use of artifice:

> We shall not cease from exploration
> And the end of all our exploring
> will be to arrive where we started
> And know the place for the first time

Nicholas is expected to 'sail after knowledge'.[2] These
statements may in fact remain as guides to Fowles's use of
narrative as a heuristic device. The reader is meant to
learn the lessons as well. In <u>The French Lieutenant's Woman</u>,
the point of departure for the narrative of Charles's self-
interrogation, and the analysis of an age, is the beginning
of a journey, both metaphoric and literal, where the plot
is grounded in the protagonist's 'voyage, journey, evolving
movement /which7 is a matter of social, emotional, and psychological exploration, carrying an obligation to discern a basis
forpersonal authenticity'. [3] Charles's one-directional journey

leads him away from his 'society' life in London, to America,
which offers him a critical perspective on English society,
and English women in particular. Finally his quest for
Sarah leads him to the confrontation with a more emancipated
figure who shares her life with the Pre-Raphaelites, who
intended their life and art to be a critique of the claustro-
phobia of Victorianism. What is to be learnt is explicitly
stated for Charles and for the reader. The process which
enables such didacticism is both archetypal and deterministic.
Grounded in a romance quest structure, whereby the ongoing
movement of plot is instigated and maintained by a male
character's pursuit of 'love' in the guise of Sarah, or Julie
and Alison in The Magus, the mode of action is largely pre-
determined by the structure of narrative. Nicholas is lured
on through the 'heuristic mill' of the psychodrama, and then
on to a dramatic confrontation with Alison which itself is
enacted, ritualistically, on the model of the godgame. Sarah
Woodruff's rebellion against society in The French Lieutenant's
Woman offers Charles a model for action, and his rejection of
convention and pursuit of her effects a denial of free will:
he is an agent who is written into a plot by her actions; her
disappearance coerces him into the quest situation; all his
actions are determined by the end and purpose of his search.
The utter subjugation of Nicholas in The Magus contrasts
markedly with the self-determined nature of his action in
the later sections of the novel. He has been 'drugged' by
the seductions of the storyteller and the lure of sexual
promise. His unique philosophical and psychological adventure
overwhelms him, and the reader, with its labyrinthine confusions
of the real and the imagined. A growing impatience to explain

everything rationally and yet a feeling that he is 'chained
to Bourani through subtle psychosexual bars', [4] characterize
Nicholas as a helpless listener and spectator, and then as a
victim of the coercions of plot.  In the end, the situation
dictates that he become his own detective.  He never chooses
the role; it is largely determined by the need to continue
the search which the psychodrama instigated.  And Nicholas
is conscious of this but helpless all the same:

> I was aware that in all this I was acting the role
> I had decided not to act: that of detective, of
> hunter ...5

His rational skepticism motivates his search for physical
reality behind the artifice of the godgame.  This soon gives
way to an obsessive investigation of Alison's whereabouts.
But his obsessive rationality confounds his apparently
amourous motives.

The archetypal love-quest structure of these narratives is
further demonstrated, and clearly explained, in the collection
of stories, The Ebony Tower (1974).  John Fowles is interested
in the storytelling origins of narrative.  His translation of
Marie de France's tale Eludic recalls what the artist, Breasley,
in the title story explains as the twelfth and thirteenth century
mania for romantic legends full of mystery, love, and adventure.
The celtic romance, its chivalric codes and its courtly love
syndrome is emphasized by the author in a personal note prior
to the translation.  It also forms the basis for Marie de France's
tale.  'It was composed not least of sexual honesty and a very
feminine awareness of how people really behaved - and how

behaviour and moral problems can be expressed through ...
dialogue and action.' [6] For the author, the 'amour courtois'
had a debrutalizing effect on twelfth century society. The
'female intelligence' is fundamental to the structure of
Fowles's narratives, as I shall argue in this chapter. Male
characters in these works have to choose between two women,
between convention and its defiance, and are meant to understand and finally transcend their selfishness. David Williams
in The Ebony Tower confronts his 'riskless' life through the
challenge offered by Breasley's art-theories, and art-work,
but his escape is in the form of the attraction of female
flesh. His failure to actually have an affaire is a symptom
of his ordinariness. In the end he is able to remain 'faithful'
to his wife: the honesty and faithfulness syndromes in Eludic
are given a modern, and less ritualised, context.

Such an archetypal basis for the structure of narrative is re-
enforced by articulate characters who themselves see the world
in terms of archetypes from literature, myth, and art. In
The French Lieutenant's Woman, the nature of Charles'
emotional and psychological exploration is prefigured, as it
were, by Sarah's experiences retold to the reader as they
were supposed to have happened prior to Charles' encounter
with her. We are told that she had read 'far more fiction
and far more poetry, those two sanctuaries of the lonely,
than most of her kind'. [7] Literature substitutes for experience:

> Without realizing it she judged people as much by
> the standards of Walter Scott and Jane Austen as
> by any empirically arrived at; seeing those around
> her as fictional characters, and making poetic
> judgement on them. [8]

Bearing this in mind, it is no surprise that she reacted to the
'charming' French lieutenant in a manner more appropriate to
a Romance novel, and received a severe shock at the sight of
his 'betrayal' of her. Sarah is seen progressively to mature
out of the limitations of her romance perceptions. For Charles,
she is an Emma Bovary in the flesh, or even an archetypal
Persecuted Maiden, and we are expected to see his self-exploration
as a part of a liberating movement away from such perceptions.
But in the end we must wonder just how far he has overstepped
the confines of too simple a literary mode of perception. Lest
we forget, a large portion of the novel is structured around the
almost stereotype Romance Quest for the lost love, which takes
the protagonist on a journey in pursuit of his Dream, or Ideal
Love. His limited and archetypal mode of understanding hampers
his final encounter with Sarah. Miranda, in The Collector,
offers herself and the reader various archetypal explanations
for her situation with Clegg. Her tormentor is the insipid
caricature of a Byronic villain, and a self-styled Caliban who
usurps the role of Prospero. The influence of The Tempest on
both this novel and The Magus enables an allegoric potential to
be contained at a structural level. In the latter novel,
Nicholas's potential 'calibanity' in his sexual attitude to
women undergoes examination at the hands of Prospero-Conchis.

According to Fiedler's analysis,[9] one can distinguish clearly
between the gothic romance and the historical romance tradition.
The difference is noticeable in the gothic implications of
The Collector and the historical romance overtones of The French

Lieutenant's Woman:

> The historical romance shares with the gothic
> a concern with the past and a desire to restore
> to prose fiction 'the improbable and marvellous',
> which the sentimental novel of contemporary life
> has disavowed.[10]

Fowles's first three novels all share aspects of this 'desire'.
But the third novel, 'contains all the characteristic properties
of the historical romance, including a Persecuted Maiden, the
motif of flight, and dramatization of "history - real history,
as distinguished from legend and myth", backed up by an impres-
sive array of documentation'. [11] Thus, for the critic too this
archetypal basis for narrative is largely enabling.

The narrator in his various guises persistently guides the
reader through possible modes of interpretation, archetypal and
more complex. Miranda in The Collector, and both Nicholas and
his mentor, Conchis, in The Magus, perform this function. Thus
the texts are largely self-interpretive. Miranda's fertile
mind attempts to make sense of the world in which she is a
prisoner, through two principal fictions. Her imagination is
dominated by literary analogies of extreme situations recalling
Robinson Crusoe, and The Tempest. But also she relocates the
story in the present day by articulating the author's own
posture, explained in The Aristos, of society grounded in the
simplified conflict between the Few and the Many. The symbolic,
mythic, and archetypal relationship between artifice and meaning is fully exploited in The Magus, where the example of one
man's life determines the course of another, and where the
history of the twentieth century is bound up with the meaning

of its art. Not only do characters offer archetypal, and
thus simplified, visions of the world and their personal
experience, but also these narratives are grounded in the
structures available in early forms of storytelling. Hence
the abiding presence of quest and voyage in Fowles's novels.

Another, and not unrelated, modelized form of understanding
the structure of these novels is the implicit relationship
between narration and the sexual act. Scholes goes as far
as to claim an archetypal status for it in relation to narration. Sex and the narrative act are connected through 'the
fundamental orgiastic rhythm of tumescence and detumescence,
of tension and resolution, of intensification to the point of
climax and consummation'. With specific reference to <u>The Magus</u>,
and to Nicholas's quest for Julie and then Alison, the following statement offers an abstract version for the reader of the
structural interplay between belief and the desire to continue
reading:

> In the sophisticated forms of fiction, as in the
> sophisticated practice of sex, much of the art
> consists of delaying climax within the framework
> of desire in order to prolong the pleasurable act
> itself. When we look at fiction with respect to
> its form alone we see a pattern of events designed
> to move towards climax and resolution, balanced by
> a counterpattern of events designed to delay this
> very climax and resolution.[12]

Both the reader and the protagonist are 'seduced' into the
continual desire to know more, and to experience more.
Nicholas is obsessively implicated in this process to the
extent that he is able to declare 'I didn't care what
happened; as long as something happened'. [13] The false climax

and the overabundance of peripetiae are the novelist-trickster's
stock-in-trade; and Conchis, author-surrogate, is a skilful
manipulator of his form. Nicholas, aware of his helplessness,
sees the magus holding him back, only to hurl him faster down
the slope.[14] In this novel, such an interpretation enables a
close approximation between the sexual drive behind Nicholas's
quest for Julie and the ongoing structure of narrative itself.
He is as seduced by the woman as he is (and we are) seduced
by the storyteller. Erotic intrigue and narrative rhythm
appear closely related in this way.

Existential journeys as a basis for narrative coherence are
symbolically correlated with spatial imagery. There is a
movement from enclosure to plenitude which is symptomatic of
the need to transcend the loneliness of the isolated self
and engage in meaningful relationships. In The Collector,
there is a polarisation of the extremes of underground entrapment in the cellar of Clegg's cottage, a crypt-like place
analagous to the effects of his damaging solipsism, and the
occasional emergence of the 'prisoner' into the fresh air.
Her forced withdrawal into 'inner space' enables the contemplation of self which the existential model of man defines as
a priori to purposeful action in the world. That stage is
denied her. The fresh air outside the cottage, the vastness
of the dark night sky, symbolizes the unused possibilities of
the expansion of self-expression. In this respect, landscape
and setting become symbolic of states of mind and situations
for the self. The novel is replete with recurrent motifs of

darkness and light, confinement and open space. The Magus,
similarly, uses symbolic settings. The island of Phraxos
isolates the self and enables rigorous examination. Nicholas's
need for 'fresh air' is most evident in the Russell Square
flat with Alison in London, and in the Lord Byron school on
Phraxos. The idea of the 'salle d'attente' continues the motif
and intimates the start of a journey, and the waiting to be
renewed. His eventual analysis and 'disintoxication' takes
place underground. In The French Lieutenant's Woman, Charles
confronts the bounds of his lonely self inside rooms which
symbolize the interior space of consciousness. The metaphor
of man as an island is reinforced, just as it is in The Magus.
He first sees Sarah, the enigma which will lead him, painfully,
to self-discovery, overlooking the vastness of the sea; the
novel ends with a similar motif of plenitude as he is on the
threshold of existential openness: 'And out again, upon the
unplumb'd, salt, estranging sea.' [15] The circularity enabled
by the recurrence of plenitude has both structural and thematic
signigicance: Charles has reached the point that Sarah reached
before him. He has begun to realise the conditions of his
existential journey. The journey for the protagonists of
The Magus and The French Lieutenant's Woman is circular in
a locational sense too: they both return to the London from
where they started. For, as Nicholas is informed, through
T. S. Eliot, the journey of exploration will end when the
explorer arrives where he started and knows the place for
the first time. [16] Knowledge will have been acquired. The
reader perceives the meaning-laden spatial images at key
moments in the text. Mirrors perform a similar function. They
are the objective correlation of self-contemplation. [17]

In Fowles's most recent novel, Daniel Martin (1977), the
evocation of place, and the journeys to and from significant
places, take on an explicit and profound importance. Literally,
Daniel Martin travels to America, Mexico, England, and North
Africa, and also goes back in time through memory in order
to find a form 'that would tally with the real structure of
being and mind'.[18] His self-conscious narrative is a bid to
establish a coherent, whole view of a life and its times.
He searches for a totality of consciousness, but his fragmentary structure, oscillating between past and present, and
even more distant past, is symptomatic of his failure to achieve
'whole sight'. If 'all the rest is desolation',[19] then his
nostalgia and eventual quest for original territory offers hope
and certainty. In the end, Daniel Martin returns to the lost
'domain' of childhood security, and retreats into the rural
simplicity of his arcadia away from the bustling commercial
world of modern urban life. The circular journey is comprehensible in Freudian terms as the search for the lost Mother
and original innocence. The terminal point of the quest is a
return to the original place with fresh knowledge, as in
The Magus, but in this case with a surrogate Mother. Narrative,
in this recent novel, is a process of self-enquiry, in a very
Proustian sense: the reconstitution of lost time enables a
basis for the history of the self. But for Fowles's narrator,
past selves are reduced to artifice in order to create the
necessary distance which would enable what he was to explain
what he has become. The instrusive sense of an articulate,
playful narrator, who switches narrative perspectives at will,
sometimes to become his own third person, sometimes to evoke a
more profound sense of self, often gives the impression of a
narrator rehearsing modes of narration. We would concur with
his assertion that 'the mode of recollection usurps the reality

of the recalled.'[20]  This reification of the past self and the
sense of the artifice of related events, is transcended by
the strong sense of place.  Writing a biography of Kitchener
is only finally possible when Daniel returns to Egypt and
seeks the place most commensurate with Kitchener's being.
The relationship between self and place (territory in the
world) is encapsulated in this journey, and it motivates
the narrator's most profound moments of insight concerning
his own 'soul-searching'.  The journey up the Nile recalls
Marlow's voyage up the Congo in Conrad's Heart of Darkness.
Dan contemplates the dark silence of the river, 'endless,
indifferent, like time itself'. [21] 'Its waters seemed to reach
not merely back into the heart of Africa, but into that of time
itself.' [22]  Both Jane and Dan experience a heightened sense
of the personal effect of Time as they pass the silent monuments
of an ancient past, and view the present day simplicity of the
peasant worker.  By the end of this symbolic journey, Dan
understands the need for man to have an ideal image of himself,
and that 'the freedom to know oneself, was the driving force
of human evolution'. [23]  And this stood against the determinism
effected on the self by time: the idea that man is written by
the past.  The barren desert strips away the veneer of outer
impression and offers the stark confrontation with the barrenness of inner truth.  In this respect, landscape and place are
once again objective correlatives for states of being.  Once
the threatening landscape and hostile weather of Syria has
enabled the final and complete exposure and confrontation of
the self and the other (Dan and Jane), they can retreat to the
calm sanctuary of Thorncombe.  The narrator has achieved his

journey of self-discovery, has learnt how to feel and how to
accept the reality of other people as both separate and
necessary to his own self.


## (ii) Adam and Eve

Fowles's novels and stories are structured on the conflict
between man and woman. A symbolism evolved in the early works,
and was explained in The Aristos in the following terms:

> Adam is stasis, or conservatism; Eve is kinesis,
> or progress. Adam societies are ones in which
> the man and the father, male gods, exact strict
> obedience to established institutions and norms
> of behaviour, as during a majority of the periods
> of history in our era. The Victorian is a
> typical such period. Eve societies are those
> in which the woman and the mother, female gods,
> encourage innovation and experiment, and fresh
> definitions, aims, modes of feelings. The
> Renaissance and our own are typical such ages.[24]

The conflict between Adam and Eve founds the mode of characterization in the narratives of John Fowles. Woman symbolically
offers a solution to the abiding 'selfish tyranny of the male'.[25]
The genesis for this relationship is initially dramatized in
The Collector, where symbolism gives way to allegory as the two
characters are polarized in their marked opposition: Miranda
stands for the Few; Clegg for the Many. The structuring of
character relationships becomes more complex, and less allegorical, in the two subsequent novels. In fact, in The French
Lieutenant's Woman, an existential and historical awareness is
achieved by both the male and the female protagonists, although
the latter becomes the initiator of the more enlightened,
critical state of consciousness. Nicholas in The Magus is

made to undergo rigorous self-examination through the very
contrastive relationship he has with Julie, Alison, and Mrs.
de Seitas, the enlightened female characters.  In fact, woman
is seen to symbolize the mysterious, enigmatic, motivating
force for the sinuous and artifice-laden sequence of events
on which the narrative is based.  Nicholas's choices for
further action are determined by the mysterious (and erotic)
lure of enigmatic women.  By constantly frustrating his quest
for them, the Magus is able to emphasize the protagonist's
essential selfishness.  If one follows the confrontation of
the sexes through to the third novel, The French Lieutentant's
Woman,one sees that the allegorical aspects of The Collector,
and the exploitation of artifice to confound any clear distinction between reality and fictionality in The Magus, are subtly
played down for the sake of the documentation of History, and
the confrontation of the collective consciousness of the
Victorian and the modern.  Charles, the Victorian Everyman,
strives to overstep the limits of his petrified existence and
become a more enlightened existential man.  In this, he follows
the model of 'rebellious' behaviour established by Sarah before
him.  The initial motivations may well be sexual and emotional:
the forbidden fruits of a very unVictorian Eve.  However, by the
end of the novel, Charles has escaped the confines of historical
determinism, transcended the identity which the past and convention has written for him, and has begun to realize the
multiplicity of situations which demand a more open-minded
consideration in life.  In existential terms, he must be
available constantly to rethink and choose independent courses
of action.  Self-awareness and self-knowledge are the necessary
prerequisites for the aristos, the elect man, to cope with the
hazards of modern life.  But Charles does not reach that

moment of awareness until he has undergone a process of inward
education precipitated by the initial confrontation with the
enigmatic Sarah, who figuratively and literally offers him the
possibility to choose an alternative mode of behaviour and
therefore to quit his rigidly determined social world.  The
quest to fulfil the romantic potential she seems to offer
him gives the plot its primary impetus, and allows Charles
to attempt to make sense of subsequent events which are
wholly inconsistent with his available patterns of language
and experience.  It is not until the end of his 'journey'
that he can reach a moment of realization of the extent of
his persistent misinterpretations of Sarah - something  the
reader has been aware of throughout, because of the extreme
limitations of Charles's previous experiences and social
existence, in a truly historical sense.

Enlightened women, and their enabling capacity as revelational
and educative forces, are thematically and structurally
pervasive in the work of John Fowles.  The young detective
in The Enigma confronts one such woman:

> He had an immediate impression of someone alive,
> where everyone else had been dead, or playing
> dead; of someone who lived in the present, not
> the past ...26

She will offer him a mode of explaining the mysteries which
will exceed the limits of his pragmatism, albeit hypothetical.
In The Ebony Tower, David, alone with another female figure,
'felt he had travelled much further than expected, into the

haunted and unpredicted'.[27] Woman inspires and invokes mysteries behind the quotidian banality of life. The French
Lieutenant's Woman opens with the vision of a muse-like,
mysterious female figure, turned facing the sea. This highly
visual inspiration instigates the narratorial quest of Charles.
In 'Notes on an unfinished novel',[28] Fowles explains how he
saw this imaginative vision as holding some sort of imminent
power, containing mysterious and romantic potential:

> A woman stands at the end of a deserted quay
> and stares out to sea... with her back turned
> she represented a reproach on the Victorian
> age...[29]

This image becomes 'the door into a new world'.[30] Charles himself meets the enigmatic Sarah in such circumstances, and is
immediately astounded by the directness of her eyes:

> ...for theirs was an age when the favoured
> feminine look was the demure, the obedient,
> the shy.[31]

Her look contains, 'no artifice ... no hypocrisy... no mask'.
Her look is a lance, and, 'he felt himself in that brief instant...
both pierced and deservedly diminished'. [32] Not only does he
feel decidedly inferior, but also in need of mystery and romance
which the iron certainties of his age have always denied.
Charles's behaviour is, therefore, conditioned by Sarah's
mystical and enigmatic presence.

Woman dominates man in Fowles's works. As the author himself
explains, 'my female characters tend to dominate the male. I

see man as a kind of artifice, and woman as a kind of reality'.[33]
Sarah fulfils this role, exposing the 'reality' behind social
convention. Alison in The Magus is the reality from which
Nicholas escapes, and he is eventually taught to return to her
and all she represents. Sarah exposes through her direct
'look' and her actions the false veneer of Victorian society,
by her very presence; she leads Charles on, away from a
restrictive society and towards a deeper experience of self
and a more enlightened self- consciousness. For Sarah is the
enabling 'device' for Charles to make his Kierkegaardian
'leap in the dark'. A dual structure poses the two conflicting
sides of Charles' predicament: the petty provincial life
offered by Ernestina and the prospect of marriage, respectability
and inevitable family connections is opposed by the offer of
the far more problematic relationship with Sarah, the social
outcast. For the intelligent young palaeontologist who is
passionately involved in one of the major Victorian contro-
versies, between the rigid Linnaean Scala Naturae and Darwin's
Theory of Evolution, feels there must be more to life than
Ernestina could offer him. But, first, Sarah must 'teach' him
to abandon the study of fossils, and attend to the more living
and vital pursuits of life in the here and now. The penetrating power of her eyes, the confrontational, intimidating
directness of her manner, are symptomatic of the challenge
she offers Charles. The effect of her look lends a narrative
impetus to the novel as she lures Charles on towards his final
encounter with her in London.

In the foreword to the revised edition of The Magus (1977), the
author mentions his deep interest in Jung, when he first wrote

the novel. This influence is most conspicuous in the structure
of male and female relationships in his works. Jung's concept
of the self is grounded in what he called the psychic totality
of I and not-I. 'What is not-I, not masculine, is most probably
feminine, and because the not-I is felt as not belonging to
me and therefore as outside me, the anima image is usually
projected upon women'. [34] The enlightened female characters
play a crucial role in the male protagonists' almost ritualistic
passage towards self. The archetypal status of the anima is
structurally legitimized in the narratives:

> ...with her cunning play of illusions the soul
> (anima) lures into life the inertness of matter
> that does not want to live. She makes us
> believe incredible things, that life may be
> lived. She is full of snares and traps, in
> order that man should fail, should reach the
> earth, entangle himself there, and stay caught,
> so that life should be lived; as Eve in the
> garden of Eden could not rest content until
> she had convinced Adam of the goodness of the
> forbidden apple.[35]

The anima is apparently able to break down moral inhibitions
and unleash forces from the unconscious; 'the anima can
appear also as an angel of light, a psychopomp who points
the way to the highest meaning'. [36] The anima, in the guise
of woman, reflects a superior knowledge of life's laws,
both for Jung and for John Fowles. This is reflected in the
structure of his narratives, and is most pervasive in The
Magus.


(iii) Enigma and Revelation

In The Aristos, Fowles describes the 'tensional nature of
human reality'. An ultimate tension is caused by the

relationship between what we know and what we will never know.
The tension between knowledge and mystery may well be 'the source
of human being' in The Aristos,[37] but it is also fundamental
to the structure of narrative.   Ironically, the twentieth century
narrative voice which frequently intrudes into the nineteenth
century reality of The French Lieutenant's Woman asks, 'Who is
Sarah?   Out of what shadows does she dome?'[38]   The mystery is
cynically unanswered.   But Charles will continue searching,
because the enigmatic question about her mysterious character
coerces his involvement.   Nicholas, in The Magus,thirsts for
mystery to release his typical ennui;  the mysteries of the
godgame cause him to seek rational answers, but the enigma of
unknown female flesh provides an even more motivating force.
As life is characterized as a conspiracy, so the mysteries of
the psychodrama collapse into the pragmatism of the detective
story.   Nicholas hunts for clues where none would explain what
has existed more in the realm of fiction than reality.   Because
he, the protagonist, is also the narrative point of view, the
enigmas seem in need of revelation.   The productive relationship
between Nicholas's pervasive rational scepticism and the mysterious
connivances perpetrated by Conchis, enables detection to appear
an inevitable consequence of narrative logic.   The narrator
clearly states the case, but is volitionless to alter the
situation:

> By searching so fanatically I was making a detective
> story out of the summer events, and to view life as
> a detective story, as something that could be
> deduced, hunted, and arrested, was no more realistic
> (let along poetic) than to view the detective story
> as the most important literary genre, instead of
> what it really was, one of the least.[39]

Despite this moment of insight, Nicholas continues his detective
work, obsessively, through Athens, Rome, and finally England.
The last sections of the novel are comprehensible in these
terms.

As the story, The Enigma, clearly illuminates, nothing lasts
like a mystery. The process from enigma to the quest for revelation is strangely reversed. Instead of trying to find out
precisely who a character is, we are made to realize that who
he is confounds the question about what he has done. Barthes
in S/Z (1970) first instigates the structural analysis of the
logic of narrative by demonstrating that the enigma, often
focused on a mysterious character, motivates the quizzical
interest of the reader. Similarly, a motivation grounded in the
solution of mystery informs the narrative of Fowles's story.
However, we are offered all the conventional information to
substantiate a knowable character, based on a recognizable model
of a socially defined person. For the detective, and the
reader of conventional realism, names, professions, and social
background are all truth-establishing sources of information.
John Marcus Fielding is a well-defined character and a highly
plausible individual. Therefore his enigmatic disappearance is
initially inexplicable. The limitations of the rational mind
exemplified by the detective are offset by the enlightened
female who, characteristically for Fowles, explains the mysteries
in terms of an escape from the 'plots' of society.

Fowles is seen to exploit the logical and enquiring nature of
reading through the tension between mystery and knowledge,
enigma and revelation. Characters in his works mime the role
of reader: Nicholas becomes a detective despite himself; the
detective in The Enigma searches for clues and explanations

grounded in all the usual avenues of enquiry - but mystery
prevails. John Marcus Fielding remains an enigma because
he has defied the rationale which made him into a stereotype.
He may be compared to the image of a cloud in the story of
that title:

> A cloud, but a mysterious cloud, the kind of cloud
> one will always remember because it is so anomalous,
> so uncorresponding with the weather knowledge that
> even the most unobservant acquire.[40]

Anomaly, mystery, enigma: the play on the inquisitive relationship of reader and protagonist to such knowledge-demanding
properties is fundamental to the structure of narrative in the
novels and stories of John Fowles. The highly defined lacks
energy. The word continually defeated before the ineffable
in Mallarmé's poetry is preferable to the precision of the
Parnassians. The case for the energy-giving presence of enigma
in the novel is clearly stated in Daniel Martin:

> ...there are some people one can't dismiss, place,
> reify...who set riddles one ignores at one's costs;
> who, like nature itself, are catalytic... His
> /Daniel Martin's/ metier had forced him for so
> long to think in terms of visual symbolisms, of
> sets, locations, movements, gestures; of the seen
> actor and actress. This psychologically obscure
> creature /Jane/ belonged, or had grown to belong,
> to another art, another system, the one he was
> trying to enter.[41]

The energy contained in mystery is poured into whoever seeks
an answer to it. These are the wise words of the magus,[42]
and they emphasize the compelling nature of the storytelling
aspect of narrative which John Fowles and his surrogate authors
manipulate. Realism is always threatened by a 'quantum of
mystery',[43] rationalism by the unexplained.

(iv) <u>Modes of understanding</u>

> The basic situation is always someone trying
> to cope with an experience outside their
> traditions and their language, having to reach
> out and call on unused resources of imagination,
> which sometimes turn out to be their and sometimes
> not.[44]

In <u>The Magus</u>, the persistence of Nicholas's rational scepticism
frustrates the emergence of meaning from the mysteries of artifice. Through the narrative perspective of protagonist-narrators,
or the access to the point of view of a central character by a
narrator, the reader is implicated in the basic situation described
above. Highly specific situations are intelligible as universal
predicaments. This is largely brought about by the persistence
of models of explanation which the predominantly artistic, or
literary, sensibilities of principal characters consistently
offer. <u>The Collector</u> achieves this collusion of protagonist and
reader in ostensible fashion by providing two views of events,
which in itself sets up two contrasting thought processes and
two writing styles, with the inclusion of Miranda's diary in
the text of Clegg's narrative. The conflict of the Few and the
Many is enacted most meaningfully at this level. Art and literature are called upon to explain life, as collectors and liberators
express themselves through opposing forms of art: in this novel
lepidoptery and photography stand against the creativity of
modern art in the form of Clegg's pastimes and Miranda's more
sophisticated artistic tastes. Patterns of literary archetypes are called upon by Miranda in her diary to make sense of
her situation. Clegg is to Caliban what Conchis is to Prospero
in <u>The Magus</u>. 'Islanded' in Robinson Crusoe  style, marooned

in Clegg's autotelic world, Miranda sees herself as the Persecuted
Maiden of the Gothic tale, imprisoned in her vault: she is the
helpless female victim of an archetypal male villain.

Unusual and extreme situations are also comprehensible in The
Magus through art and literature.  The use of classical mythology,
modern poetry, masque, autobiography, history, as well as intimations of theatre, quest romance, and detective stories are
all present in some form in the text.  The discussion of theatre
and the novel, history and literary criticism, as well as the
indulgence in artifice in order both to dramatize the consciousness
of the protagonist, and at the same time enable modes of explanation
for that consciousness, these are all fundamental aspects of this
novel's intelligibility.  In this respect, narrative is manipulated
to express ethical truths, but also to stage a self-interpretative
mode of articulation on the aesthetic level.  A logic of narrative
is grounded in a 'mise en abyme', a mirror-like self-reflection
of the process of writing and the modes of its interpretation.
Fictionality is seen to be the underlying potential of narrative,
the source of its energy; it is also the principal constituent
of social life.  The relationship between the aesthetic and the
ethical, art and life concerns, in Fowles's work is comprehensible
at this level, as protagonists attempt to give order and form
to the chaos and confusion which results from their confrontations
with unusual and extreme experiences.

In The French Lieutenant's Woman, Sarah Woodruff has to create
the fiction of the French Lieutenant in order that she may become
the outcast which her feelings about society demand.  Charles
initially sees her as the Persecuted Maiden who contains the

mysteries that were banned by Victorian morality. Dr. Grogan
gives Charles an explanation of Sarah's attraction for him in
the La Roncière story about the machinations of a young,
frustrated virgin. Immediately, life is a conspiracy, a
'dark machine'; he is determined, and destiny will not be
defied. But on further contemplation he sees Sarah for what
she is: the possibility for him to step out of the 'suffocating
banality of ordinary life' into a 'far deeper and stranger
reality'.[45] His symbolic interpretation of Sarah as instigator
of a new eden restricts his understanding, and he must overcome
these limitations in order to be able to confront life in its
multiplicity.

The basic situation of trying to cope with extreme and unusual
experiences is focused more sharply in The Ebony Tower. In the
title story, David, like Nicholas before him in The Magus, enters
the strange private world of an eccentric artist-figure, who
'lives' with two young women, and who has fashioned his world
after his own desires. The literal and figurative journey of
the central character examines his own powers of comprehension
and enables a process of self-examination. He not only enters
the debate in modern art between Realism and the Abstract, but
also questions his own ordinariness next to Breasley's eccentricity, and the artist's promiscuity next to his 'safety' in
the one marriage. The highly literate writer who nears the
completion of his life's ambition - 'a definitive biography
and critical account of Thomas Love Peacock' - in the story,
Poor Koko, attempts to use all the articulate resources available
to him to make sense of the enigma of a burglar's behaviour
towards him: the total destruction of his manuscript. The

confrontation between class-distinct beings, similar to that
Clegg-Miranda contrast in The Collector, is dramatized through
attitude, behaviour, and most of all, language. The literacy-
gulf between writer and burglar is offered as an explanation for
action. The Enigma is more ostensibly about limited understanding. The articulate female character explains the disappearance of the M.P. in terms unavailable to the quizzical
detective. The story records the exhaustion of his resources
of logic and language, and offers a hypothetical interpretation from a more literate source.

Daniel Martin's narrative persistently arrests its flow to
analyze its operation and to assess its intentions. John
Fowles's narrator wants to produce the 'real history' of
himself, exculpate his past selves in order to create a future.
As author of his own life, he becomes his own third-person.
He, in the line of other wise authors (the narrator of Balzac's
Sarrasine, for instance, as explained by Barthes in S/Z), constantly resorts to gnomic statements, which establish a level
of credibility in his truth-seeking venture. The narrator
makes sense of himself by employing traditional devices of
characterization, referring to images of modern man in literature
(especially Beckett), typifying the whole narrative venture as
a Freudian search for the lost Mother, parodying Marlow's journey
up the Congo to the heart of darkness, discussing Realism and
Modernism in the novel through the work of Lukacs, quoting
Gramsci for political comment. Ancient Egyptian civilization
and culture is compared to the modern world: the state's art
and its extreme functionalism is a symptom of the lack of
models for artistic activity in the pharoah's world.
Their equivalent in the modern world is Socialist Realism:

life for the future. This he accomplishes by retreating
into the privacy of Thorncombe with Jane.

Daniel Martin's perceptions of himself produce the very
structure of narrative:

> Above all, he felt determined ... the illusory
> pursuit of lost innocence, the seeking, or
> fascination, for situations that carried their
> own death in them from the beginning, that
> ensured an eventual determinism in the process ...
> the very perception of this was itself a crystal,
> and of the kind that profoundly structures all
> narrative art; without which it collapses both
> internally and externally.[51]

The determinism of his life, coupled with a profound sense
of loss, encourage a process of retelling which would seek
out that lost innocence and understand wherein lies the act
which would overcome his determinate being. By recreating
what might have offered a different story of his life, his
love for Jane which was so swiftly abandoned in the Oxford
days, he belies the determinism of his life since, and
creates a new beginning. Story for Daniel is a mode of
discovering through retelling: narrative is his own mode
of understanding.

Conchis in The Magus, knows the usefulness of story in advance.
As he tells his eager listener:

> It will take me a long time to define what I mean.
> It will take me the story of my life.[52]

Similarly, Daniel Martin enigmatically poses the essential

problem of his narrative in the first lines: on the one hand
the author of his life must attempt to encapsulate the vast
panorama of that reality which itself can only be 'that ultimate
ambiguous fiction of the enacted past';[53] on the other hand, the
evocation of a 'lost paradise' in the country is the place that
he will return to - it will take him the length of the story
of his life to reach that point which is the beginning.  'Story,
narration, history, lay imbricated in the nature of things.'[54]
This declaration in The Magus may, thus, stand as a slogan for
the persistence of storytelling as mode of apprehending the world.

The narrative imagination understands that story gives both order
and meaning to the chaos of life's perceptions.  The process
offers a conceptualisation of the narrational act.  Kermode
has defined this as: 'the tension... between paradigmatic form
and contingent reality'.[55]  Such a relationship consists of
the events of life and the possibilities conventionally available
for their representation in literary form.  Because form is
grounded in models, or paradigms, it possesses ready-made
structures which provide the order the storyteller requires
to make sense of his chaotic perceptions of his life.  Eidetic
images, images persisting from past perceptions, enable the
storyteller to organize and make intelligible his sense perceptions for both himself and for the reader.  As Barbara Hardy's
thesis would endorse, this process of apprehension applies to
all our generalizations and patterns of understanding our lives.
In this respect, we are all authors of our own lives, whether
we embellish or fictionalize the past or not.  The works of

John Fowles dramatize this 'narrative imagination'.[56]

Principal characters comprehend their life through modes of
narration of their own past. The novels and stories are replete
with images of the artist. Clegg in The Collector is the
perverse artist-collector, image of the gothic tyrant, who
creates a world after his own image, determines the fate of
those he manipulates, and therefore destroys the possibility
of creativity. Nicholas in The Magus, has to learn to overcome his potential for the 'calibanity' of a Clegg. Conchis
offers himself as example of the artist as liberator, wise
old man, who presents story as mirror for self-realization.

The narrator of The French Lieutenant's Woman skilfully switches
guises when it best suits him: lay-preacher or impressario;
Victorian gentleman novelist, or post-Freudian, post-Modernist,
self-conscious author. Narrating the events of a strange
burglary in Poor Koko causes anxious moments for the 'honest'
author-surrogate:

> But what concerns me far more than one or two
> minor misinterpretations or inaccuracies of
> memory is my continuing inability to make sense
> of what happened.[57]

And, Daniel Martin, playing with time-perspectives and point
of view, characterizes himself in the past, foreshadowing the
possible writing of a novel based on those events of his life:

> Already his dialogue-inventive mind, the monster
> that then still seemed a joyous gift, was secretely
> rehearsing various amusing ways of telling what
> had happened...[58]

The Hollywood scriptwriter is well skilled in producing
'special effects' and appropriate scenarios. But his intention
is a serious one as he searches to reconstruct the vanishing
past and prepare the way for a tangible future.

The centrality of storytelling as a way of making sense of
life is exemplified in the terse 'fairy tales' which
characters resort to in moments of insight. They also
enable a 'mise en abyme', a mirror image, of the meaning of
the main story in which they are contained. Miranda
composes a strip cartoon about Clegg: 'The Awful Tale of a
Harmless Boy', a nice little clerk who becomes a horror-
film monster. Nicholas discovers a fairy story written by
one of the sisters, entitled 'The Prince and the Magician',
which reflects the notions of truth and fiction, and the
need to be one's own magus which the novel itself dramatizes
through the 'godgame'. Dr. Grogan in The French Lieutenant's
Woman offers Charles the story of La Roncière, albeit misleading. In The Cloud, Catherine tells the child, Emma, the
story of the princess who eternally waits for her vanished
prince, just as she, Catherine, senses the eternal absence of
her recently deceased husband. The tale within a tale reflects
the moral within the story. Storytellers, wise magus-figures,
characters as listeners who become themselves storytellers,
are symptomatic of narrative as an imaginative heuristic
process. These artist-figures significantly seek situations
that carry 'their own death in them from the beginning'. [59]
This is the conventional sequential structure of narrative:
a point of departure that seeks its own ending.

## CHAPTER FIVE

Structure as 'verbal and psychological
coherence' in John Hawkes's Novels

In what follows, I shall firstly look at Hawkes's precise theory
of narrative 'structure', and then discuss its manifestations in
a selection of his novels taken from both the earlier works and
the more recent ones. The second part of this chapter comprises a
detailed formal analysis of the structure of <u>Second Skin</u> (1964),
where the aim is to probe the intentional relationship between the
psychology of the first-person narrator-protagonist and the unusual
complex structure of his narrative. In this way, following Hawkes's
theory of structure, I shall describe the logic of narrative which
both underlies and is partially 'foregrounded' by the structure
itself. It will be seen that precisely because of connections
between narrative logic and psychoanalytic revelation, the critic,
in his attempts to offer a formalistic analysis of the text,is
forced to mediate between conventional 'point of view' analysis and
a more formal logic of narrative method.

(i) <u>Narrative Structure as Verbal and Psychological Coherence</u>:
    <u>The Structure of Motifs</u>

The works of John Hawkes have always offered the critic the
possibility of interpreting narrative structure from an approach
through psychology.  It is the principal contention of this
chapter that psychology and form are necessary constituents of the
same problem:  the problem of narrative discourse.  Hawkes has
clearly outlined his particular definition of narrative structure
in terms of 'verbal and psychological coherence':

> Related or corresponding event, recurring image and
> recurring action, these constitute the essential sub-
> stance or meaningful density of my writing.[1]

Hawkes claims to be holding in balance 'poetic and novelistic
methods in order to make the novel a more valid and pleasurable
experience.'[2]  The new validity he wishes to bring to the novel
concerns the discovery of the appropriate form that can create the
images which correspond to that 'whole panorama  of dislocation and
desolation', and that nightmarish and violent conflict between the
disruptive needs of the 'visible' world and the unconscious desires
of the solitary will, which I have described above.  As this chapter
aims to demonstrate, Hawkes's works employ devices of modern poetry;
and  language and structure are comprehensible through poetic questions -
rhetoric, and tone in language,  complexity and paradox in structure.
Hawkes appears to transcend such conventional realist problems as
verisimilitude, and allows recurring images, motifs, patterns of
behaviour and  action to **imply** meaning.  Apparent textual incoherence
in highly fragmentary narratives demands to be understood not from

the norms of a representationalist aesthetics, but rather from
within the bounds of their own theory of narrative structure.
Psychological coherence functions as a mode of recuperation for the
dislocated narratives. The resonance of images and motifs, landscapes and recurrent patterns of action, offer the novel a mode of
coherence which relates language to psychology. In this respect,
form is manipulated, through poetic means, to encapsulate problems
of the self. This mode of narrative becomes problematical, in a
self-conscious way, with the use of first-person narrators.

Before analysizing the narrative structure of Second Skin (1964)
in some detail as a way of illustrating Hawkes's definition, I
shall look at some of the recurrent patterns and motifs in his
works in order to underline the type of coherence they give to the
text. In The Cannibal the narrative begins in 1945, returns to
1914 ( and briefly recalls 1870), and finally moves back to 1945
and the uprising perpetrated by Zizendorf and his small band of
neo-Nazis. The various crucial historical moments comment on each
other figuratively.    Recurrent actions and their consequences
are reversed,so that the effect of war in 1945 stands as an implied
critique of the idealistic fervour prior to the previous World War:
the descriptions of war-ravaged Spitzen-on-the-Dein, a desolate
landscape of insanity, peopled by the mentally and physically
maimed;  the memories echoing in the now silent, derelict Beer Hall
guide our response to the Brauhaus festivities and the nationalism
and dreams of glory, heroism and duelling which the following
section in the novel describes. The critical use of hindsight
is enabled by the actual narrative order grounded in an intentional
dislocation of temporal sequence. The dead of 1870, 1914, and then
1945 are seen as the result of idealism. By the time we reach
part three of the novel, the reader's response is governed by the

preceeding sections, and the failure alluded to by Zizendorf in the
italicized prologue ('I was forced to leave the town') is seen to
be inevitable because of the pattern of behavioural repetition,
despite the lessons offered by history. Significantly,    Zizendorf
declares in his prologue, 'at present... I am waiting, and at the
first opportunity I will return.' This pattern from idealism to
purposeful and violent action, and then through destruction to death
and failure, will ceaselessly recur.  The structural juxtaposition
of the two historical moments emphasizes the underlying irony in the
historical investigation:

> /Hawkes's/ concern is where events flow from, causalities
> (or causal illusions);  his concern is one of narrative...
> with story:  from a mad  "once-upon-a-time" to a horrific
> "the end"  3

The aetiology of behaviour in an historical  context is not only
crucial to the investigation of history itself, but is also, in
this historical novel, central to the logic of sequence in the
narrative:  the author's dislocative structure enables him to remain
detached and to allow the text to create its own mode of explanation,
structurally.

The transformation prefigured in the character, Ernst, serves as an
example of more widespread historical changes.  The once proud
duellist and chivalric suitor becomes a feeble, ill,  uninterested
and bedridden husband;  and this is a symptom of the wider
disintegration of the 1914 world in Germany.  For  not only is
Stella's family gradually destroyed, but also society in general is
seen to break up.  That world is described as  'sinking downwards
in a landslide ... that would never end.' [4] The town is gradually
corrupted by war, and streets fall into ruin;  birds cease their

singing; death and prostitution become widespread. This process
of disintegration is echoed in the recurrent, figurative references
to horses. Stella once loved 'white prancing horses, square
shouldered men with spikes rising from their helmets.'[5] But, at
the outbreak of war the 'horse' is described as black, old and
decrepit, and '"you could count his age on all the ribs".'[6] The
horse now belongs to the 'lower world', while the honeymoon takes
place in the cosmopolitan 'upper world', itself a kind of haven, a
retreat full of joy, a fleeting escape from a hostile world
(symbolized by the 'snarling dogs /which/ ran under foot'[7]). We are
told that the black horse 'thrived better in the lower world. He
was the same horse the students rode, shivering with the cold, tied
alone to suffer the night.'[8] The same black horse had shaken off
his 'coat of white'[9], transformed its symbolic reference. Equally,
the university is described, like the Asylum (both centers of
'revolution, dogma, and defeat') as drawing 'the city into its walls
with a crushing will.'[10] The transformed image of the horse, and
the university, imply in their very transformation the historical
process itself, the movement towards defeat. This process is tersely
indicated through the meaning enabled by the recurrent horse imagery.
A significant historical moment is indicated when a child cries out
"the old horse is dead".[11] Thus the text produces a fundamental
level of coherence through such recurring patterns of images and
motifs. The horse is manipulated in this novel as a figurative
correspondence to the 'essential substance' of the narrative, and
to relate the progressive movement towards destruction and death.
Dogs are used in a similar way, although their symbolic status is
more ambiguous. However, their recurrent presence does generate an
overall atmosphere of menace, violence, and impending death. Dogs
prowl the landscape from the time of Stella's return from the
honeymoon until the death of the American, Leevey, in 1945, and are

characterized as forces of evil. Both kinds of animal imagery
prevail and enable an ironic relationship between two historical
periods to be implied progressively through the narrative.
Significantly, the horse occupies a prominent place in the town
centre of 1945. The statue of a horse is in bad repair, and
Zizendorf plans, after the murder of Leevey, to 'put the old horse
statue back on its feet,'[12] a symbolic gesture which would restore
the novel's most fundamental symbol of Prussian militarism and
national pride. The use of such resonant motifs is symptomatic of
a narrative structure which achieves its coherence through a
general pattern of renewed hope and idealism followed by more defeat.
Furthermore, the wishes and 'disruptive needs' of the solitary wills
in The Cannibal are ironically encapsulated in this structure of
recurrence, juxtaposition, and resonant motifs.

John Hawkes has recently reiterated that language is used to enhance
the structure of his novels. For him this is a poetic method:
'Words, images, symbols are thematic carriers'[13] burdened with
psychological implications. In The Lime Twig (1961), the preoccupation with that 'terrifying similarity' between unconscious desires
and disruptive needs is dramatized through images and symbols, as
well as recurrent action. The possibility for fantasy-escape from
the dreary daytime world in The Lime Twig, and the enactment of
unconscious desires in the 'visible world,'is initially associated
with horses in Hencher's description of the gilded cherubim which
is as 'big as horses that fly off the top of the Dreary station
itself.'[14] This reference foreshadows the function of the horse,
Rock Castle, as an embodiment of unconscious desires, and an
instrument of their enactment in the world of gangland intrigue and

violence. The horse is harmless as a symbol in Michael's fantasies.
Once it enters his life through Hencher's involvement with the
gangland, it precipitates violent disruptions. The stallion becomes
the symbol of hitherto suppressed violence which Hencher has unwittingly unleashed. The violence contained in repressed fantasies
is irrevocably associated with the image of the horse, whose power
is also an indication of its focus as an illusion of sexual power,
a release of his frustrations prefigured in his impoverished dull
life. The actual horse, Rock Castle, causes involvement in intrigue
and death as well as fulfilment of his sexual fantasies during the
orgiastic night before the great race. The horse lures Hencher
and Michael into the plot, and significantly it is the instrument
through which Michael can destroy that plot. Therefore, the horse
functions as a motif for sexual power and violent destruction, but
it is also the motivation for the plot, in both the senses of
narrative structure and intrigue. It is the unifying element in
both the narrative and the thematic structure, and is associated in
one way or another with each character and their fate. For 'clearly
the horse is the product of wishes and desires.'[15] The horse is the
most powerful lime twig in the novel, entrapping those who are
attracted to it. Through making conscious their darkest fantasies
and desires, they become ensnared like birds stuck to the lime.

The structure of The Lime Twig is grounded in recurrent images and
modes of action referring to luring and entrapment. Through the
sustained realism of Hencher's prologue, and through our early
encounters with the life of the Banks, a forceful level of recuperation is established for the subsequent action. Impoverished lives
conceal repressed desires, the people who live with such impoverishment are easily manipulated, and in fact seem to desire it. Hencher's

initial story, and his need to assert his will, sets in motion a
pattern of behaviour that foreshadows the subsequent patterns of
obsession and entrapment.  A sense of dullness and boring conventionality is emphasized in Hencher's 'circling' around the dreary
station area for fifteen years.  Later, Banks and Hencher wander
around in the fog, apparently circling in a nebulous maze of
unreality.  The race-track also is a circuit, underlining the
circle as a primary symbol of repetition, which in a more universal
application points to the cycle of human failure that pervades
The Cannibal, and is seen here, in The Lime Twig, in the degradation,
squalor and corruption of war-torn England.  The image of repetition
also indicates the entrapment in fantasy of which it is the cause.
The structure of enticement is set in motion by Hencher through
leading Michael into the intrigue surrounding the horse-stealing.
Michael is limed by his fantasy-desire.  Both he and Margaret are
finally 'lured to a lime twig and  stuck fast for destruction.'[16]
Hencher's action foreshadows Larry's role, as he further entraps
Michael and Margaret in a night of violence, orgy  and assault.
Hencher's death mirrors  the death of Michael by the powerful destructive force of the stallion.  Finally, the structure of recurrent
motifs surrounding luring and entrapment is exemplified at the moment
when Michael and Margaret's capture is related to limed birds:

> Even two oven tits may be snared and separated in such
> a dawn. [17]

This recurrent image enables an explanation of the temporal dislocation between chapters six and seven, whereby the brutal beating
and rape of Margaret in chapter six is seen as a direct result of
Michael's sexual exploits and Larry's consequent anger in the following
chapter.  The oven tit that stirs on a branch at four o'clock is the

mate of the oven tit described towards the end of chapter seven.
The motif of birds and lime twigs function as both thematic carriers
and, in this instance, as structural indications. Michael's moment
of decision to act purposively is echoed in a further use of the
motif. A bird is seen 'flying straight up from the thick brown
tree with its song turned into a high and piping whistle.'[18] Later
Michael 'saw a dove bursting with air on a bough'[19] at the point
when he is about to stop the race.

A poetic structure grounded in words, images and symbols as thematic
carriers is consistent in the works of John Hawkes. The complex
patterns of motifs and images in The Blood Oranges (1971) draw
attention to possible meanings. However, in this novel, and in
other first-person narratives by Hawkes, the issue is complicated
because the narrator himself interprets images and symbols to his
advantage: Cyril in The Blood Oranges interprets motifs as signs
of hope for the 're-establishment' of his 'ultimate harmony'. In
any one scene, flamboyantly described by the narrator, the oblique
and highly figurative manner in which he 'writes' undermines his
reliability. The complex imagery patterns have to be understood if
the scenes he describes are to make any sense. Some of these are
directly concerned with Cyril's view of himself and his determination
to reassert harmony:

> Obviously the two birds mating on the horizon were for
> me a sign, an emblem, a mysterious medallion, a good
> omen. They augured well for the time I had spent with
> Catherine and for my own future in the electrified field
> of Love's art'[20]

However, this statement, and its pompous rhetoric, its egotistical
tone, is immediately disabled by Cyril's doubts about the symbolism

of the birds. Some of the scenes and their patterns of images
and motifs are directly concerned with the central themes and with
the conflict on the level of characterization. For, as I described
in the _Part One_ above, the novel is structured on theme and
character constrasts grounded in Cyril's view of the fundamental
conflict between his 'sex-singing' and Hugh's 'medievalism'. The
chronology of events is dislocated and scenes are related through
recurring images and motifs. Mythic and Christian symbols are
given unconventional meaning enabling the elaborate structure of
implied motifs to imaginatively create a new moral order which aims
to supersede a sterile Christianity. Unfortunately, any psychological coherence is attained at great effort by the reader. For
he is initially at the mercy of Cyril's rhetoric. Not only is
Illyria a place where time 'melts and flows', where precise
definition is significantly absent, but also Cyril talks of 'an
undying unity' where 'everything coheres'.[21] We must be readily
critical of Cyril's fictions.[22] His self-conscious artificiality,
his lyricism, his ritualizing of the most banal events, despite
the destruction he has caused, serve to allow a critique of the
narrator. His idiosyncratic use of images and symbols, and the
distance the reader obtains from the persuasive force of Cyril's
assertions, enable two levels of psychological coherence: the
one Cyril would like us to accept; the other, the one we are able
to perceive behind the torrent of words, so to speak. In understanding the motivation for Cyril's art, we understand his
psychology. The interplay between language and images, and the
intentionality which they contain, gives the novel a structural
coherence.

In <u>Death, Sleep and the Traveller</u>, once again a fragmentary mode
of narration, dislocating time and fragmenting event into a series
of recurring patterns, gives the lie to the obsessions of a
narrating consciousness. Intentionality is partially revealed by
the narrative structure where sexuality is fetishistically dominant
and yet meaninglessness is the lesson to be learnt. Allert's
narrative is characterized as 'concreteness rotating toward illusion.'[23] Just how much is 'fact' and how much fantasy is difficult
to assess. The two triadic relationships which reflect each other
may well be projections of the narrator's fantasy. Nevertheless,
they do produce a set of recurrent patterns of action consistent
with the Hawkesian desire for verbal and psychological coherence.
Allert's 'triangle' on the cruise enables him to assert his sexual
prowess in compensation for his inadequacies in the other triadic
relationship with wife and her lover. The narrator's accumulation
of words cover up the pain of his isolation and remorse. Psychology
explains structural framentaries, as it did more especially in
Hawkes previous two novels, and the narrator's intentionality is
revealingly foregrounded through his insistence not to tell the
story directly.

In the novels and stories of John Hawkes, landscape is used to create
tone, atmosphere, and meaning. As I showed in the previous section,
landscapes of desolation, destruction, death-ridden hostile places
of decay symbolized the view a world in the aftermath of war. But
landscapes are also used as correlatives for states of mind. For
instance, <u>The Beetle Leg</u> (1951) is characterized by its desolate,
arid and noxious land of anti-growth. The people are equally sterile
and unproductive. The sheriff who narrates the beginning of the

novel exposes his restictive and noxious mentality in his
explanation of the 'lawless country'.  Insects plague the people
of this barren wasteland, and the motifs of barreness and
suppressed hostility recur throughout the novel, giving the text
a coherence of tone and atmosphere.  The landscape recalls 'The
Burial of the Dead' in T. S. Eliot's The Wasteland.

Landscapes in Hawkes's work not only create a world, but also
create 'the shape of the satiric writer's meaningful psychic
paradox (Hawkes).'[24]  As his works are replete with portraits of
the artist, landscape either gives the cause for the artist's impotence, or offers a critique for his delusional and 'dishonest'
assertions.  Cyril's paradise in The Blood Oranges is a place of
destruction, decay, and death;  Skipper's Spice Island in Second
Skin is a land of tropical swamps and rotting vegetation which he
learns  to accept as a better alternative to the barren, cold and
desolate Atlantic Island.  The islands are both correlations for
his states of mind.  Allert in Death, Sleep and the Traveller creates
the sun-drenched island which he visits on the 'cruise' as a distinct
contrast to the cold, snowy Northern  place where his friend, and
wife's lover dies in the Sauna.  'Hawkes creates atmosphere through
locations that recur and meaning by juxtaposing these locations.'
Conceptual patterns (life versus death, for instance), and
psychological revelation are implied through fragments of recurring
descriptions:

> The author's world therefore has psychoanalytical
> validity and carries the reader beyond outer actuality
> to inner reality, an inner reality whose instability
> is symbolized by Hawkes's landscapes and settings.[25]

The juxtaposition of fragments creates the 'associational flow'
characteristic of much modern poetry.  The relationship between
recurrent images is not arbitrary but, conversely, masks a highly
'shaped', highly 'textured' work, based on what Hawkes has called
'controlled chaos'.[26]  The party scenes in <u>Charivari</u> (1949) are
noted for the hurly-burly commotion and tumult, and this wildness
creates an absurdly confusing atmosphere.  The bizarre juxtapositions
of violent fantasy and absurd reality establish a surrealistic text
the   destructive landscapes and repressed sexuality of which are held in
balance by the chilling comedy to which the title refers.

The haunted world of oppression is a feature of the Grotesque in
art and literature.  Disharmony;  the comic side by side with the
tragic; exaggeration and extravagance;  abnormality and the tension
between horror, pity and mirth define the Grotesque.[27]  Hawkes's
early work resembles the grotesque perspective formally, with its
fragmentariness, its bizarre juxtapositions, and thematically, with
its demonic vision of the insane, the maimed, and the violent
manipulators.  Wolfgang Kaiser defined the nature of the Grotesque
in art and in literature as nightmarish and ominously demonic,
'the medium through which some horror, anguish, or fear of the
incomprehensible is expressed.'[28]  Among its most persistent motifs,
we find human beings reduced to puppets (manipulated victims), and
man reduced to caricature.  'The encounter with madness is one of
the basic experiences of the grotesque,' and insanity is related
to the artists state of mind, his mad fantasies and dreams.  As I
have argued, the early works contain damning parodies of the writer
as manipulator and fascist dictator; the violence he perpetrates

is echoed in the landscapes of his world. But the later writer-
narrators are also fantasists who delude themselves with their own
ornate rhetoric. Kayser tells us that the Grotesque 'instills fear
of life rather than fear of death,' and there are many examples of
this in Hawkes's work. 'The loss of identity ... the destruction of
personality, and the fragmentation of historical order,'[29] recall
both the themes and the structure of The Cannibal. The world of
the Grotesque appears in 'the vision of dreamer or daydreamer.'
It often appears in two basic modes, and Hawkes seems to combine
them in his works:

> ...the "fantastic" grotesque with its oneiric worlds
> and the radically "satiric" grotesque with its play
> of masks.[30]

Laughter is cynical and mocking as the form plays on the absurd.
Many of Hawkes's characters are absurdly comic or foolish; some,
in the later works, self-consciously so, others, in the early works,
unself-critical, rigid and narrow-minded, and therefore more severely
criticized. However, Kaiser's conclusion that the invocation of
demonic forces in the world effects both a liberation and a subduing
of those forces is not born out in Hawkes's grotesque 'worlds'.
Such horror and helplessness, violence and absurd destruction is
indeed liberated, but from within the minds of those who secretly
harbour repressed terror. Nothing in the end is subdued. The
irrationalism of the Grotesque is partly mitigated in these novels
by the play on psychological coherence. This accounts for the
structural as well as thematic manifestations of the Grotesque,
prefigured in 'suddeness and surprise', pregnant moments, and
situations 'filled with ominous tension.'[31]

The essential incongruity of juxtaposed elements are held in
balance in novels like The Blood Oranges, where Cyril, as artist-
surrogate, describes the essential features of his art as

> Grace and chaos, control and helplessness, mastery
> and collapse. [32]

The baroque structuring of paradoxical elements is a formal reflection of the fundamental conflicts on a thematic level. His
'tapestry' contains 'several different modes of incongruity.'[33]
The pervasive symbol of the blood orange itself reflects the
structural and thematic coherence of this novel:

> The fruit is sweet, but it's streaked with the colour
> of blood, which ... is a paradox. It means that the
> blood is real but also sweet; it means that no sweet-
> ness is ephemeral but on the contrary possesses all the
> life-drive seriousness of the rich black flow of blood
> itself. It suggests wound invading desire, desire
> "containing" agony. [34]

Unresolved contradictions permeate Cyril's assertions: love and
death, the illusion of altruism and the desolation of solipsism,
harmony and discord; this multiplicity of contradiction is not
just a symptom of Cyril's narrating consciousness, but is contained
in the paradoxical structure of fragmented movement between desolate
present and idealistic past in the narrative discourse. The agony
caused by Cyril's play on desire is absurdly contained in his
pompous, self-abnegatory narrative. The timelessness of Illyria
is invaded by Cyril's 'weekly ritual of hope and fidelity,'[35] and
by the presence of death in his paradise. The forty-two scenes
in the novel appear arbitrarily juxtaposed, yet thematic and image
patterns relate them. The frequent movement between present and
past belies any precise chronology of events in that past. The

present, however, is characterized by its 'weekly ritual'.

(ii)  The analysis of structure:  towards a logic of narrative.

Psychological coherence is achieved through a play on images, resonant motifs, symbolic landscapes, and recurrent patterns of behaviour.   The narrative form has been described as a juxtaposition of fragments which cohere in an overall structure grounded in 'verbal and psychological coherence'.  Since Second Skin (1964), Hawkes has been more exclusively concerned with the manipulation of narrative structure as a mode of foregrounding the psychological problem of unreliable, impotent narrators.  The problematical inter-play between narrative logic and psychoanalytic revelation is the subject of this particular section.  I shall focus more sharply on the question of structure in Second Skin.  In this work, Hawkes has written both a parody of the novel in general, a self-conscious and self-critical artifact, and also his most thoroughgoing parody of the writer.  He is able to sustain this level of self-awareness because of the unifying device of a first-person narrator in what amounts to a play on the autobiographical mode.  Through the relationship between narrative structure and psychoanalytical revelation, this novel is able to ground its perspective in the normally unifying and reliable unity of the single narrating consciousness, while at the same time, through structural dislocations, emphasizing fragmentation and chaos in both the narrator's mind and also in the world of his apparent experiences.  The consolations of form (the narrator, Skipper's particular version) are in the final analysis only Skipper's consolations, not the reader's, as structure enables a critique of his deceptions.  By the end of the novel the reader is fully aware that Skipper is a victim of solipsism, of the

limitations of his view of himself and others. He thrives on
his delusions of courage and heroism. Yet the same reader must
also be conscious that the protagonist narrator has survived the
traumatic events of his past, and is narrating through carefully
selected episodes and with a particular order of revelation from
the tranquil vantage of his 'paradise' island. It is the manner
of his narration, the order  through which the events are told and,
of course, the exclusiveness of his viewpoint which enables his
successful self-affirmation.

There is, therefore, a clearly defined situation whereby Skipper
'writes' his 'naked history' from the comparative peace of his
new life and thus is able to come to terms with the brutal events
of his past through the distancing effect of his present 'reality'.
In his mind there are two separate realities, the one being characterized by 'nakedness', the other by his clumsy entrapment in oilskins, for instance. Skipper's second skin is a metaphor for the
order of his new-found reality and new identity, and this differs
in his mind significantly from the first skin of his past identity.
One of life's failures is seen to create a second chance for himself.

The antipodal nature of these two realities is expressed in terms of
two islands. This mode of thinking about, and giving order to,
experience founds the narrative structure: a pattern of alternation
between the brutal acts of the 'first skin' world, and the paradise
world of picnics and artificial insemination on the Spice Island.
Skipper literally embarks on a voyage that takes him through a time-
bound barren rocky island in the Atlantic, a focus for the hostility
and deaths which concern him in the past, and then onto a more
imaginary, timeless tropical island where he literally has the time

to procreate, in one way or another, and through love come to terms
with death. In many respects, this is a novel about man's time-
bound existence in a world of chaos and violence where suicide is
a feature of Skipper's involvement with those he 'loves'. But the
novel is also about the possibility available in art to reshape,
refurbish a world elsewhere where love and procreation dominate and
transcend the 'seeds of death'. This is the way Skipper would
encourage the reader to see his 'serpentine tale', and his Spice
Island alternative. Moreover, the idea of Second Skin refers to the
activity of writing, the artificial but affirmative manipulation of
words to design a surrogate identity and a self-styled world. The
narrator self-consciously mediates between the experiences of both
islands, between past and present, outlining a conflict between the
two, yet the reader at least is able to understand by the end that
both islands are part of a total order of experience which the narrator
tries to come to terms with. Understanding Skipper's 'schizophrenic
flesh'[36] enables us to account for structural features.

The principal characteristic of the narrator's voice is a fumbling
attention to detail, especially at crucial moments from the past.
Skipper apparently needs to convey the 'true tonality' of events,
and this obsessive quest for authentication masks a profound fear
of complete revelation both to his daughter, Cassandra, and to himself:

> The truth. Yet wasn't I deceiving her even then?
> Wasn't I sparing her certain details, withholding
> others, failing somehow to convey the true tonality
> of the thing? [37]

The narrator overindulges in his apparent love of detail, and yet
he spares certain other details. This latter 'prerogative' creates
suspicion in the reader about his reliability. The narrator's

speaking voice is characterized by 'the suave relishing of words
and rhythms: a prose of delicate balance.' His mode of description
is impressionistic, 'with its controlled wandering of memory and
nuanced foreshadowing of later incidents /with/ . . . elaborate
reasonings /and/ composed classical allusions.'[38] Through the
poetic balance and rhythmic flow of words, Skipper attempts to
persuade the reader through his version and through the control he
exercises over form, that he is indeed reliable: he aims to engage
our attention compellingly through his elaborate reasoning. Naming
names and manipulating classical allusions give the lie to the
credibility of his articulate assertions.

The narrator claims that he 'matured into a muscular and self-
willed Clytemnestra',[39] the cause of murder and revenge. This
illusion of a positive trait is tempered by the idea that if he
had been born his mother's daughter he would have become 'a large
and innocent Iphigenia betrayed on the beach.'[40] The final image
of Skipper's character is one which combines both allusions, but
with a bias towards the Iphigenia. We might conclude then that he
is more like his mother's daughter, and he does indeed exhibit an
effeminate walk. This, coupled with his ineffectual nature, is
fundamental to his evidently repressed homosexuality.

Classical allusions foreshadow the revelations of events and
Skipper's involvement in them, but also they emphasize his unreliability through the misleading use of such allusions. He equates
himself with Hamlet because of his wish to portray an heroic stature.
Yet it is the morbid connections with death that truly relate Skipper
to Hamlet. The self-deceptive use of allusions is exposed in his
descriptions of the crucial figures in his life. Cassandra is the
BVM (Blessed Virgin Mary), although we realize her sexual complicity
with the crew of the Peter Poor is obvious to everyone except Skipper.

He even mitigates her willing involvement with the three soldiers
in the desert incident.[41]   Miranda is described as Venus, although
she appears frequently as the 'dark lady'.   Not a young and innocent
lover on the enchanted island of her namesake in The Tempest, this
Miranda is associated with Skipper's impotence and 'castration fears'.
Her overbearing sexuality expose Skipper's inadequacies.   Tremlow,
a young sailor from the past who mocked and even sexually assaulted
Skipper,is always used as the satanic figure who can be blamed for
all the 'brutal' acts  which the narrator tries to control through
his narration.   Names and allusions are initially misleading, then,
but the subsequent revelations obliquely correct these initial assertions.   Dishonest statements about other people lead us to suspect an
equal dishonesty about himself.   His version rewrites his role in
the past, elevates his personality above that of a mere figure of
fun to the level of the heroic.   He characterizes himself as a
courageous but helpless victim of brutal maliciousness.   Furthermore, his self-conscious articulation of words and images demands
that his narrative be read in a certain way:

> High lights of helplessness?  Mere trivial record of
> collapse?  Say, rather, that it is the chronicle of
> recovery, the history of courage, the dead reckoning
> of my romance, the dance of shadows.   And all the
> earmarks of pageantry, if you will, the glow of Skipper's
> serpentine tale. [42]

Skipper   is  not only conscious of the need to justify to
himself, at least, his version of his personality and the view
of other characters that he allows, but he is also highly aware
of his role as self-styled chronicler of these 'dreams', the
'cameo profiles of my beribboned brooch,'[43] and also of the
'neutralizing'[44] effect of his writing.   It is his attitude to his

writing that enables him to succeed in exorcising the traumas of
his past.   He can impose a structure which will effect a beginning
('because I suppose that names must precede these solid worlds of
my passionate time and place and action.'[45]) and an end ('because
now I am fifty-nine years old and I knew I would be.'[46]).   The
main content of his tale is intentionally encased in all the evidence
of his 'success', qualified as it may be.   He can hold the horror of
the past, and the pain of its revelation at a distance by inter-
spersing recollections of that past with accounts of the 'evidence,
proof, the exhilerating images'[47] of his present life.   Yet,
significantly, this very structure is precisely the evidence available
to the reader of the narrator's partially concealed psychology:   it
reveals the necessary quota of intentionality which will permit the
reader to respond with a certain critical awareness to that gulf
between word and deed through which an implied author builds in a
subtle and pervasive critique of his narrator.

The direct division between past and present, paradise and 'hell',
life and death, black and white, proposed by the self-conscious
narrator, testifies to his inability to cope with fragmentation and
ambivalence at any level.   The abiding need to organize, to simplify,
the multiplicity of experience is fundamental to his use of antipodal
islands.   As Hawkes himself has recently commented:

> The juxtaposition of the two islands, the juxtaposition
> of Cassandra's death and the eventual birth of Catalina
> Kate's black child, these are the essential opposites of
> Second Skin. [48]

The novel portrays two dominant landscapes, the one a barren, rocky,
windswept and sombre Atlantic island noted for its desolation, decay
and death;   the other, a tropical island described as a paradise of
fruit, gentle winds and fertility.   Cassandra and her mentor,

Miranda, are the human embodiments of that destructive potential which
reverberates through the hostile landscape of the Atlantic island;
Catalina Kate symbolizes the life-force of the alternative island.
She, in her simplicity, naked and pregnant, is apparently able to
defy the miasmic landscape of the tropical swamp by her very presence.
The islands function as symbolic focii for Skipper's attempts to make
sense of his life.

The Atlantic island is a death-ridden landscape, a place of rotting,
rusting, disintegration, and barrenness.  It is a wholly necessary
landscape through which Skipper can explain the violence and apparent
maliciousness of his experiences.  The place of darkening storm, chaos,
and hostility, is viewed from  the calm and friendliness of the tropical
island:

> In the sun of the tropical island the dangerous death-
> ridden landscape of the Atlantic island loomed with a
> beauty quite the equivalent of the Caribbean island
> paradise. [49]

These words by Hawkes describe his own situation, writing Second Skin.
They do underline the necessary distance that such alternatives create.
Skipper, his narrator, is not just retelling the events which took
place on that Atlantic island, using it as a focus for an extreme
psychological state, but also he is writing the characterization of
himself, emphasizing his courageous role despite his 'victimization'.
Recalling the past through the tranquillity of the present (and even
Cassandra's death is apparently seven years from that present time of
narration), he is quite distanced from those circumstances.  His
'distant shore' is a measure of his ability to fictionalize those
'highlights of helplessness' and to render the most effective
characterization of himself through his persuasive rhetoric.

The Atlantic island is, then, a focus for the past, just as the
Spice Island is a focus for the present.  The clear distinction

between the two islands is symptomatic of his need to emphasize the transformation in his circumstances.   If at the start of his tale he claims that it will soon be clear that he is a man of courage, and a courageous victim, we must realize immediately that whatever really happened, so to speak, the narration of those events contains prior intentions, and Skipper makes no attempt to conceal the fact.   Moreover, frequently he seems to have to remind himself not only of his primary intention to justify his past failures and emphasize the positive nature of his survival, but also of the difference between past and present circumstances and identities exemplified in the division of experience into two opposing island worlds.   Herein the structure of the narration is explained:   a first chapter functions as a microcosm of the essential features of the work, introducing characters and foreshadowing events.   Then ensues a pattern of two sections consisting of highlights of brutal acts from the past followed by a Spice Island section.   In this way, the narrator appears to create an interlude for recovery before returning to the 'painful' narration of more brutal acts from the past.   In the tropical island scenes, Skipper reminds himself of his intentions as narrator, and also congratulates himself on the success of his new life.   Towards the end, as he prepares to recount the traumatic episode of Cassandra's suicide and his ineffectual efforts to save her, he indulges in quite a long section, from his Spice Island haven, building up his ego with descriptions of his role as artificial inseminator and as leader of his small community.   After this he feels prepared to go on 'to the dead reckoning of (his) romance,'[50] to narrate Cassandra's suicide. His apparently simple, archetypal mode of ordering experience in narrative is both a weakness and a strength:  by proposing such a direct division between past and present, in all its manifestations, he gives the lie to his inability to cope with life's multiplicity; but, this is also a saving inadequacy and the foundation of his

survival.   The psychological urgency to absolve his involvement
with the 'seeds of death' through retelling the content of the
most painful events in the manner described above, is the basis for
a logic of narrative.   The self-conscious artificer exorcises through
art:

> for it is clear from start to finish that Skipper,
> feet propped on the rotted sill, is contentedly writing
> his own history, is (at least after the fact, as artist)
> arranging the events of his life in the order, and with
> the emphasis, that is most pleasing to himself. 51

A principal aspect of Skipper's attempt to understand and control
terrifying events through his narrative structure is the use of
colour imagery.   The manipulation of colours will be seen to be a
symptom of the narrator's search for order and stability in his
process of comprehension, but also evidence of fragmentation.   An
abiding paradox in this connection is that Skipper survives on the
'wandering' island, itself noted for its spatial and temporal
uncertainty, and fails hopelessly on the stable, solid, time-bound
'Gentle' island in the Atlantic.

Colours are used as objective correlatives for Skipper's states of
mind and also as thematic carriers.   The major colours that focus our
attention structurally and thematically are yellow and green, and black
and white.   They depend for their meaning on the dictates of locale
and mood.   During the scenes of his experiences in the past, yellow
is emblematic of pain and of painful situations.   When his wife,
Gertrude, dies, her room is described as a 'pure lemon colour';   the
dance-hall in the high school and the tattoo-parlour are both
characterized by their yellow glow, thus linking them in a situation
of pain and humiliation.   Miranda wears yellow slacks when she
sexually confronts Skipper and this, through cross-reference to other
images of destruction, points to her 'destructive' sexuality.   On the
'Peter Poor', oilskins are yellow, and by implication serve as a

warning of impending danger. The traditional associations of black
with death are maintained on the Atlantic Island and during any
reference to his childhood: his father's black limousine, the
mortician's vehicle, is a prime example. Thus black is instantly
associated with death and suffering. The island itself is characterized by its sombreness, a dark place of pain and suffering, and
Miranda's influence on Cassandra is seen in terms of the black yarn
she knits with. It is an image of their dangerous entanglement,
as Skipper points out:

> Between the two of them always the black umbilicus,
> the endless and maddening absorption in the problems
> of yarn.[52]

A climax in this black-imagery is reached with the obsessive
recurrence of Miranda's totemic black brassiere which looms larger
than life, and functions to stress Skipper's fear of her sexuality
which threatens to expose his impotence and to destroy the 'innocence'
of Cassandra, in his estimation. Thus far, traditional concepts
prevail, but with the use of white and green these are disrupted.
White is normally an emblem of ambiguity and green an image of life
and fertility. In the scenes from his past white is evoked in
refering to his mother's demise (she is dressed in white) and
subsequently white, along with black, refers to death. Skipper's
white naval uniform becomes sullied in time after much suffering;
Miranda places it on a tailor's dummy and he eventually discards it
completely, evidently a symbolic act in his exorcism of the demonic
Tremlow. Cassandra's face reminds Skipper of Pascal's white death
mask, and yet he prefers to associate her with the virginal whiteness
of the Blessed Virgin Mary.[53] But there is no confusion here, because
white has been already firmly associated with lack of innocence and
with death on the Atlantic Island. The colour green is used
untraditionally to refer to humiliation and death, prefigured in the

painful tattooing in green of Fernandez's name on Skipper's chest:
significantly it is Cassandra who forces him to be subjected to this
torture, and also it is Fernandez whose ill-fated marriage to Cassandra
finally ends in his violent death.  It is Fernandez's green car which
is used on the honeymoon, as is his green guitar, its strings being
eventually used to strangle him.  Green, slimy lizards are another
colour-cross-reference, beginning with the soldiers in the desert
described as 'deadly lizards', and culminating in the iguana on the
Spice Island, 'thirty pounds of sprawling bright green putty'[54] which
eventually crawls away.  Therefore, in all this, colour is given
significance through its thematic centrality, and through the narrator's
efforts to order a very disordered and fragmentary experience.

However, a certain amount of confusion is initially caused by the
reversal of these colours-as-emblems on the Spice Island;  and this is
more especially the case when we consider that the narrative frequently
alternates between these two orders of experience.  The four major
colours thus fall into two distinct sets of references.  'Order' is
maintained however because these two sets are as consistently maintained as the islands are separated.  Skipper himself celebrates this
fact:

> Because I know and have stated here, that behind every frozen
> episode of that other island . . . there lies the golden wheel
> of my hot sun;  behind every black rock a tropical rose. . .55

For, here black is associated with romance, life, and procreation in
the various shapes of Sonny, Sister Josie, and Kate, and finally
embodied in the black baby, which counteracts all the prior images of
sterility.  Yellow becomes a triumphant golden, the colour of
Skipper's skin enriched by the sun, which helps to fade the green
tattoo.  Green is re-established as the emblem of romance and
fertility and both Skipper and Sonny wear white, while the former
artificially impregnates cows, and the latter makes love to Kate.

The conscious use of colour-imagery is consistent with Hawkes's
theory of structure. Verbal and psychological coherence within a
single totality was seen to be central to his idea of structure which
was defined as 'related or corresponding event, recurring image and
recurring action'. Thus, psychological coherence is conveyed in
this novel by Skipper's colour insistencies, once the reader is aware
of the two different sets of colour relationships, and once he realizes
that both sets comment on each other in the same way the islands do.
Skipper's final triumph is symbolized in the normalizing of traditional references of colours to their appropriate themes, but it is
also symptomatic of the necessary requisite that he accept the
possible ambiguity inherent in meaning at any level. The fact that
he explains and excuses the past through an archetypal pattern of
intelligibility is evidence of his avoidance of ambivalence. At
least the ongoing conflict between Thanatos and Eros is in the final
analysis partially transcended by the ritualistic celebration of
birth amongst the graves. Structural coherence is conveyed through
colour imagery, but its idiosyncratic use by the narrator indicates
the extent of his desire to influence opinion.[56]

Once the narrative structure is explained, then the problem of
intentionality can be seen to be crucial in the set of problematical
relationships between narrator, reader, and a detached but implied
author. How, then, does the reader respond to Skipper's histrionic
sensibility, the sensibility of a narrator who wants both to express
the 'true tonality' of event and yet seeks to mystify through the
purposeful complexity of his highly structured narrative. The
sometimes frantic quality of his voice undermines his confident
claims for self-justification. Hawkes has recently stated that in
Second Skin he wanted to create the kind of novel that would allow

for 'the dramatic interplay between what a narrator perceives and
what the reader perceives.'[57]   This dramatic interplay leads to
a tension between the credibility which the reader seeks to determine from the narration of events, and the strangeness of the
narrator's inconsistent voice (self-justificatory, egotistic, and
confident tone, punctuated by moments of hysteria), and the anomalies
of his narrative structure.   The most traumatic moments (the murder
of Fernandez for instance) are conveniently enveloped in brutal events
which render the notion of helplessness on the part of Skipper, and
those events themselves are mitigated by descriptions of an alternative mode of existence on the Spice Island.   Such narrative anomalies are related to the reprehensible, yet comic, nature of Skipper's
character which is revealed gradually and indirectly by the implied
author's play on the reader's search for explanation.

The structure of Second Skin can be described in a more formal,
schematic manner deriving from Mukarovsky's notion of 'foregrounding',
as a paper by R. Imhoff has clearly demonstrated.[58]   Hawkes has
claimed that he has abandoned familiar ways of thinking about 'fiction'
and that 'totality of vision or structure'[59] was his principal concern.
How does Hawkes demonstrate his transcendence of familiar ways, or
conventions of writing, in Second Skin? The novel is based on a
first person narrator's unreliable tale, and this is a very
traditional literary device.   The text begins with a conventional
exposition of characters, narrator's self, and the foreshadowing
of events.   Skipper is located in the present narrative mode, and
the narration proceeds through the oscillation between flashbacks
and present situation.   This mode of narrative is quite normative.
But a careful analysis of the structure reveals a more complex and
less normative mode.   Hawkes's fracturation of the norm his own

work establishes at the outset is intelligible through the notion
of 'foregrounding.'

Mukarovsky investigated the fundamental nature of poetry from the
point of view of the intentional violation by poetic language
of normative, everyday language. Poetry's systematic violation of
the standard usage of such normative language foregrounds its very
claims to be poetry:

> The function of poetic language consists in the maximum
> foregrounding of the utterance. Foregrounding is the
> opposite of automatization, that is, the deautomatization
> of an act; the more an act is automatized, the less it is
> consciously executed; the more it is foregrounded, the more
> completely conscious does it become. Objectively speaking:
> automatization schematizes an event; foregrounding means the
> violation of the scheme. [60]

The poem thus draws attention to itself through its play on language.
By extension of the analogy, a certain normative idea of poetry can
be violated itself by disturbing the poetic components, and therefore
the reader's expectations. The maximum foregrounding of the poetic
utterance would draw attention to the very relationships between
components by distorting their normative organization. The component
of the work which sets it in motion and gives it direction will then
influence our awareness of any consequent distortion. The argument
extends from the level of language to that of the 'aesthetic canon',
which Mukarovsky defines as 'the set of firm and stable norms into
which the structure of a preceding school of poetry has dissolved
by automatization.'[61] Therefore, every work of poetry is comprehensible against the background of a tradition, a set of conventions,
from the point of view of which it may constitute a distortion. New
trends in literature are clearly defined by the extent of their
violation of accepted aesthetic norms from whatever history of
literature that standard emanates.

The interplay between foregrounding and that from which it deviates within any work enables a definition of structure. Mukarovsky concludes that:

> The mutual relationships of the components of the work
> of poetry, both foregrounded and unforegrounded, constitute
> its <u>structure</u>, a dynamic structure including both convergence
> and divergence and one that constitutes an indissociable
> artistic whole, since each of its components has its value
> precisely in terms of its relation to that totality. [62]

As Imhoff claims, this notion of structure 'as an interplay between different parts of the artistic work has a striking applicability to <u>Second Skin</u>.'[63]  In this respect, an analogical shift comes into operation, whereby the analysis of language components in poetry becomes the relationship between narrative units and materials in the novel.  Hawkes claims to be critical of familiar ways of writing novels and therefore appears to want to violate the conventional norms, and 'deautomatize' the novel.

The standard, or norm, from which the violations in <u>Second Skin</u> may be judged, is established at the outset of the novel.  A narrator uses the narrative-with-flashback from the position of the present narrative mode, which itself disrupts the expectations invested in the autobiographical intimations of Skipper's initial statements:  recollections of past experiences would normally succeed one another in chronological order.  The first norm is replaced by a more complex norm, but this 'flashback' technique is still itself a standard novelistic convention.  Thus the text establishes a logic of structure which creates expectations of continued movement into more flashbacks or returns to the present mode.  A pattern appears to have been established.  However, this current norm of oscillating between present and past is usually foreshadowed by Skipper's anticipatory remarks.  But once he begins to mention the death of

Fernandez he then avoids the expected section concerning that memory. The pattern is disrupted. There appears to be a gap in the text's 'continuity'. This problem recurs later in the text after Skipper should have continued the description of life on the Atlantic island. He continues to omit the story about Fernandez's death, and instead indulges in a lengthy recollection of his daughter's honeymoon with Fernandez. This is followed by descriptions of the aftermath of Skipper's wife's suicide. Thus the 'flashbacks' now appear to occur anywhere, and the carefully controlled and ordered narrative is becoming more arbitrary in its logic.

The structure of a work is perceived cumulatively as the reader follows the sequence of narrative units. He relates components as he comes to them, and in this way he attempts to render the structure intelligible. The process is described thus:

> (1) The perception (decoding) of the work of art is a linear process which runs through time. Only when the total meaning has been perceived, is the work of art complete for the perceiver.
>
> (2). . . Each new sign, or partial sign, i.e. each part of the work of art of which the perceiver becomes aware during the process of perception, not only joins these parts which have penetrated the perceiver's consciousness before, but changes, in major or minor ways, the meaning of everything that has preceded it. On the other hand, everything that has preceded, affects the newly perceived parts. Each component of the work bears partial meanings, and the totality of interrelationships of these partial meanings is the work of art as a complex semantic whole. [64]

This process of decoding applies significantly to the reading of Second Skin which has already been described. Adjustments are continually required as modified norms develop new expectations for parts to be perceived. The play on expectations was seen to be a feature of the thematic, schematization of colour imagery in this novel. It is with 'The Brutal Act' section that a major break in the 'normative' pattern most radically occurs. This section contains a collection of disparate past events, partially recalled, and all vaguely related to the title. Suicide, violation, and victimization are almost hysterically related. This section is highly foregrounded by its disruption of the narrative norm, and by Skipper's indirect and almost evasive recollection of the murder scene, which finally is seen to draw attention to itself in every way possible: constant postponement; framing by reference with other 'disappointment' scenes concerning Cassandra; near-hysterical tone of Skipper's preface to this crucial event. Structurally, therefore, the text foregrounds the significance of Fernandez's murder. This unfamiliar mode of narration enables Hawkes to fulfil his aims of disrupting conventional novelistic technique. Moreover, it allows for the insertion of psychological problems into the explanation of narrative structure. Through the first-person narrative mode, as I have argued, the motivation for structural anomalies is intelligible and thus recuperable through the unusual character of Skipper. As Imhoff rightly claims:

> Whatever dark significance the murder scene possesses
> for Skipper, there is little doubt that he avoids
> recalling that traumatic moment from the past; and the
> consequence is the convoluted and unconventional
> structure of his story. 65

Hawkes foregrounds both the underlying structure of his text and the psychology of his protagonist-narrator. Verbal and psychological coherence is thus maintained. The controlling functions of convergence and divergence revolve around the dominant event of Fernandez's murder. Resonant correspondances and a general backward and forward movement enable the crucial murder, the sexual assault, and the suicide to reverberate throughout the novel. These are Skipper's traumas, and they cause, in ways described above, the necessary series of dislocations and transformations which

disrupt the automatization of narrative norms, and foreground the
process of resonant images, motifs, and events which are fundamental
to Hawkes's theory of narrative structure.

The above analysis of narrative structure verifies the manner by
which Hawkes's fulfils his theoretical propositions:

> I'm concerned with the creation of new forms of fiction.
> If you view these forms in the light of tradition, I
> suppose you could say that they destroy many expectations
> that earlier forms created in readers .[66]

In a more obvious way, The Lime Twig plays on the reader's
expectations by establishing the norms of realism in Hencher's
prologue, and then violating that norm by having the narrator killed,
and changing the mode of narration.   Early works were even more
disruptive of the aesthetic norms and technical standards of
conventional realism in the novel.   The use of personalized narrators
is itself tempered with the presence of an implied author evident in
the manner by which the reader's need to recuperate structure finally
enables a critique of the narrator's psychology.

The novels and stories of John Hawkes create not only their own
unusual logic of narrative sequence, but also the laws and 'morality'
of their own world.   Just as structure is comprehensible only in
its own terms, as the analysis above has demonstrated, so the moral
perspectives are initially understood in terms of those created
worlds.   But as Kuehl has rightly asserted, in The Lime Twig,
'inexplicable things often occur to subvert the logic that
characterizes detective fiction.'[67]   These works are related to
novelistic conventions which are sometimes clearly defined, as in
The Lime Twig's parody of a certain detective story genre, or they
are general parodies of writing seen through the organizing consciousness of the surrogate artist-narrator.   The disruption of
conventional novelistic expectations formally duplicates that

disruption of conventional morality discussed in __Part One__ of this
study.   Finally, 'those nightmarish inventions of a single,
suffering psyche'[68] implicate the reader in a complicated sympathy
in those first-person narratives characterized by unreliable and
reprehensible narrators.   These figures are ironic parodies of the
writer as liar in novels which evince a marked predeliction for
criticism of conventions of all kinds, including the convention of
realism itself.   Hawkes's theory of structure demands that the
critic mediate between conventional 'point of view' analysis and a
more formalistic description of recurrent patterns of motifs and
images, as the logic behind strangely dislocative narratives is
grounded in the aberrant psychology of an unreliable narrator.

## CHAPTER SIX

'Generated' structure and the self-referential

text in Claude Simon's works.

### (i) The possibility for the structural analysis of the self-conscious text.

In     Part One of this study, the novels of Claude Simon, and especially those published between 1957 and 1967, were interpreted thematically, taking the content of the works as the primary subject for description.  Character, the principal mode of reference to the world in conventional realism, was seen to be reduced to a mere stereotype.

The concepts of self and other, on which character is traditionally founded, were themselves seen to be undermined in these novels, from an epistemological point of view.  If the analysis of these texts from a psychological and a philosophical perspective reached the conclusion that the self  and Other are unknowable because language fails to reconstitute them in any complete, and not fragmentary, way, then perhaps these texts are more concerned with the problematical status of language itself as a mode of representing the world.  The movement away from a Subject (narrator)—centred novel to a more structural, analogical, linguistic text, witnesses the lessons of Simon's novels up to Histoire (1967).  For not only is the traditional narrating Subject denied its epistemological status in narrative, but also the conventional idea of subject-matter (the world, society, a story of individuals, intrigue ) is itself denied its primacy. The subject of the novel is the possible genesis of that novel, itself an interrogation of its own form.  It is the reading of Simon's later novels, la Bataille de Pharsale (1969), Les Corps Conducteurs (1971), Triptyque (1973), and Leçon de Choses (1975), which appears either to force us to conclude that his

work is marked by a radical change of style, or that his
earlier works (from 1957 to 1967) may well be susceptible to
the kind of reading which these more recent works necessitate.
The apparent progressive effacement of personalized narrators
up to Histoire, and the disappearance of the narrator as
anxious interrogator, searching for 'truth', in the later works,
bear out the claim that his works do undergo a radical transformation, a relocation of emphasis. But how much of the
semantic polyphony, the paronomasia, the homophonic relationships between words, so evident in the later works, are present
in these earlier novels? Furthermore, if there is an emphatic
play on words, precisely how far can language been seen as a
source of structure, as well as an evocative 'generation' of
fiction?[1] A recent analysis of L'Herbe by Gérard Roubichou [2]
offers an alternative interpretation of Simon's work, character-
izing the author's investigation into the possibilities of
narrative structure and the logic of narrative, as a self-
conscious exposure of the practice of writing (écriture).[3]

Roubichou formulates his interpretation of Simon's work through
a fundamental comparison between perspectives and narration
technique in Le Vent and L'Herbe. He claims, and persuasively
demonstrates, that the explanation of narrative structure through
the analysis of the vagaries of a personalized narrator-protagonist may well be feasible in Le Vent, but not in L'Herbe nor
in any of the subsequent novels. What he calls the 'memory'
thesis, whereby the structural idiosyncracies are recuperated
by organizing the text as evidence of the vacillating memory
of the narrator-protagonist, is an inadequate mode of interpretation for L'Herbe. The first indication of this apparently

radical dissimilarity between the two novels is that the narrator
of Le Vent is personalized and this allows for a more normative
level of intelligibility. He attempts to give narrative
order to the disparate, and often unreliable, sources of
information about the enigmatic Montès. The narrator is also
a character in the novel, and his is the focal perspective,
the synthesizing point of view, albeit a confused and inadequate formulation in the end. Despite claims to the contrary,[4]
Roubichou contends that if we read the narrative of L'Herbe as
the property of Louise's consciousness, then ambiguities and
inconsistencies arise at certain crucial points in the text.
A key question may be asked about the following extract: Who
speaks?

> ...et plus tard, quand Louise se rappellera cette
> période—les dix jours qui s'écoulèrent ainsi dans
> la tiède agonie de l'été moribond - elle lui
> apparaîtra non comme une tranche de temps précise,
> mesurable et limitée, mais sous l'aspect d'une durée
> vague, hachurée, faite d'une succession, d'une
> alternance de trous, de sombre et de clairs ...[5]

For the reader is confronted with a dual perspective: he is
asked to imagine Louise remembering certain days from a point
in the future. The narrator is clearly distinguished from
Louise, although she is endowed with a point of view, a memory
which the narrator conceptualizes for the reader. This may
well indicate that we are in direct collusion with a narrator,
and at one remove from Louise, who thus becomes comprehensible
as an enabling, characterized point of view. This ambiguity
is emphasized by the changes in temporal perspective, as in
the extract above, whereby an 'unpersonalized' narrator interrupts
the flow of words which apparently stem from Louise's consciousness.

Such a hiatus in the text undermines the kind of interpretation
which is grounded in viewing the text as the product of a single
memory attempting to reconstruct the past.  Furthermore, this mode
of analysis, so familiar in the many critical works and papers on
Simon's novels, enables a more conventional analysis of themes, as
I demonstrated above.


L'Herbe is readable sometimes as the direct view of Louise,
and at other times as a view of Louise in the process of
thinking, which itself creates a certain distance.  The
narrator appears to play freely with the use of perspectives,
and Roubichou claims that herein lies the foundation of an
alternative reading of Simon's novels:


> Ces variations continues de la 'vision' rappellent
> la liberté traditionelle du narrateur omniscient,
> libre de se déplacer à son gré dans l'espace de sa
> création.  Pourtant, certains éléments épars dans le
> texte témoignent que nous avons autre chose que
> cela; c'est que si le narrateur paraît entièrement
> libre dans ses mouvements narratifs (ruptures de la
> vision, glissements, etc.), il ne cherche pas à nous
> cacher son travail d'invention: parenthèses, incertitudes,
> digressions font, semble-t-il, participer à l'élaboration
> patiente du texte et de la scène, comme si à chaque
> instant la scène evoquée glissait, à l'occasion d'un mot,
> d'une remarque, vers une autre scène possible.


The wealth of evocations themselves seems to call on the
reader to assist in a sort of visualisation of narrative
possibilities on the fictional level.  Thus scenes are
created through a process of writing grounded in a system
of elaboration.  The modality of such a narrative movement
is aptly exemplified in the more questioning, tentative
moments in the text:

... devant une table, absorbe tout entier dans
quelque minuscule tâche - écrire, compter? - à la
fois énigmatique et angoissante, probablement parce
que ... donc, derrière le massif de fleurs aux
teintes chaudes (rouges, jaunes, brunes et orangées) ...
et peut-être, plus tard, une femme pourtant une
ombrelle - Sabine - apparaissant sur le perron,... la
forme lourde et lente d'un homme - Pierre?'

A principal feature of the composition of narrative here
is the perpetual fragmentation of the flow of words by
parentheses which pose questions, offer alternatives, or
elaborate the words and images of the main text. Given the
presence of a narrator who exposes his evocative work of
narration, these textual anomalies are not fully accounted
for through the 'memory'-thesis.

The use of tenses in L'Herbe is the crucial support to
Roubichou's claims for a re-interpretation of Simon's work.
As we saw above, perspective is transformed by visualizing
Louise thinking in the future about the present ('et plus
tard, quand Louise se rapellera cette période'), Simon's
massive use of the present participle has an analagous effect
on perspective. As Roubichou claims, this verbal form enables
a mode of self-exposition of the creative process itself.
Claude Simon himself has emphasized that, contrary to
the conventional Realist writer who described action in the
simple past which effectively postulates an a priori status of
action in relation to text, the present participle allows
the reader to visualize an action in the process of its
taking place. It is not being recreated, but rather
is seen to be created, evoked in the text, so to speak.[8]
I shall have recourse to a further discussion of the
use of present participles below when I concentrate on
the play on language as a structural phenomenon. In

L'Herbe, however, the author mixes participles with the more
traditional verbal forms, and thus frequently creates the
illusion of an authentic novelistic world of characters and
events.  Indeed, the novel is intelligible on the fictional
level in more traditional terms.  But to interpret the text
only in these terms is to effect a reduction of the meaning
contained on the narration (discourse) level.  For it is the
case, as Roubichou argues, that inside a narrative completely
in the past, so to speak, the reader is allowed to see precisely
how the novel is elaborated in and through the process of narration: 'nous sommes, en quelque sorte, à la naissance du récit'.[9]
In other words, what was comprehensible as the attempts of a
personalized narrator to re-construct the story of Montes in
Le Vent, is now seen, in L'Herbe, as the efforts of an anonymous
narrator-author to show a narrative in its process of formulation,
never complete, always setting up possible stories, descriptions,
characters - all the usual ingredients of a conventional novel -
yet problematically and intentionally 'inachevé'.  The narrator
in L'Herbe is not a protagonist, but rather the image of the
writer himself engaged in the act of creating the novel.  We
witness him in his essential function: manipulating language,
attempting through words to evoke a fictional world.  He is
not telling us a story in the conventional sense of an anecdote,
because this itself is traditionally anterior to the act of
writing which constitutes it.  Rather, he is fundamentally
giving the reader the illusion of participating in the process
of creating a novel.


If the mode of interpretation formulated by Roubichou is
argued through to its logical conclusions, then narrative
coherence transcends the bounds of psychological relativism,

and demands to be understood as a self-conscious interrogation
of its own compositional phenomena, its practice of writing.
What then happens to the more conventional thematic interpretation of Simon's novels? Accepting this re-interpretation as a premise, fictive events, leitmotifs, and imagery
are seen to echo the narrative problems which formulate
them. For instance, the epigraph which heads le Vent describes
the world as threatened by two dangers: order and disorder.
The structure of narrative itself oscillates between the
'extremes of utter dispersion and implausible compactness'. [10]
The attempts to describe minute details are tempered by the
accumulation of alternative words, and the very disgressive
movement of the text away from the sequential order of conventional narration. Dispersion, disorder, the 'va-et-vient' of
movement in the 'world', in nature, which I described in the
previous section above, may be understood as symptomatic of
the structural problematic. 'Cette interminable chevauchée
nocturne',[11] which describes George's sexual exploits with
Corinne as well as his rememberances of the eternal wanderings
of the Cavalry in 1940, is also an image of the structure of
that narrative itself in La Route des Flandres, with the
straddling of one part of the text over another. (Clearly, the
use of word-play on the level of the works total structure is
fully in evidence in these early novels, and I shall discuss
this in more depth below, where much of the punning as part of
an erotic substructure will be seen to be a consistent feature
of Simon's work).

A web of images and motifs are structurally related, just as
images from previous novels are reiterated in subsequent

texts. The whole 'oeuvre' is characterized by a mosaic of
texts which repeat dominant motifs and images, comprehensible
on a thematic level. It is precisely this ostentatious display
of technique which allows for the alternative interpretation
exemplified by Roubichou. Even the epigraph which heads
L'Herbe may be re-interpreted, where the meaning of 'personne
ne fait l'histoire' indicates the self-generative text
(histoire= story = fiction). The fictional level arises out of
the rich connotations, the semantic polyphony of words themselves, and not out of a process of re-presentation. But
contrary to all Roubichou's claims about the radicalisation of
form in L'Herbe, one can see the evidence for the primacy of
structure over theme also in Le Vent, albeit    recuperable
through psychology with reference to our appetite for logic
which can only produce a derisory, incoherent result.[12]  This
is the ultimate realization of the anxious Realist writer who
confronts the impossibility of re-presentation. Georges in La
Route des Flandres continues this anxious quest, but is no more
successful. The dispersed debris of images from the 'world'
are a derisory attempt to ground narrative in a conventional
realism. In these early novels, Simon investigates the fundamental basis of Realism, its representationalist aesthetic,
and clears the ground for his later works and their effacement of
the Subject (in both senses explained above) in favour of the
play on language and its generative potential. The genesis for
this mode of composition is contained in these early works,
as Roubichou's analysis of L'Herbe, and its radical critique
of more thematic, psychology based interpretations, has demonstrated. The novels of the period 1957 to 1967, however, are

susceptible to two interpretations, if only because of their
density and the proliferation and evocation of a world of
themes and motifs. To understand the progressive radicalisation of Simon's novels is to organize the narratives in
terms of the demands made on the reader, and the increasing
withdrawal of modes of recuperation. Analysing narrative
structure in Claude Simon's works becomes an increasingly
complex search for a logic of narrative.

(ii) Structural phenomena: towards a logic of narrative

> 'Arrangements, combinaisons, permutations'.(Le sacre
> du Printemps p.36)
>
> ... on doit se figurer l'ensemble du système comme
> un mobile se déformant sans cesse autour de quelques
> rares points fixes (La Bataille de Pharsale p.186)

The very precise geometrical connotations of structure in these
quotations guide us towards a descriptive mode of discourse
which will always keep us within the bounds of the type of
structuralist analysis exemplified by Gérard Roubichou (among
others). It will also enable us to go some way towards an
understanding of the crucial opposition in structuralist literary
theory, and in the work of the writers and theorists of Tel Quel,
between production and representation. Arrangement and rearrange-
ments, permutations of images and evocative words, abrupt disruption of the flow of words into parentheses, and the to-and-fro
movement around deminant motifs, characterize the Simonian
narrative as a 'baroque' structure.

Sturrock refers us to the seminal work of Heinrich Wölfflin which

first described the style that abandoned 'straight lines and
plain surfaces ... for a great amount of ornamentation and
tension between structural elements.'[13]   Quoting Wölfflin,we
may see the analogies between a mode of architectural design
and Simon's narrative composition:

> Unlike the contour, which gives the eye a definite
> and easily comprehensible direction to follow, a
> mass of light tends to a movement of dispersal,
> leading the eye to and fro; it has no bounds, no
> definite break in continuity, and on all sides it
> increases and decreases. [14]

In the baroque, form is overtly unstable, it appears forever
on the point of disintegration.  The ceaseless movement, the
two dangers of order and disorder, the quest for the exact
description and the doubts and uncertainties cast on that
conventional narrative operation, all characterize the
Simonian text as markedly analogous to the description of the
baroque above.  The connotations of disintegration on the
formal level typically reverberate on the evoked, thematic
level:

> The baroque never offers us perfection and fulfilment,
> or the static calm of "being", only the unrest of
> change and the tension of transience. [15]

Passing time, death, decay, are all essential themes contained
in the allegorical potential of the baroque in art and literature.
As Walter Benjamin asserts:

> ... the baroque, earthbound exposition of history
> as the story of the world's suffering - is the very
> essence of allegorical perception; history takes on
> meaning only in the stations of agony and decay.
> The amount of meaning is in exact proportion to the
> presence of death and the power of decay, since
> death is that which traces the jagged line between
> Physis and meaning.[16]

The instability on the fictional level in Simon's novels
(especially from 1957 to 1967) is a product of the baroque
structure. But in these novels there is also an abundance
of baroque themes which revolve around one of Simon's central
preoccupations discussed in the previous section: the tension
of transience. Up to **Histoire** (1967) these works purposively
offer the reader an explanation and recuperation of the baroque
structural anomalies, which falls under the sign of the tension
of transience:

> ... d'une combinaison, d'un ombreux et fulgurant
> enchevêtrement de lumières et de lignes où les
> éléments éclatés, dissociés se regroupent <u>selon</u>
> <u>le foisonnant et rigoureux désordre de la mémoire.</u>[17]

These pecularities of vision evoked through recurrent motifs,
and through the attempts of a narrator-author to persuade the
reader to visualize a process of recollection, always revert
us back to the function of narration itself. For it is in the
narrative structure that the essential oppositions, which
enable the conceptualization of a baroque form, are visibly
in evidence: 'between order and disorder, space and time, unity
and dispersion, continuity and conflict.' [18] These in turn are
mediated on the fictional level by the oppositions of the seen
and the imagined, and noise and silence,which give an anthro-
pomorphic presence to the text, albeit it an illusive, anecdotic

phenomenon. Chaos and order coexist in texts that are

characterized by a 'contained mobility,' [19] figuratively

encapsulated in the words of Valéry which head La Bataille de

Pharsale (1969): 'Achille immobile à grands pas.' For

temporality is frozen (figé) in the spatiality of the continual

present moment of narration (exemplified in the proliferation

of past participles). The illusion of simultaneity is created

by the agglomeration of words, [20] at the same time as the

structure of narrative creates the illusion of temporality.

For as Barthes asserts, the critic has a well-defined task:

> ...la tâche est de parvenir à donner une description
> structurale de l'illusion chronologique; c'est à la
> logique narrative à rendre compte du temps narratif...
> La temporalité n'est qu'une classe structurelle du
> récit (du discours), tout comme dans la langue, le
> temps n'existe que sous forme de système. [21]

It is time to be more precise about that structural description

of the illusion of temporality which may well be the fundamental

issue in the formulation of a logic of narrative.

## (a) The principles of organization

The structural analysis of narrative has clearly demonstrated

that to investigate problems of coherence in writing is at the

same time to analyze the whole compositional phenomenon of a

text in terms of the narrative structure. Simon's novels are

constituted by a movement of proliferation, reiteration, and

combinations of words, images, motifs and series of 'events',

which condition the very notion of development in the text.

The anxious quality of many of Simon's novels has been well

noted.  For example, in <u>Histoire</u> we find:

> ...les mots se pressant se précipitant se bousculant
> avec cette espèce d'intolérable maladresse des infirmes
> comme si leur accumulation leur afflux pouvait suppléer
> à l'absence de gestes l'immobilité forcée  du corps
> disant ou essayant de dire et plus que dire persuader
> mais comment peut-on...22

Also, the baroque tension described above is contained in the
perpetual coexistence of immobilized images, fragments of a
continuity that can only be re-presented in that static form,
and the accumulation of words themselves.  The 'foudroyante
discontinuité'[23] contrasts sharply with the sinuous flow
of words into parentheses and then back to the principal focus
of discourse, a compositional principle grounded in elaboration
whereby the text plays on the tension between the structure of
development on the one hand, and the more liberating tendency
towards digression.  But the digressive parenthesis is never
divorced from the main narrative continuity which it apparently
fractures.  This structural situation can be schematized as
follows:[24]

phrase porteuse

(parenthèse)    phrase porteuse (modifiée)...

The relationship between apparent digression and principal thread
of discourse often depends on what Ricardou calls the 'calembour
producteur.'[25] A productive play on words, often resounding
with erotic connotations, is an important compositional principle,
and I shall discuss this in more depth  below.  Parentheses serve

to break up the rhythm of the continuous prose, slow up the
rapid accumulation of words momentarily; but, contrary to
their conventional usage, they reorientate the narrative,
giving possible meanings a further density by evoking further
connotations of images, words and motifs. The principle of
proliferation is further enhanced, therefore, by the massive
use of parentheses, especially in those works written prior
to 1969. Roubichou goes further in his claims for the
importance of the parenthesis when he describes Simon's
radical use of such a potentially digressive device:

> Chez Claude Simon, au contraire, elle (la parenthèse)
> est un des éléments essentiels du "discours" (au
> sens où l'emploie Fontainier) et, loin de détourner
> l'attention de son object principal, la parenthèse
> a tendance à devenir elle-même le centre de la
> narration. [26]

For parentheses give the illusion of digression when in fact
they function as linkages which enable modifications in the
narrative flow. Any part of the text may be schematized as
follows: [27]

(A) → parenthesis → (A') → parenthesis → (A'') → parenthesis → (B)...

The composition is grounded in a perpetual fracturation of
the text. However, the parentheses act as both guides to
the narrative development and its possible modifications, and,
consequently, as evidence of an anonymous narrator-author who
continuously exposes the process of textualisation.

( b) <u>temporality explained by structure</u>

The apparent confusions in the reading of a Simon novel are caused by attempts at recuperation through the level of 'histoire'. But such incoherences are essentially explicable through the level of 'discours' (narration). Such a fundamental problem of intelligibility which the reader is faced with (the temporal anomalies) is to be accounted for by structure itself. As one critic has recently indicated,[28] in <u>La Route des Flandres</u> there are four different chronological periods discernible on the level of 'histoire' and they invariably merge with one an other:

(1) Georges and Blum attempt to reconstruct the fragments of Sabine's tales of Ancestral intrigue.

(2) The search for the truth about De Reixach (Suicide?/Accidental ambush?) and the speculations of Corinne's infidelity with Iglésia.

(3) Georges's recollections of wandering with the remaining Cavalry troops in Flanders, and his journey to the prison camp, and the conversations there with Blum and Iglésia.

(4) A recent past in a hotel bedroom with Corinne from which all the memories seem to radiate.

One pervasive account of this structure is the 'memory'-thesis which creates plausibily on this level of 'histoire'. But when invention and speculation blur the truth-potential of such re-creation, levels of plausibility are undermined. Elements of (1) and (2) above are contained in the chronological sequence of (3), and all the chronologies are contained in (4). In such apparent confusion of event-series and chronologies, the novel offers us various fixed points of reference: (1) The

ambush and death of De Reixach, his statuesque, futile
gesture. (2) The dead horse by the side of the Flanders road
seen four times, each time in a more advanced stage of
decay. (3) The journey to the prison camp. (4) Blum and
Georges incessantly arguing. (5) Georges and his Mother,
Sabine and the gossip around Ancestral intrigues. (6) The
passionate and violent love-making with Corinne. Claude
Simon himself has referred to this structure in schematized
fashion as shaped like the sign of the 'clubs' in cards,
whereby the whole design may be drawn in one continuous
movement, passing through the same fixed point (symbolic of
the movement through references to the dead horse, Corinne,
and so on). [29] In fact Simon sees the novel as highly
symmetrical in structure, with the ambush at the very heart
of the novel, closely related to the other 'charge' of horses,
at the Races.[30] The author's claims for symmetry and intricate structures in his novels are born out by the structural
analysis of chronology. The illusion of amorphous, intermingled
chronologies is belied by the description of narrative logic
not through the story-element, but rather through the narrative
structure itself. Our search for an organizing principle in
the midst of such apparent amorphism may well be satisfied by
reading the work in its own terms as a permutation, combination,
and arrangement of words and images which generate a structural,
ongoing narrative movement through the play on the semantic
connotations of key words. If the text is only organized as
the relationship between micro-texts to give the illusion of
the completed text, and the anomalies of fragmentariness and
the merging of micro-texts recuperated through the 'memory'-thesis,

and these readings are possible in these earlier works,
then a limited reading of structure is offered taking its
criteria from the norms of realism in the traditional novel.
If, however, coherence is based on an understanding of
structure in less normative, less psychological, and more
formal terms, then the reader would be equipped to understand
the later novels and their perpetual play on modes of recuperation, exploiting the organizing principles from which the text
may or may not be generated, without the enabling presence of
a narrating consciousness through which to reduce the text.
An interesting example of this mode of analysis is available
in a recent paper on Leçon de Choses (1975).[31]

( c ) The play on modes of recuperation

Reading a narrative is conditioned by the desire to organize
the text according to a certain logic. Simon's work has
always been preoccupied with this operation. From the appetite
for logic, and the derisory, approximative results in Le Vent,
to the accumulation of the causal conjunction, 'de sorte que'
in La Route des Flanders,[32] to the relationship between the
'Générique' of Leçon de Choses and its 'Expansion' and
'Divertissement,' the search for the organizing principles
on which the work is grounded has become increasingly problematical. The progressive withdrawal of a focal narrating
consciousness, and the consequent fragmentation and dispersal
of the multiple aspects of the text through La Bataille de
Pharsale, and Les Corps Conducteurs, to the play on micro-texts
and their recuperative plausibility in terms of modes of representation (the cinema, the picture-poster, for instance) in

<u>Triptyque</u> (1973), together prepare the reader for the neatly organized, apparently self-generated, anecdotic structure of <u>Leçon de Choses</u>.

The novel begins with what Jost calls the explicit metaphorisation of description, whereby a whole level of story will be evoked. A deserted room, full of debris and fragments coated with the dust of time, contains the apparent credit-titles, as well as the generative starting-points for the composition of a text. It is from this room that descriptions expand into possible episodes which may or may not be related to each other, but which all, in the end, appear to be evoked by these initial descriptions. At first, this kind of structural affinity of parts to the whole, and the beginning to the subsequent text, offers a simple logic of narrative grounded in an anecdotic structure. The anecdotes themselves are partially constituted, only to be abandoned after a few lines, and then to be returned to later. From a more normative point of view, the question arises: is the structure abitrary or is it motivated? The initial pages of the 'Générique' create the illusion of a simple mechanical structure which would follow, causally, those initial descriptions. But this illusion is soon undermined by the assertion that such descriptions, such a textual composition could continue indefinitely in a kind of ongoing movement of metaphors and partially described objects, 'sans compter les divers hypothèses que peut susciter le spectacle.'[33] Thus the text apparently has the possibility of following multiple lines of expansion. The logic of narrative appears arbitrary. This undermining of a narrative

logic is analogous, as Jost points out, to the change from
the reassuring 'how I wrote certain of my novels' (referring
to the author's comments on his early works in interviews),
to the more disturbing, 'how I could have written Leçon de
Choses'. The'Générique' rewrites, in its own way, the preface
to Orion Aveugle (1970), which I shall refer to, briefly,
below. It is from what it does not say (for example, 'Ainsi
il n'a pas été dit'; 'il n'a pas non plus été fait mention
de...')[34] that the novel will develop. The schema of motivating generator no longer suffices as a model of structural
explanation. The 'Expansion' does not seem to develop
directly from the initial descriptions of 'Générique', but
rather pursues the hypothetical directions a narrative may
take. However, on closer inspection, all the episodes seem
to be related to each other in some way or another. The
masons working in a room (the room?), and the soldiers
 taking cover in a room (the room?) are associated, figuratively,
by the notion of DEMOLITION, the destruction of a building
(through war, or by the work of the stone-masons). This would
seem to belie the claims for arbitrariness.


Rejecting the 'vraisemblable' (implicit and external motivation),
without ever explaining its orientations (explicit and internal
motivations), this recent Simon novel creates a mode of ambiguous
motivation for a composition which has totally effaced any of
the more relativistic psychological levels of plausibility.
The interlacing of anecdotes undermines the normative consecu-
tive demands of narrative, creating the illusion of simultaneity.
The fiction level is reduced to the anecdotic in the play of

narrative structures which exposes the possibilities for
the production of text. Jost concludes that:

> L'arbitraire du récit est donc neutralisé par
> une motivation structurelle externe à l'histoire
> racontée mais pourtant intra-textuelle.[35]

The textual motivation, then, whereby events are structurally
related, is grounded in a non-chronological interlacing.
Jost formulates a schematic version of this account, demonstrating that the relationship between episodes can be
viewed from any one episode taken as a starting, and focal,
point.[36]

The structure of Simon's Leçon de Choses is built on the
changing of event-sequences, whereby there arises a continually productive interaction between them. The implications
of this priority of narrative structure over episodic content
(level of 'histoire') is seen, rightly, by Jost as a foregrounding of the production of a text:

> Leçon de Choses oblige à considérer les structures
> narratives en elles-mêmes, non plus comme simples
> matières originelles déjà constituées mises au
> service de l'agencement,c'est-à-dire du récit,
> mais comme un matériau au travaux.[37]

An intentional ambiguity is therefore built into the narrative.
Connections between episodes are suggested, both figuratively
and evocatively, and may well enable the motivation of a
structural logic. But these connections are hypothetical,
and are never firmly asserted. Just as any possible

chronology of events (the masons seem to reach the end of
their day's work near the end of the novel) is disabled
by the man's 'c'est promis ce soir' on the last page,
which may well refer to the coupling which has been described progressively throughout the novel; so also the whole
series of episodes could stem from the newspaper which the
soldier reads.  Furthermore, if the theory of textual
generation is both established and frequently threatened
by the movements of the narratives, then nothing precedes
the production of narrative, and the fiction is seen to be
produced, not re-produced:

> Motiver l'expansion d'une structure narrative,
> c'est la désigner clairement comme résultat
> arbitraire et non comme apriori  contraignant.[38]

Thus, the argument would continue, the 'générique' must never
be the a priori constraint on subsequent narrative possibilities,
but only a tentative beginning whose static nature is continually
disrupted by the fluidity of expansions and digressions.  For
to situate the narrative generators at the beginning of a text
which it produces. is to conceive of the writing activity
itself according to the linear, progressive schema which it
is supposed to be criticizing (the a priori subject which a
text will then represent or express), instead of the step by
step production of text.  The whole 'fugue'-like structure,
and the 'court circuit' which brings the anecdotes and
generators of the text together for the last time (but
significantly modified), enables the novel to contest its
own theory of primary generators.  The search for the principles
of composition bring us, therefore, to the realization that
Leçon de Choses is a novel primarily about its own creation.

The difference between the self-consciousness of this recent
novel, and that of Le Vent, say, are fundamental to the
understanding of the radical changes which mark Simon's
oeuvre. For while we were able to characterize his earlier
works (and especially Le Vent) as critiques of realism in
terms of what Barthes has called 'L'effet de réel,'[39] with many
of the conventional aspects of realist novels very much in
evidence, in this most recent novel we may, in analogous
fashion, characterize the anti-representationalist aesthetic
as the 'effet de production'.[40] Leçon de Choses creates the
illusion that the reader is himself in the very process of
producing a narrative text, of holding the pieces together
in a narrative which is highly self-enclosed and eventually
short-circuited (all levels of structural, and fictional,
recuperation are withdrawn). Thus all formulations of
logical connections in the pursuit of intelligibility and
meaning are condemned to failure, because the very notion
of narrative derivation is exploited. This novel, more than
any of its predecessors, is comprehensible as a truly post-
Modernist, subversive text.


(iii) Language as a structural phenomenon


> Il me semble que le livre se fait au niveau
> de l'écriture, du langage. Celui-ci n'est pas
> seulement un moyen, mais un moteur. Il est
> créateur lui aussi (Simon).
>
> Réduire la narration à une vision, ce n'est pas
> s'apercevoir de l'existence de l'écriture (Todorov).
>
> ...cette dynamique du langage, des mots qui en
> entraînent d'autres..(Simon).


'La phrase simonienne' is the subject of this section, its

lyrical qualities and the implications of its massive proliferation, its 'entassement' in the earlier works; but
also the 'transforming power of the word,'[41] language as
the very creator of structure through the play on words,
the paronomasia which establishes a mosaic of connections,
even an erotic substructure in certain novels. This 'pro-
liferating style of writing' makes the reader conscious of
the 'inadequacies of language as a weapon to immobilize
reality.'[42] Yet, at the same time, there is a continual
'mise en spectacle' of writing through a play on the figurative potential of words, the evocative power, 'l'incontatoire
magie de langage'[43] whereby the text exploits the
semantic field of words whilst it creates the 'effet de
production' discussed above. As Roubichou so rightly claims:

> ...pour Claude Simon, c'est bien dans la mobilité
> interne de la phrase que se produisent les trans-
> mutations à partir desquelles s'élabore aussi le
> roman. Par sa structure, par son mouvement, par
> son rythme, la phrase simonienne est un système
> proliférant, signe visible de la création dans
> et par le langage.' 44

The massive use of the present participle has been mentioned
above, in relation to the baroque structure in particular.
This verbal form is comprehensible in novels that directly
interrogate the representational problematic insofar as
the use of the participle undermines the notion of represented reality. It plunges action into an indefinite state
with no apparent beginning and no visible end. It suppresses
a conventional linear time sequence, because what is described
is always happening, and has not happened prior to the description. It renders the idea of fixed moments within

mobility, preserving the impression of stasis and undermining causality. The memory-thesis accounts for the
present participle as the symptom of the discontinuity of
the reflecting consciousness. As Sturrock suggests, the
present participle

> ...has the effect of diminishing the importance
> of the agent in any action. By using it Simon
> withdraws the primacy from the agent and gives
> it to the act, which is thus partly depersonalized.[45]

It has also been suggested that description as a dominant
mode of representation 'is the sign that some vital
relationship to action and to the possibility of action
has broken down... Thus description begins when external
things are felt to be alienated from human activity, come
to be viewed as static things-in-themselves; but it is
fulfilled when even the human beings become themselves
dehumanized, become lifeless tokens, mere objects in
motion to be rendered from the outside'.[46] The image of
man and the reduction of action to derisory gestures were
discussed in the previous section. The implications of
the use of participles on this more thematic level must be
tempered with the structural significance of both proliferation and self-consciousness (what Simon has called the
process by which the reader is asked to visualize something
happening[47]).

The lyrical power of 'la phrase simonienne' returns us to
the seldom discussed aspect of the almost obsessive descriptions in many of Simon's novels. It is those novels

with a perceptible narrative Subject who attempts to be a reconstituter of events from the past (a potential Realist novelist), that allow description to be explained as a compensation for the solipsistic act of writing, or as a symptom of inaction, or as part of a general epistemological problematic. The desperate rage to describe has been attributed to the personal anguish of Claude Simon, a failed painter, whereby the novel evinces a certain nostalgia for the directness of paint as opposed to the inadequacies of language, which, it would seem, 'destroys and disperses what it creates.'[48] Furthermore, failure is a permanent and intentional feature of the period of his work which directly questions the possibilities of realism. The novels, and especially the later ones, abound with descriptions of photographs, post-cards, paintings, statues, all those 'fixed' images which have already represented the world. His representations of them are at one remove from the 'world'. The key word here is 'IMMOBILE'. The description of movement itself is not characterized by continuity, but rather by a succession of 'instantanés', the static images which fill the pages of his later novels. But, apart from these implications of the failures of descriptions, the recuperation of its often urgent quality, description is no longer illustrative, as in the conventional novel, but rather creative. For Simon, description can no longer be reduced to an auxilliary role:

> ...la description pourrait bien devenir au contraire
> l'élément dominant, l'action' ne servant plus alors
> que de prétexte à les accumuler.49

The fiction is to be generated from description itself.[50] The 'transforming power of the word' takes on a progressively

important role as language appears to create narrative
structure.

The apparent grammatical incoherence of the Simon novel is
defined within the bounds of the 'lisible', as the play on
language contests preconceived notions of the readable and
the unreadable. Such a complex language-construct demands
to be made intelligible in terms of the relationship between
words and other words through contiguity and propinquity in
the psychological approach,[51] and through the productive
word play, the paronomasia, which creates a certain 'polyphonie
sémantique', whereby the word-play itself is not just a cause
of expressivity but rather the very generation of structure, [52]
in the structuralist approach. Thus, the logic of narrative
is to be understood as the logic underlying the connection
between the words themselves:

> ...chaque mot en suscite (ou en commande) plusieurs
> autres, non seulement par la force des images qu'il
> attire à lui comme un aimant, mais parfois aussi par sa seule
> morphologie, de simples assonances qui, de même que les
> nécessités formelles de la syntaxe, du rythme et da la
> composition, se révèlent souvent aussi fécondes que ses
> multiples significations.[53]

For Simon, the 'sentiers de la création' are grounded in this creative
use of language through which the textual continuity obviates the
apparent grammatical anomalies, substituting a 'scriptural'
coherence. In the earlier novels, narrators (images of the
artist at work) appear to manipulate language in this process
of creation, and this establishes a Simonian norm for textual
coherence even when the collusive narrator disappears behind the

narrative, so to speak.  As Roubichou states:

> c'est son maniement visible du langage qui est le
> moteur d'élaboration du roman.  L'histoire progresse
> par les lois et constantes de sa narration et de
> son écriture. [54]

Multiplicity and juxtaposition describe structural features based
in this use of language: witness the accumulation of possible
descriptions joined thus: ' et...et...et'; the proliferation of
the 'comme si...' of simile which serves to inundate the text
with equivalent figurative expressions, as if selection as a
principle has been left to the reader; the causal conjunction,
'de sorte que', ironically used in texts that undermine causality,
as the use of participles clearly demonstrates. For, herein lies
the radical nature of Simon's manipulation of language.  In the
conventional novel of realism, the reader appears more aware of
themes than of language itself, whereas in Simon's works language
draws attention to itself through the dislocative syntax, the
massive continuity through proliferation,  the play on words rich
in semantic connotations, and finally the creation of structure
itself from the figurative and homophonic relationship between
words.

Jean Ricardou has clearly demonstrated how narrative continuity,
traditionally understood as a line from beginning through the
middle to the end, has its unity contested frequently in <u>La Route
des Flandres</u> by the violent use of 'calembour' (play on words)
which burdens the word with the function of a 'charnière
structurelle' (hinge, point of contact).  Thus one can speak of

the <u>structural metaphor</u> grounded in the semantic irradiation
connoted in certain key words, which lends the text an 'ordre
morphologique', replacing conventional narrative chronology.
<u>La Route des Flandres</u> and <u>La Bataille de Pharsale</u> are works
which are particularly rich in evocative images irradiating
from key words which consequently act as sources of generation
on both the structural (narrative) and the fiction levels.[55]
The punning surrounding horses, riding, and sexual activity
has been well-noted in <u>La Route des Flandres</u>, as the following
example clearly demonstrates:

> de Reixach...a voulu lui aussi monter cette alezane,
> c'est-à-dire la mater, sans doute parce qu'à force de
> voir un vulgaire jockey la faire gagner il pensait
> que la monter c'était la mater, parce que sans
> doute pensait-il aussi qu'elle...(cette fois je parle
> de l'alezane-femme, la blonde femelle...)[56]

The play on the word 'alezane' (chestnut mare) and the associations
of riding and sex, Corinne and Iglesia's apparent infidelity, and
de Reixach's possible jealousy, are made explicit here. The
exploitation of erotic connotations invested in 'chevaucher'
performs a similar function, as I pointed out above. In <u>La
Bataille de Pharsale</u>, the word, 'jaune' opens up the semantic
field with its frequent recurrence and its connotations in this
text of sexual jealousy and infidelity.[57]   In this particular
novel the story level is radically subsumed into the discourse
of words and into the reiterated and juxtaposed textual fragments,
which together effect an extreme form of dispersal. Thus the
evocative power of words and the subsequent connoted substructure
plays a primary and vital role in the composition. In this novel,
more than any of those which preceeded it, reading is not just a

search for themes, even partially evoked ones, but rather
an analysis of the very generation of such evocations
through word-play. For as Simon himself clearly indicates,
quoting Lacan:

> ...le mot n'est pas seulement signe mais noeud de
> significations.[58]

These centres of evocation are productive on the semantic
and on the structural levels as they produce transitions
in the narrative:

> ...la gloire, sur l'acier virginal...Seulement,
> vierge, il y avait belle lurette qu'elle ne l'était
> plus...[59]

Here the transition from sword to woman effects a structural
modification and also contains sexual connotations, evoking
speculations about a death and sexual jealousy. In this way,
emphasis on the play on key words and images draws attention
to, and defamiliarizes, the narrative surface, undermining the
conventional mirror-language of Realism which represents the
world, in order to represent itself. For as Jameson rightly
claims:

> In modern literature, indeed, the production of
> the sentence becomes itself a new kind of event
> within the works, and generates a whole new kind
> of form.[60]

Language as a representation of reality demonstrates its own
impossibility in many of Simon's earlier novels, while at the
same time language as creative force and structural phenomenon

clearly demonstrates its function and its evocative force.
It is this latter use of language which dominates the later
novels. Jiménez-Farjardo has pointed out the intricate
erotic substructure of Triptyque; there is a play on the word
'bassin' for instance, 'which in French means both basin
(trough) and pelvis [which] anticipates the back and forth
movements of fornication, while being an image of the vulva,' [61]
in a novel which moves in and out of episodes often concerned
with forms of sexuality, including intimations of voyeurism.


The transforming power of the word and the manner by which language
thus draws attention to itself has been the subject of this section.
Mention must, finally, be made of the increasing use of the overt
defamiliarisation of normative language through the subversive
intrusions into the text of foreign language words (Spanish,
English, Greek, for instance); reversed words; capitalisation;
ideograms; half-completed words; fragments of newspaper headlines;
political and advertising slogans. Also the idiosyncratic use of
punctuation (especially brackets, and the absence of full stops).
On a more general level, and especially from Histoire onwards, the
novels often quote fragments of previous novels as if exploiting
ready-made perspectives. The examples of this defamiliarisation of
language are many and varied. To choose but one novel, Les Corps
Conducteurs (1971) reiterates long sections of Spanish with an
appended translation, taken from a writers' congress; and the
novel is also replete with capitalized fragments of advertising
slogans, and various other 'disruptive' uses of words. [62]


Jean-Marie Benoist in La Révolution Structurale (1975), encapsulates
the conclusions that this analysis of language in Simon's novels has

attempted to formulate, in the following words:

> La Route des Flandres... mène le jeu d'une prolifération,
> d'une arborescence du langage qui vient subvertir la
> clôture de la notion traditionnelle (et récente) du roman.
> Celui-ci n'est plus le miroir promené le long d'un chemin,
> mais sa route, ou si l'on veut le miroir à facettes tendu
> au langage par le langage même. 63

## (iv) The novel as a critique of representation

The principal and most abiding characteristic of Simon's whole
'oeuvre' has been the progressive radicalisation of an avowed
subversion, and critique, of conventional Realism in the novel.
It is clearly demonstrable, as this chapter has shown, how a
more formal analysis of his works enables us to understand
texts on their own terms as structural phenomena, and precisely
how the onus is firmly placed on language as a many-sided mirror
reflecting itself. It may well be that Simon's most radical
critique of conventional Realism is grounded in the manipulation
and exploitation of the full potential of the word itself. This
point in his progressive research into the properties of the
'romanesque' is reached after investigating all the possibilities
for telling stories, prefigured in the frustrated efforts of
'narrators' to re-present Reality and know the world, the Self,
and the Other. This 'presence' enables a recuperation of the
'méticulosité dans le détail'[64], the overwhelming need for a
totalising description. The failures of realism in the novels
from 1957-1967 are indicated to the reader by a state of
uncertainty contained in doubts cast on the very operations of

re-presentation, especially in <u>Le Vent</u>, <u>La Route des Flandres</u>,
<u>Le Palace</u>, and to a certain extent, <u>Histoire</u>.[65] The world
of people, matter, and objects is seen to be unorganizable
and, finally, unknowable in the language-construct of the
text. Once this is accepted, re-presentation is abolished
in favour of a series of projections evoked by the creative
use of language as described above. In the later works,
the anxiety to describe the world and to reconstitute
lost time disappears; there are, generally, shorter sentences,
fewer parentheses, and less conventional modes of recuperation. The 'effet de réel', caused by the continual descriptions of perceptions, memories of the seen, the heard, the
felt, becomes less intelligible as an attempt by a narrating
Subject to reconstitute an order out of the chaos of the
mind. Rather, the effacing of such recuperative logic
enables the existence of 'micro-texts', anecdotes, and
fragmented episodes, apparently generated from the very
words they contain, to be comprehensible only as the laying
bare of the constituent parts which are available to produce
the text. They give the reader not the illusion of reality,
but rather the illusion of producing the text. This we have
called: 'l'effet de production'.


The true source of text in <u>La Bataille de Pharsale</u> is other
texts, 'groups of signs that give the illusion of nature
and life'.[66] From <u>Histoire</u> onwards, Simon purposively used
extracts from previous novels to create a kind of intertextu-
ality which would underline his belief in a total 'oeuvre',
whereby his works ceaselessly modify each other in a never
ending research into the possibilities of narrative. Simon

insists that one cannot ignore the importance, in our
apprehension of the world, played by the totality of texts
(literary, pictorial, philosophical, mathematical) which
have already been produced.[67]    The notion of 'work in progress'
which underlies all his novels gives them an unfinished,
tentative, experimental quality:

> ...j'essaie de composer un texte qui se tienne
> à peu près debout selon une certaine conception
> de la littérature que je me suis faite peu à peu, et
> qui d'ailleurs se modifie sans cesse. [68]

The feelings of unrest, change, incessant modification of
parts within each novel is echoed in this statement by the
author about his movement from one novel to the next.  But
the illusion of fragmentation and chaos masks a highly
structured series of artifacts, each in turn reverberating
with aesthetic and theoretical implications about the novel,
representation, the structure of narrative, and the recuperative
logic of the reader's search for the principles of coherence.

Perhaps Les Corps Conducteurs is the least recuperative text,
as its litany of descriptions stems from a selection of
identifiable art works, first described in Orion Aveugle, and
here acting as 'generators' for more descriptions.  If the
text is organized according to the normative principles which
previous novels have established, then the result would be a
misrepresentation.  It seems ironic that the author who spent
many years producing novels that demonstrated the impossibility
of a representationalist aesthetic, should then produce a
novel grounded in the apparently 'objective' description of

representationalist works of pictorial art. But then one
could hastily add that it is not unusual to witness the
presence of immobilized pictures of a represented reality.
For this may well be Simon's ultimate comment on the failure
of representation in the novel: the author is only able to
describe the captured, fixed 'reality' of the canvas, itself
another text which already exists, and which may therefore
act as a basis for our apprehension of the world.

Triptyque, with its mosaic of fresh combinations of previous
scenes, motifs, and images, exploits, more radically than
previous works, types of representation in a bid to confound
the search for a guiding logic of composition, in its play
on recuperation. Postcards, film strips, cinema, circus,
bill-board signs, paintings, and engravings abound, and the
text moves in and out of these different orders of representation, either halting the narrative in a 'fixed' image, or
turning it into the wild charade of a filmed scene, or
the clown's act in a circus. Once an order of 'reality' is
firmly established, it regresses into another (circus into
poster, for instance), thus defying the recuperative potential
of each mode of representation of an action or a scene. Because
of the continual modification in status of elements of narrative,
the reader is directly confronted with questions of continuity
and composition. There is no personalized narrator on which to
focus the problem, and therefore the whole novel stands as a
collection of anecdotes which may or may not be related to
each other, and which may well be generated from a poster on

a wall, or be part of a film shown in a cinema which the 'audience' appears to leave at the end of the novel. This kind of exposition of artificiality, illusion, and technique is continued in the highly structured recent novel, Leçon de Choses, which I discussed above. The multiple sequences in Triptyque give the narrative a continuity, but they also serve to cancel each other out in the exposition of the very activity of creating structure, in a text that denies all the usual recuperative aids.[69] As Loubère argues, the reader is brutally interrupted as he attempts to make sense of the scenes he views 'not only by the destruction of the "story" but by the breakdown of the viewing mechanisms and by violent changes of focus that makes it impossible to "recuperate" the anecdote by ways of dreams, imagination, or madness. The "story content" of Simon's novel resists explanation except as a metaphor for its own resistance to explanation.'[70] Just as in La Maison de Rendez-Vous (1965), so in Triptyque; both Robbe-Grillet and Simon allow no 'correct' version of events to be discovered. The reader is confronted with the very act of creating text and story. The artificiality of the illusion of representation is central to the meaning of Simon's narratives. The presence of art, cinema, and types of theatre was noted in Part One of this study in another connection, and, as one critic has rightly claimed,[71] all forms of 'spectacle', of theatre, are seen to be derisory, and inadequate, in their very modes of representation.

In this analysis of the whole question of structure in
Simon's works, a more formalistic methodology has been
invoked, and the narratives appear wholly intelligible
in this way. Stylistic anomalies are not always adequately
accountable through a psychological relativism. This applies
especially to Simon's later works.

Finally, the analysis of structure in Claude Simon's
narrative fiction has revealed the fundamental anti-
representationalist poetics which they progressively
formalize. In this respect, the following words by
Benoist seem apposite:

> L'œuvre devient l'aventure d'un sens ou des
> sens qui n'en ont jamais fini de se dire tant
> que le texte n'est pas achevé, qui se trouve
> engagé par la lecture dans l'aventure d'un
> avènement dont l'échéance toujours est repoussée,
> auquel conspirent et n'ont jamais fini de
> conspirer tous les lecteurs disséminés qui par
> leur acte de lecture sont en quelque sorte les
> coécrivains du texte.[72]

Thus, the tentative unfinished nature of these texts demands
a more creative reader, whose role is no longer to consume
the ready-made artifact, but rather who is in the position
of co-ordinator of the fragments of text in his search for
wholeness.

Conclusion

A formalistic analysis of narrative sequentiality and
logic in the work of John Fowles would want to emphasize the structural centrality of the Quest, the process
from Enigma to revelation, and the catalystic function of
the Jungian Anima. Protagonists journey towards self-
discovery, both figuratively and literally. They
oscillate between states of mind prefigured in movements
from Enclosure to Plenitude. Appropriate imagery
symbolizes states of emotional and psychic impoverishment.
The quest for knowledge about the self, the world, and
Other Minds focuses on wise artist figures, themselves
ideal models of man, and the enigmatic Anima, the driving
force of plot. The tensional interplay between Adam and Eve,
Animus and Anima (the Jungian components of the self)
found the mode of characterization and the being-for-others
of characters. Mysteries exhaust rational logic and call
on unused resources of the imagination. The lessons of
these novels finally demonstrate that, for Fowles, man must
become the author of his own life in order to escape the
determinism of the plots of others, or of society itself.
Art and literature are historically bounded modes of knowledge, and self-conscious artist figures infuse questions
of the literary process, its rationality grounded in a
dialectical relationship between a self-conscious fictionality and an enabling realism, with the logic of narrative
itself. As the above chapter on structure and interpretation in Fowles's works has implicitly reiterated, a formalistic
approach to these texts must be limited to the principles
of coherence on which the works themselves are based. The

literary critic will always have to account for the relationship
between art and the world as a fundamental assumption of Fowles's
self-conscious realism.

A formalistic analysis of narrative in the novels and stories of
John Hawkes is possible, albeit because the author incorporates a
clearly defined notion of structure in those works.   But, as with
Fowles, the object-in-itself is not comprehensible without reference
to a more transcendent logic, acknowledged as the process of mediation
between the art-work and its referentiality.   For, in Hawkes's works
there is an arguable relationship between myth or aberrant states of
mind and the search for structure in narrative.   Clearly the Fascist
myth in some of the early novels and stories is a case in point, as
life is given the order and structure of 'fiction', and chaos is
apparently mitigated by such 'clear vision'.   In the later first-
person narratives, the relationship between states of mind and the
order of narrative structure becomes more problematic.   The perplexing
contradiction between Skipper's highly structured narrative in Second
Skin and his refusal to tell a tale in any straightforward manner,
enables the reader to perceive a more disquieting and perplexing
connection between states of mind and the structure of narrative.
Psychotic narrators and their obsessions with order and structure are
made intelligible by those myths of order to which they adhere, or by
those Freudian models of the self which are implicit in the text.
We are thus able to explain the apparent refusal of a narrator to
engage in a chaotic multiplicity by his ordering of experience in terms
of myths, symbols, motifs and essential opposites within the bounds
of any given narrative structure.   The fundamental interplay of recurrent motifs, symbolic landscapes, and the psychological states
they evoke found Hawkes's notion of structure.   Psychological
'coherence' is an intentional mode of recuperation for such apparently
unconventional narratives.   Their implicit critique of conventional

novelistic forms is grounded in the uses of inference, terse poetic
imagery, structural anomalies, and the foregrounding of crucial structural principles in a self-conscious disruption of the normative logic
of possible narrative sequences.  Psychological explanation of
structural idiosyncracies, then, becomes more pervasive in first-
person narratives, where the manifest unreliability of narrators is
foregrounded by the problematic relation between claims for truth and
the near-hysterical insistencies on those claims.  The convergence and
divergence of narrative around key images and events allow the reader
to formulate a critique of the narrator.  Structural principles reveal
questions of intentionality, and this founds the critique of conventional realism in texts which exceed the normative bounds of narrative
sequentiality in order to defamiliarize notions of the self based on
naive and less 'problematical' psychology.

Formalistic analysis of narrative is most apposite for the works of
Claude Simon.  Once the transcendent mode of explanation of narrative
logic is intentionally rescinded, the text as a source of epistemological anxiety no longer explains structure.  In fact, as I have
argued after Roubichou, the kind of structural analysis of the later
works enables a re-reading of the earlier works.  Once the question
of the conventional Subject as a source of narrative, and its explanation, has been effaced from Simon's work, then the onus falls on
language as an explicit source of narrative structure.  Semantic
polyphony, digressive flow of words, and the use of parentheses, for
instance, serve to fracture the notion of a unified and finished work.
This traditional idea of the literary text is replaced by the emphasis
on the production of the text, whereby its process of textualisation
is only knowable in its immediately apprehended yet never finished
state of becoming.  The use of the present participle undermines the
agent's importance in any action, and also, because of the state of
continual process which that verb form evokes, it enables the principles
of production to be related to its linguistic realization.  Such a

radical, self-conscious critique of the representation of reality
as a compositional principle for the novel causes an increasingly
complex search on the part of the critic for the logic of narrative.
The evident structural phenomena of order and disorder, fixed points
of reference and the utter dispersal of fragments, combine to undermine the initial impression of formlessness, and to reveal highly
structured texts. Arrangements, permutations, and combinations are
the structural principles which intentionally allow a play on modes of
recuperation. This play is foregrounded to the extent of a perpetual
rescission of an intelligibility which derives from the rationality of
conventional realism. The nearest Simon allows narrative to become
'realistic' in this sense is the use of the 'reality-effect' itself,[1]
which is always overshadowed by the 'effet de production', the illusion
of a text in the process of its tentative formulation. Finally, Simon's
texts are primarily about their own narrative problems in a more radical
and exclusive manner than those of Fowles and Hawkes. They are subversive of conventional realism to an extent which exceeds Hawkes's
works. They contain an implicit critique of the assumptions within
which Fowles's novels remain, and hover on the edge of comprehensibility
precisely because they test our norms and conventions of reading and of
writing. They ultimately articulate a poetics of refusal that derives
from a gallic tradition which emphasizes the problematics of language
in its assertions of knowledge and being. The denial of transcendent
understanding is part of that tradition, exemplified in the formalism
of French literary structuralism, and the disruptions of the nouveau
roman and Tel Quel, which all deny the primacy of the Subject. The
final part of this study will be more explicitly concerned with the
manner by which the post-Modernist novel evinces degrees of subversion precisely in the kind of relationship it intentionally has
with novelistic conventions.

PART THREE:

Parody, pastiche, and the manipulation of the reader's expectations in self-conscious narrative fiction

Toute véritable transformation de forme romanesque, toute féconde recherche dans ce domaine, ne peut que se situer à l'intérieur d'une transformation de la notion même de roman...

Michel Butor

CHAPTER SEVEN

(i) INTRODUCTION

So far in this study I have described those devices in the works
of the three writers which raise questions about the structure
of narrative, its modes of intelligibility, its characters and
the models of persons, which serve to define levels of the comprehensible and the incomprehensible. The reader brings a set
of implicit assumptions to his activity of understanding literature. A level of coherence is attained in the novel precisely
because it is read in a certain way. The connections between
structure and the logic of narrative are fundamental in this
process. Writing narrative fiction engages the author in an
implicit tradition of literary forms. The work characterizes
itself historically through tacit, and often problematical,
relationships with past forms. The literary historian tells
us that new forms derive from past traditions, and the extent
of a work's modernity, its newness in any historical period,
is contained in the kind of relationship it has with those past
forms on which it is founded. In this sense, a work is always
the product both of available notions of form and often a transformation of those notions. The text effects an intentional
mutation of given formal conventions.

Genres invoke sets of expectations grounded in certain implicit
assumptions, and, if this is indeed the case, then the transformation of archetypal forms (the quest romance, or more recently,

the detective story, for instance) may well be most effectively
achieved by the play on the reader's expectations. The purposes
of such a strategy are both self-interpretation and criticism.
Conditions of meaning in narrative fiction are often seen to be
based on the tacit relationship to past forms, where historical
redefinition of the possibilities available to the novel in
any era is to be discovered precisely in that transformation
and implicit questioning of the assumptions of traditional
forms and conventions:

> A cluster of conventions determines the medium of
> a literary generation - the repertory of possibilities
> that a writer has in common with his living rivals.
> Traditions involve the competition of writers with
> their ancestors. These collective co-ordinates do
> not merely permit or regulate the writing of a work.
> They enter the reading experience and affect its
> meaning. The new work is both a deviant from the
> norm (as a crime is based on attitude toward
> accepted social custom) and a process of communication
> referring to that norm. 1

In order to construct a methodology which would account for the
historical foundations and underlying assumptions of generic
models, the literary critic needs to avoid foreclosing the text
by imposing assumptions which derive from different traditions.
One familiar pitfall in literary history is that of misinterpret-
ating one literary tradition by imposing upon it from the outset
norms that have been derived from the study of another. There
can be little doubt that contemporary American fiction needs to
be related to a literary tradition in which romance has played
a much larger part than has been the case in England. Similarly
the attempt to clarify the emergence of self-consciousness in
English novels will run serious risks of distortion if it seeks

definitional clarity in relation to the French <u>nouveau roman</u>.
If indeed there are signs of the growth of a 'critical' novel
in England (and the work of John Fowles is a prime example),
it is not a critique conducted at the level of the production
of language, and the epistemological status of the literary
text, in the way that Simon's work is.  Contemporary experiment
in France evidently owes much to a tradition influenced firstly
by the poetry of Mallarmé, perpetually defeated before the
ineffable, and the sinuous narrative discourse of Proust, for
instance.  The aesthetics of representation are simply not
problematized in contemporary English writings in the way that
they are in the novels of a Robbe-Grillet or, differently, a
Claude Simon.  The starting-point for useful comparisons is the
understanding of national traditions in their own right, as
influencing and constricting literary forces.  Having acknowledged
the inherent bounds of given traditions, it falls to the comparatist to broaden the perspective by placing such trends and
limitations side by side in a more general poetics.  For, as
this study persistently maintains, the investigation of certain
methodological positions is always related to the implicit poetics
of any text, but this factor alone does not in any way preclude
the eventual critique of one text by another, or of one tradition
by another.  The interpretive operations themselves should
enable an understanding of precisely those conditions of meaning
on which the more challenging texts of recent literary 'experiment'
rely for their optimal effectiveness.  Describing the strangeness
of such texts is therefore more appropriate than recuperating
them into schemes which comply with presuppositions stemming

from given historical models.  In any case, such works play on
recuperative procedures.  What must, however, be clearly stresed
is the extent to which a dialectical process of refinement needs
stable literary models as norms from which to deviate.  The
reader also needs such knowledge in order to act as mediator
between the text and its critique.

Todorov tells us that each literary work modifies the totality
of possibilities, each new example changes our notion of the
literary type, or genre.  'Pulp' literature, the mechanical
reproduction of soporific plots, adds nothing to our understanding
of genre, if only because of its stereotypicality.  But today
it is difficult to defend the thesis which wants to claim the
'individuality' of a work of art.  The Romantic notion of the
work as the unedited production of personal inspiration, made
without any relationship to past works, must be rejected.  Genres
enable us to approach the new text with certain presuppositions,
and new texts may enable a closer understanding of genre.  It
is doubtful whether contemporary literature is more or less
exempt from generic distinctions; only, these distinctions may
no longer correspond to notions bequeathed by past literary
theories.[2]  In Todorov's argument, then, works that intentionally
modify original types of plot, structure, and the relationship
between Histoire and Discours, not only allow us a fresher perspective on the past, but significantly specify their own implicit
modes of understanding which are contained in that very difference.
What the literary critic must never fail to recognize in this

process of accounting is precisely how far these rearrange-
ments of interests and emphases are an historical problem.
The evolution of narrative forms from oral narratives to
written epics, from medieval romance to the nouveau roman,
is related to man's understanding of the world and of himself,
and of the very idea of literature.

Given the overwhelming presence of recalcitrant phenomena in
modern art and literature, and the necessity for a recuperative
rationality by the reader and critic alike in order to make
sense of such works, we will always look to the past for
guidance. In this respect, we would agree with Kermode when
he claims that we may well find that, in understanding the
great novels of this century, they may all contain certain
qualities of Balzac's Sarrasine, as defined in Barthes's S/Z ,
but also certain qualities of twelfth century romance, as
exemplified in the work of Marie de France.[3] We have been
made aware by critics and writers alike just to what extent
the nouveau roman is indebted to the novels of a Balzac.
Fowles, Hawkes, and Simon have built their texts on a discourse,
both implicit and often more overt, with traditional paradigms.
It remains to be seen in this chapter precisely how far their
works can be assessed through their relationships to past
forms. This approach will enable an analysis of both the
critical and the historical dimensions of the works under
scrutiny. How far do Fowles, Hawkes, or Simon define their
implicit idea of the novel through differentiation with
commonly received notions of what the novel is; how far do

they effect both a critique and a transformation of the conventions norms?  Whether it be any one recognizable genre (the
detective story; the romance quest novel, for example), or a
more generalized relationship to the novel of Realism in the
nineteenth century (particularly in the case of Simon, but,
differently, in Fowles's The French Lieutenant's Woman), the
centrality of criticism in their works is a crucial aspect of
their relationship to literary tradition and its underlying
assumptions about what the novel today may be.

My intention in this section is to discuss in some detail one
work by each of the three writers in order to determine the
kind of attitude to the novel they contain.  An historical
awareness of formal problems in connection with given interpretations of reality, and the interplay between the literary
text and the world, is clearly fundamental to all three writers,
as the preceding sections have argued.  Another form of historical
consciousness needs to be analyzed by the critic: the attempt
in each novel to distinguish itself from literary tradition.
Those texts which I shall discuss here offer different degrees
of critique through their uses of parody and pastiche to effect
disruptions of the reader's conventional expectations.  That is,
they all evince degrees of modernity in one very specific sense:
they are constructed, in part, at least, in terms of an in-built
aesthetic discourse with the literary tradition which defines
and constricts them.  Such novels represent this relationship
with past literature and established conventions in terms  of
parody and pastiche - modes which function as a means of self-

conscious interrogation of each work's indigenous tradition,
but also with more universal questions about the convention
of realism itself.

One of the fundamental purposes of parody in literature is that
of literary criticism. That is to say, the literary technique
of parody often pre-empts the activity of the would-be literary
critic by offering degrees of self-interpretation; it focuses
on the limitations of past forms, often by suggesting the
inbuilt historicity, and hence obsolescence, of 'previous' styles.
Analysis and critique of underlying assumptions, as well as the
process of undermining the absence of self-awareness in the
original type, may be effected by the mode of criticism available
in parody. Examples in English literature alone are many and
varied: Fielding's Joseph Andrews (1742), and Jane Austen's
Northanger Abbey (1818), are classic examples of either the
critique of another writer's work, or even the newly perceived
'absurdities' of a genre. These works offer an orthodox
definition of parody. By it, parody is seen as a 'subversive'
mode of imitation, and is to be distinguished from pastiche,
which implies a non-subversive form of imitation, usually
depending on systems of borrowing: patchworks of quotations,
images, motifs, mannerisms, or whole episodes may be borrowed
untransformed from the original. Pastiche may be the result
of a conscious recognition of influence; it may also be a
kind of immature pre-emption which indicates the lack of any
distinctive originality in a work. Deliberate pastiche, however,
is often a far from negative device; it may be used to stress

the ironic awareness that language, literary form, themes and
motifs regularly come to a writer in second-hand form, so to speak:
the writer is influenced, albeit unconsciously, by tacit knowledge
of the literature of the past.   The deflationary use of pastiche,
highlighting ambiguities in the original, for instance, underlines
the difficulty in clearly distinguishing between pastiche and parody,
especially in self-conscious literature and its less orthodox uses
of such modes.   For, the _conscious_ recognition of conventional and
non-conventional novelistic practices, which exist in history and
stubbornly refuse to be forgotten, is fundamental to such self-
conscious literature.   The contemporary novelist recognizes the
anxiety of personal signature in connection with the persistence of
literary realism and the understanding of the text which it demands;
but also in connection with the profound questioning of such aesthetics in the modernism of the late nineteenth and early twentieth
centuries.

The complex interrelationships between past convention and present
narrative fiction is indicative of the stage of self-awareness and
self-criticism which many recent works have attained.   In a sophisticated combination of literature and criticism, these novels address
themselves to a highly 'knowing' audience whose sensibilities and
expectations are accustomed to the vagaries of the French _nouveau_
_roman_, or to the kind of 'experiment' in American, or English novels.
Such a 'modern' reader is asked in various ways to be aware of the
anxieties involved in creating novels which are thoroughly modern,
when many of the ways of being modern have become established
conventions.

Parody, then, is to be understood as a mode of aesthetic foregrounding in the novel.   It defines a particular form of
historical consciousness, whereby form is created to interrogate

itself in relation to significant precedents. This kind of self-
consciousness requires careful understanding because it is a traditional strategy of crisis in the face of the persistence of
literary forms from the past. The uses of such modes of critique
in the works of Fowles, Hawkes, and Simon clearly enforce their
specific attitude to the past, and especially to the critique of
realism. The reader is asked to participate in the act of creating
story in Fowles's The French Lieutenant's Woman, and, with very
different results, in Simon's Le Vent. Hawkes's demands on the
reader are initially more disturbing as he disrupts the norms of
the detective thriller and asks us to peer into the strange psychological and moral world this formal disruption creates. John Hawkes
uses parody far less for the purposes of burlesque, as a Jane Austen,
or a Fielding, would have done. For one must see in many recent
parodic narratives that instead of merely caricaturing the 'original'
style with the intention of analytical mimicry, the 'modern' writer
offers, 'a mirror of a mirror, a critique of a view of life already
articulated in art.'[4] The critique of literary paradigms may also
be extended to a complex and profound questioning of the assumptions
on which the original was founded and the worldview (its ideological
character) to which it refers. Even in the more orthodox uses of
parody in Fowles's novel, the text is largely intelligible through
its critical, self-conscious investigation into the possible connections
between conventions of writing in the novel and socially accepted
attitudes in both Victorian and contemporary English society. We
may well then find a need to disagree, in part, with the function of
parody implied in the following statement:

> In calling something a parody we are specifying how it
> should be read, freeing ourselves from the demands of poetic
> seriousness, and making the curious features of the parody
> intelligible. [5]

Needless to say, if we know in advance we are going to read a parody
a certain expectation would be invested in our reading, and the
established conventions of parodistic writing would serve as a
powerful recuperative device in accounting for the apparent anomalies
of such texts.   However, given the complex set of relationships
between The Lime Twig (1961) by John Hawkes and the conventions of
the detective story and the thriller, or those between Fowles's
The French Lieutenant's Woman (1969) and Victorian novel conventions,
or even on a more general level those sets of relationships between
the novel of realism (as in a Balzac) and the abortive attempts to
tell the story of Montès in Simon's Le Vent (1957), one cannot see
parody as always freeing us from the demands of 'poetic seriousness'.
These novels will be seen not just to engage in a critical discourse
with past forms and the very idea of the novel, but also to force
the literary critic to rethink his orthodox categories of explanation.
Concepts as well as forms change with history, as the former is
derived from the latter.

In The Situation of the Novel (1970), Bergonzi asserts that:

> No matter how unflinchingly the novelist may try to
> deal with wholly new kinds of experience, he cannot
> escape from being influenced by the novels that have
> been written before him;  to this extent writing any
> novel is an implicit literary-critical act. [6]

Although one may well wish to disagree with the implication that all
novels are critical of their heritage, because many are obviously
parasitic in a very uncritical way, this statement does focus
attention on the markedly self-conscious nature of many novels today,
itself recalling the comic awareness of craft and convention in much
of the literature of the eighteenth century.   Allusions to past
works have always been commonplace in the history of poetry and drama,

but the novel, as its name indeed suggests, has always been
committed 'to originality and the immediate unique response to
individual experience.'[7]  The contemporary novelist, faced with
the traditional, post-Romantic premium on originality, and yet
fully aware of the overabundance of 'originals' and their various
derivatives which already exist in history, may indeed be in a
state of anxiety in his search for his own style.   This problem
has always been acute for the creative writer.   But the serious post-
war novelist is also a post-modernist writer;  that is to say, he
can never ignore the lessons of modernism, and the work of Kafka,
Proust, and Joyce in the novel.   For their implicit critique of
the kinds of authority embedded in the representationalist novels
of the nineteenth century, in particular, called for a re-evaluation
of the founding relationships between text and world, and text and
knowledge.   It is precisely on this level that parody in the three
writers may well be understood.   Even the avowed realism of Fowles's
novel still acknowledges the modernist critique of the status of
the text.

Parody may well be born of a self-conscious awareness of the
constrictions of established forms, but often it is also a product
of a radical scepticism about the relationship between language and
truth.   The work of Claude Simon grounds its critique of Realism
precisely in the connections between rhetoric and epistemology in
the storytelling process.   Hawkes's quest for psychological
coherence necessarily disrupts the soporific plot and surface
psychology of the detective genre.   Fowles continues to utilize
modes of realism, but uses a post-Marxian, post-Freudian, twentieth
century wisdom to characterize the degrees of authority in pre-
modernist novelistic practice.   As   subsequent analyses will endorse:

> The parodistic novel, exploding the absurdities of
> previous literary conventions as it unfolds, effects
> a kind of dialectical refinement and correction of
> lying, edging us towards the perception of certain
> truths about the manipulation of language, about
> character, about human nature, perhaps even about
> the kind of social world we inhabit. [8]

A work may indeed indicate the precise historicity of literary

forms by acknowledging the unconscious and conscious influence

of the past both as a source and as a constriction.

(ii)  John Fowles, <u>The French Lieutenant's Woman</u>

Novels written in the mid-nineteenth century evinced a marked
documentary bias, founding a relevance in a highly developed sense
of social history and gnomic statement which relied for authenticity
on the right-sounding, authoritarian voice of a knowing, collusive
narrator.  The apparent height of the novel's development out of
various pre-novelistic narrative forms is reached in the nineteenth
century, a 'progress' well surveyed in Auerbach's seminal work,
<u>Mimesis</u> (1953).  The major characteristic of realism in the novel
of that period is  'a serious representation of contemporary everyday
social reality against the background of a constant historical
movement.'[9]   An acute sense of the deterministic force of history,
the malleability of man and his need to protect his 'individuality'
against the coming commercialization of life, and a zero degree of
self-consciousness define the dominant features of the type of novel
that would have been written in, say, 1867.  The date is specific
and significant, for it is the date that locates <u>The French</u>
<u>Lieutenant's Woman</u> (1969) firmly in a time, depicts the scene to
flesh out a real historical situation, that of life in the Lyme
Regis of the winds of late March, and invites the reader to collaborate
with a narrator in the guise of a typical Victorian gentleman novelist
opinionating about the world on which he castes his knowing eye.  The
reader is asked to participate in the educated view of the world
offered by a narrator who steps out of the past.  But we realize that
1867 is an historical perspective, and the narrative voice a contrived
guise, when the illusion is momentarily fractured by the casual
intrusion of knowledge from the twentieth century:  Henry Moore is
very much of our time.  Apparently unperturbed, the narrator
explicitly compares the Lyme Regis, and the Cobb in particular, of
1867 with his twentieth century image of it: 'the Cobb has changed

very little since the year of which I write'.[10]   The circum-
locutionary eloquence of the Victorian novelist maintains its
poise even when the reader's suspicions have been aroused concerning the evident use of hindsight and invention masquerading
as Victorian social document;  and this, despite the wealth of
detail about current fashion (1867).

In these early pages of the novel, a heightened sense of a
Victorian reality is evoked through circumstantial detail imparted
by the typical voice of the knowing narrator who indicates his
equality with the educated reader.   Into this 'proper fragment
of the petty provincial day (p.9)'in 1867 erupts a brutal intrusion
of mystery not so unlike the enigmatic presence of Conchis in
Fowles's previous novel, The Magus (1965).   Already the reader
suspects a novel concerned with Victorian society, but in terms
of both the Victorian novel of realism tempered with the force
of history,and also the informed hindsight of the historian
privileged to interpret 1867 in terms of the intervening 'progress'
in thought, art, and society.   These suspicions contained in the
first brief chapter are swiftly confirmed.

The essential questions for this chapter are those which focus
on the aesthetics of the novel in the nineteenth century and the
elements of parody, pastiche, and imitation which serve critically
to establish a dialogue with literary tradition.   The various
levels on which the work may be read and interpreted are never
satisfactorily divorced, and this is a consistent factor in all
Fowles has written.   To make sense of the aesthetic preoccupations
is at once to acknowledge the intentional fusion of art and life-
concerns:  dominant contemporary ideologies which encapsulate the

sum of social life-worlds historically defined may never be separated from the production of works of art, and for Fowles the Victorian novel, its literary styles, are intricately inter-woven with the dominant ideology of its time just as the world of 1967 demands an apparently more enlightened (if less 'sincere') ethical and aesthetic fusion in the novel.

Thought and literature, science and social document provide sources by which Fowles footnotes the mid-nineteenth century. Quotations from the key figures of the age function in the first instance as epigraphs to the chapters they head.  As well as enabling the evocation of a real historical period, these references sign-post the principal thematic concerns in the portrait of an age and its fundamental crises.  The epigraphs are comprehensible in three major categories:  quotations from Marx delineate the plight of the working class and generally refer to the dehumanized nature of the human condition;  Darwin is often cited, supported by quotations from both physical and social scientists, and these together define a certain perspective on history as a determinant force, whereby the rising middle-class are seen to be more apt for survival than the outmoded aristocracy symbolized in Charles Smithson (much emphasis is placed on fossils as a source of motif). The third category, and the most predominant, is that of Victorian poetry.  Tennyson's Maud reflects the anxiety-filled situation of a man's love relationship which conflicts with social propriety, and In Memoriam significantly encapsulates the doubts, fears for change, and the basic insecurity of the age.  Clough's poetry evoke the ideas of duty (social conformity) and introspective self-analysis demanded by love.  Hardy's verse evokes scenes of the late 1860's, but the poet's 'presence' behind the novel, so to

speak (cf. p.236), as another self-interrogating lover who collides
with the constricting morality and social demands of the age, is
even more significant.    Finally, Arnold's poetry reinforces the
existential anxiety of the sadness and isolation of continual
introspection:  man     must acknowledge his isolation in such a
vast and depersonalized age.[11]

The connections between these selected epigraphs and the thematic
preoccupations of the novel, its dominant motifs, its central action
and the crisis-filled relationship between Sarah, Charles and the
age against which they react, need not be dwelt on here.   More
significant as far as this chapter is concerned is not only the
evocation of an historical period in terms of ideas and anxieties,
but also the stylistic commensurability of epigraphs and subsequent
narrative in the adopted pose of the Victorian novelist.   The
epigraphs serve to heighten the illusion of reading a novel of a
clearly defined historical period.

Fashion, descriptions of place (especially the Dickensian scenes
in London), the de-sentimentalizing of Dickensian stereotypes
(Sam, Mrs. Poulteney), the more generalized references to the
fiction of Hardy, Dickens, and occasionally to Jane Austen's
Persuasion, and the crippling behavioural prescriptions of a
stifling society, all contribute to the tissue of references which
found the mosaic of a world and its culture, heavily authenticated
by these various reality-effects encapsulated in a prose style which
mimes the literature and the historical and social reality which it
claims to represent.

To state the centrality of the documentary presence of a well-
delineated historical period does not in itself account for the

conditions of meaning of the novel as a whole.  A cursory glance
at the first few pages above raised the question of a certain
gamesmanship on the part of a narrator who, ariel-like, can adopt
the guise of a type of historically defined novelist, only to
break the illusion at will, and in so doing introduce another
historical dimension:  not only does the narrator want to play
at being a Victorian novelist, with all the attenuate reference
to the ambient society, but also he wants to be the historian
calling on his powers of hindsight to judge one age in the terms
of another.  Acknowledging this, the question of the <u>function</u>
of the mosaic of references must be answered.

The function of the historical perspective can be illustrated
by reference to three passages in the novel.  In chapter three
(especially pages 15 and 16) the reader confronts the first lengthy
intrusion of the narrator's  twentieth century knowledge.  The
very mention of the aeroplane, the jet engine, television, and
radar breaks the illusion of a Victorian novel.  Yet the most
significant aspect of this hindsight is its use as a means of judgment
on the twentieth century:  the great misery of our age is the lack
of time (p.15); life is less leisurely.  The narrator evinces a
certain regret for something lost in the acceleration of the modernization of life, despite our increased enlightenment.  Wealth today
is seen in terms of destructive neurosis (a post-Freudian perspective),
whereas the only ill effect of Charles's wealth was tranquil boredom
(p.16).  This same mode of criticism is manifest later (p.115) when
the nineteenth century is seen to have had qualities now regrettably
lost, where the individual was more individual for being more
distanced (without radio, television, cheap travel) from his fellow

man.  Strangeness is defined as a now lost, but once exciting
factor of existence.  The most overtly satirical pages in the
novel are contained in chapter thirty-five which states its
intention in the first line:  'What are we faced with in the
nineteenth century (p.231)?'  We see an age where the apparent paradoxes
in its attitude to woman and sexuality are indicative  of its
fundamental hypocrisy.  The work-ethic is partially explained by
the post-Freudian narrator in terms of sublimation;  but at this
point, once again, the critique of Victorian life is tempered by
a more sympathetic account of sexuality and a  denigratory view
of modern sexual mores.  In fact, the Victorians, we are told,
were more serious about something we openly enjoy.  For them the
mystery of sex increased their pleasure, suggests the narrator.

The use of an ambivalent historical perspective is initially
perplexing in The French Lieutenant's Woman.  In chapter thirty-
five the type of modality has changed from one of confidence and
certainty in gnomic statements (when the pose of the Victorian
novelist is in operation) to the more questioning modality of the
modern writer.  Where then does the bias in historical interpretation lie?  It is evident from the text that one of the central
issues is the writing of history as interpretation, and this implies
bias.  The perspective oscillates between complete criticism and
rejection of the constrictions and hypocrisies of Victorian society,
and a sympathetic account of a certain lost depth in poetry and
personal relationships.  Hardy's situation as both romantic poet
and frustrated lover in conflict with the age is cited as a
powerful referent (cf. pp.235-7).  The romantic power of poetry
and its evocation of the mysteries of love are seen to give way to

a more scientific, clinical Freudian view.   This is both criticized and also called upon to strengthen hindsight.   At the same
time the whole novel is a eulogy for the enlightened post-Marx,
post-Existential world-view, and the two central protagonists
both search for self and emerge as post-nineteenth century figures.

To understand fully the apparently ambivalent function of historical
perspective is to appreciate the inherent narrative logic contained
in the interweaving of what we may call the modality of 1867 with
that of 1967.   As chapter thirty-five intimates, the whole narrative
is founded on a complex set of interrelated confrontations between
two historical periods, two ideologies, and two possible literary
styles and conventions.   To demonstrate the extent of this confrontation, to see both sides of the historical difference, so to speak,
the narrator employs the present, and occasionally the conditional
tense to underline the need for a certain objectivity (cf. pp.231-233).
He calls on the reader's involvement by speaking directly of the
contemporary 'we', forcing us to contemplate our own sexuality.
What is involved, then, is a confrontation of modern and Victorian
consciousness.   The changes of style from the Victorian literary
convention to the post-Freudian voice indicate a far wider confrontation, one that functions on the aesthetic level.   But before
discussing this aspect, I shall briefly refer to the presence of
history as a force in the novel.

History in this novel is a powerful deterministic force, and the
allusions to Marx and Darwin are symptomatic of this concern.   In
the following quotation, the narrator refers directly to Charles's
perplexed consciousness faced with the enticement of Sarah:

> There was no doubt.  He was one of life's victims,
> one more ammonite caught in the vast movements of
> history, stranded now for eternity, a potential
> turned to a fossil. (p.289).

The narrative itself progresses from this fateful view of history
to the more existential realization of personal choice and response-
ful actions whereby life is defined in Marx's formula, 'the actions
of men in pursuit of their ends (p.398)'.  The principal action of
the story centres on Charles's education towards a more ambivalent
view of the world.  But he has to struggle against the predominant
idea of cosmic determinism, the grand design which belittles man in
the great march of progress.  Part of the problem is indicated in
an earlier reference to Marx:

> The bourgeoisie. . . compels all nations, on pain of
> extinction, to adopt the bourgeois mode of production;
> it compels them to introduce what it calls civilization
> into their midst, that is, to become bourgeois them-
> selves.  In one word, it creates a world after its own
> image. (p.244).

Mr. Freeman is the representative of that man who creates the
world after his own image, and Charles is in danger of extinction
as represented in the rise of commerce and the middle-class
business-man, and the cognate threat to the 'parasitic' aristocrat.[12]

Charles does indeed understand his plight in the face of the inevitable historical process.  His membership of the fated
aristocracy defines him as ill-equipped for survival in the
coming consumer society.  He can understand this in the terms
of the great natural scientist of the age whose ideas he accepts:
Charles Darwin.  At first feeling himself to be 'naturally
selected', Charles's confrontation with 'Freemanism' coerces

him towards positive action; but the process is a slow and painful
one.   It is Sarah's initial rebellion against the propriety and
cant of the age which leads Charles to his more enlightened self-
awareness.   In order to survive, like any species threatened with
extinction, he must adapt to the new order of things.   At the end
of the novel his changed attitude to Sarah is symptomatic of his
new-found capacity to survive:

> . . . for he has at last found an atom of faith in
> himself, a true uniqueness, on which to build;  he
> has already begun . . . to realize that life, however
> advantageously Sarah may in some ways seem to fit the
> role of Sphinx, is not a symbol, is not one riddle and
> one failure to guess it, is not to inhabit one face
> alone or to be given up after one losing throw of the
> dice;  but it is to be . . . endured.  (p.399)

The recognition of hazard, plurality of situations, and the part
that the individual will can play finally destroys the myth of
a powerful determinant historical force, albeit in the guise of
the dominant bourgeois middle-class and society's condemning
morality.

The post-Darwinian fatalistic view of history, with man as the
inevitable victim, is reminiscent of Hardy's naturalistic fictional
world, or even Zola's more politicized historical forces (exemplified in Germinal (1885) for instance).   The characters of the
cosmic plot are pre-determined because of the rigid class system
which imposes a fossilized stratification.   Towards the end of
The French Lieutenant's Woman that system is threatened by the
coming middle-class domination and the general levelling of society
by economic prosperity and consumer production.   At the same time
Charles, through his personal crisis is able to see the possibility
of breaking free from determinism by imposing his own will.   The
view of history in this novel echoes another pattern of determinism

and free-will which is dramatized on the aesthetic level: Fowles
wants to say something about the potential for over-determining
characters in the novel, the power of the novelist, and especially
the convention universally accepted in the nineteenth century, 'that
the novelist stands next to God'.  He wants to include a more post-
Modernist attitude to 'authority', to create a situation whereby
characters may appear to be less determined:  and the various endings
offer choices which dramatize this need for the reader as well.

A close reading of chapter thirteen reveals the extent of the
novel's implicit modernity, its intentional dialogue with the
conventions it apparently parodies.  Uptil this point the novel
has been a conventional historical novel written in the leisurely
grand style of a Victorian 'god-novelist'.  Suddenly the work is
transformed into a metacommentary on the theory of the novel from
a modern perspective.  The challenge is directly offered to the
reader:  to be involved in the assembly of a novel that wishes to
be more than the Victorian work that was never written.  It wishes
to be a thoroughly conventional novel of a  certain era and also to
manipulate those conventions, in both the aesthetic and the ethical
sense, so as to analyse self-consciously the conventions of mid-
nineteenth century realism and the society to which it refers.[13]

The brief intrusions prior to this chapter of hindsight founded
the suspicion in the reader that a certain critical task was in
process, that mere pastiche as skilful imitation, or parody as
burlesque, although evident, were not central to the overall intention.
The manipulation of past convention is now seen to be more widespread
and deep-seated, and is addressed directly to the knowing reader.

The novelist's dialogue with the reader in this intrusive section
(pp.85-87) initially recalls Fielding's posture in Tom Jones (1749),
but the narrator swiftly clarifies his difference from the eighteenth
century writer. Fowles acknowledges that

> . . . a novelist has only to pull the right strings and
> his puppets will behave in a life-like manner; and
> produce on request a thorough analysis of their motives
> and intentions. (p.85)

Clearly, this position is rejected, for omniscience takes on a new
theological image, 'with freedom our first principle, not
authority' (p.86).

Chapter thirteen is the first major defamiliarization of the
conventional Victorian novel within the text. As well as
declaring the intention not to over-determine his characters,
the twentieth-century novelist informs the reader that his expectations of passivity and uninvolved observation, germane to the
leisurely prose and anecdotal detailed descriptions of a nineteenth
century novel, will be denied. The reader is to be as committed
to the conditions of meaning, to the various levels which are
interconnected, as the central protagonists must be to their own
existential crisis.

Self-consciousness is the most un-Victorian element in the style
of The French Lieutenant's Woman. The representation of contemporary everyday social reality, against a background of a constant
historical movement,is the principal character of nineteenth-
century Realism, and is also the extent of the realism in Fowles's
novel.[14] The self-consciousness indicates the extent of the work's
critical intentions, and is therefore a measure of its modernity.

I have outlined above the ways in which the narrator resorts to his
twentieth century knowledge for historical interpretation, whereby
commentary through hindsight enables reciprocal judgment of two
historical periods.   This is one of the ongoing modes of self-
consciousness in the novel, and it is not unrelated to the kind of
intrusion effected in chapter thirteen.   The reader is active on
the ethic and the aesthetic levels.   He is asked to judge his
society and himself, as well as the constrictions of a previous
historical period.   The novel is an attempt to dramatize the need
for active transcendence of the 'iron certainties and rigid
conventions' (p.315) of the Victorian age, both in its social reality
and its art.   The type of novel of which __The French Lieutenant's__
__Woman__ is a skilful imitation and a critique is seen to be limited
in both its fundamental aesthetics and its view of man and the
possibilities of his relationship with others (particularly women).
The massive gulf between then and now is indicated at every instance
in the text, and on various levels.   But  the defamiliarization
of such an historically defined convention of realism is intelligible
for Fowles within the bounds of his existential philosophy, which he
wishes to dramatize for the reader as well as for his characters.

Lest we forget the post-Modernist lessons of chapter thirteen,
where the twentieth century narrative voice undermines ostentatiously
the authority of his Victorian counterpart, the author characterizes
himself, so to speak, appearing in the novel as firstly 'a successful
lay preacher — one of the bullying tabernacle kind' (p.346), and
later as a rather foppish, 'Frenchified' and successful impresario
who 'looks very much as if he has given up preaching and gone in for
grand opera' (p.394).   The moral dimensions of the narrative have

always been more readily intelligible, but the aesthetic, formal
lessons are harder to grasp.    In a final gesture, with a slight
element of gamesmanship, the narrator, with all his twentieth century
cunning, offers the reader three endings.    The first is the conventional, expected ending of the kind of novel which is being
imitated (p.282).    This ending is rescinded in order to move out
of the constrictions of a literary convention and also its cognate
social conventions.    Fowles as existential novelist wants to
dramatize the need to exist within the potential anxiety of choices
and the burden of responsibility for choosing.    This is accomplished by offering two final endings, one similar to the conventional
ending (a 'happy-ever-after' situation, but this time with Sarah and
their child), the other with Sarah's ultimate rejection of Charles
and his final realization that life must be endured in all its
multiplicity.    The text creates the necessity for the last ending
through its thematic concerns, and through the aesthetic imperative
to undermine determinism at all costs — Charles is, after his
lengthy ordeal (and education), able to survive, to endure.    He
stands on the threshold of the hazards of the modern novel.

The French Lieutenant's Woman richly documents the world of 1867.
The Victorian world is intensely realized by detailed physical
description and characterization which both create a sense of
realism and historical authenticity.    I have implied the extent
to which the novel is a patchwork of allusions not only to specific
character stereotypes, but also to a specific style of writing.
But I have also suggested that the novel is a critique of the
constrictions of conventions, both social and literary.    Parody

was defined above as a mode of literary criticism which focuses on
the inherent limitations of past forms and serves to underline the
historical character of modes of writing.   In The French Lieutenant's
Woman, parody, manipulating the expectations of the reader, and also
utilizing elements of pastiche, transcends the comic playfulness of
burlesque for more serious intentions.   In Fowles's novel we may
locate the parody of a past convention in the disruption of expectations exemplified in all the various intrusions of hindsight, the
direct addresses to the reader on the confrontation of traditional
and modern theories of the novel, and the intentional rescissions
of expected endings (the Victorian and the modern happy-ever-after
situations).   The parody in this self-conscious narrative fiction
is located in the oscillation between implicit and explicit
critiques of a literary convention and its founding world-view
(ideological substructure).   It is a critique of a view of life
already articulated in art, and is also then a critique of that art.
The novel significantly ends in the company of the Pre-Raphaelites
who intended their art to serve as a profound critique of their age,
and who desired to bring life and art into closer proximity.

The work of John Fowles as a whole testifies to the view contained
in The French Lieutenant's Woman that past conventions and attitudes
are never completely rejected, that realism is a viable form but should be
tempered with a questioning self-consciousness which may enable a
transcendence of past constrictions, and re-aligned with a post-
Darwin, post-Marx, post-Freud existential world-view which must be
dramatized in the form of the novel.   The impossibility of writing the
Victorian novel in 1967 is underlined by the implicit relationship
between conventions of writing and historically defined imperatives,
the novel and its implicit view of man and consciousness.

(iii)  John Hawkes, The Lime Twig.

The past as a neurotic constriction is central to the intelligibility
of Hawkes's novel.   The relationships between psychological preoccupations and the concern with form and narrative technique per se
are fused through the essential parodic structure.   Disruptions of
conventional morality through what the author has called the
'terrifying similarity between the unconscious desire of the solitary
man and the disruptive needs of the visible world'[15] are echoed in
the intentional disruption of the expectations invested in those
conventions of the novel upon which this work is founded.   The
centrality of criticism in this novel relies for its comprehensibility
on the marriage of considerations of conventional morality and
conventional realism.

The Lime Twig (1961) is a very specific kind of pastiche,rooted in
such fiction  of English gangland as Graham Greene's Brighton Rock
(1938) for instance, but also enhanced by its use of the desolate landscape
of a
/war-ravaged London.   The novel is characterized by an image of
dreary and impoverished lives, which, typically for Hawkes, is
symbiotic with the landscape.   The gangland world appears typical,
and engenders the potential for violence and terror.   The novel
founds a wholly recognizable and credible world revolving around a
gambling syndicate's efforts to abduct a famous race-horse and disguise
it as an outsider,in order to win a vast sum of money in an important
race.   It is peopled with gangland crooks and thugs, a ruthless
'boss', prostitutes, and the inevitable forces of law and order.
After killings and 'muggings', the narrative reaches a thrilling
climax enhanced by intrigue and suspenseful action.   Hostages are
taken to ensure the success of the 'plot', however one of them

manages to wreck the plan by giving his life in a dramatic and
purposeful gesture of defiance.  All the stereotyped ingredients
of the conventional thriller are in evidence, but all the expected
ends of this convention are denied. The innocent die;  the
crooks are never caught;  the police are totally powerless;
commonly accepted notions of justice, rightness, and reason are
significantly absent.   This renders an acute sense of dislocation
and disruption in a novel which seems to have reversed the traditional
morality of good and evil/the same time as denying the outcome of
detection customary in        the specific type of novel of which
The Lime Twig is a pastiche.

If the disruption of expectations is fundamental to the definition
of parody, then, as well as being a specific type of pastiche,
Hawkes's novel is also a parody of the detective and thriller
conventions.   Locating these conventions will enable me to discuss
precisely how the parody is made available to the reader and what
its wider implications are.

In order to find a basis for these assertions one could look
primarily to the fundamental ingredients of the thriller:

> Usually they /suspense stories/ find the principal
> character, often against his will, in conflict with
> inimical forces, personal or natural, which he must
> overcome in order to save his life . . . The suspense
> turns on developments and the decisions he makes to
> work out his own salvation. 16

Evidently this formula may be applied to The Lime Twig, with Michael
Banks as the protagonist, and the inimical forces stemming from the
machinations of Larry and his gang.   Salvation is obtained in
Michael's redemptive act as he stops the race, kills himself in
the process, and foils Larry's plan.   On the level of the suspense-

plot, this is an adequate mode of accounting for Michael's
involvement in the action.

Essential to the suspense story is the unity of perception which
precipitates sympathetic identification of the reader with the
plight of the protagonist.[17]   Remove these elements and suspense
would not be effected.   The novel begins with the narrator-persona
of William Hencher uttering what amounts to a prologue, delineating
a whole world of dreariness and loneliness in war-torn London. However the
initial expectation of his centrality in the plot is denied in the
first chapter proper,where he is kicked to death by the horse, Rock
Castle.   Hencher evokes sympathy in his short-lived role as first-
person narrator, through the underlying rhetorical possibilities of
that conventional mode of narration.   However, in the first chapter
he is relegated to the status of character, as the narrative perspective moves to an omniscient and unidentified third-person mode.
Literally, he is a member of Larry's gang, and his connection with
both the underground world of crime,and the daily, banal existence
of the Banks, as their lodger, enables him to function as instigator
of Michael's involvement with the intrigue.   Hencher's usefulness
as narrator, and then as solely a character in a narrative,ends with
Chapter one.

I dwell on this point because it is precisely the change in narrative
mode between the prologue and chapter one, the figurative and literal
death of Hencher, which primarily indicates the extent of the novel's
intentions.   The disruption of the unified point of view into a more
fragmented, disjunctive narration is a measure of the novel's distortion of the essential elements of the formulaic, stereotype model
of a thriller.   I shall be concerned implicitly and explicitly with

this distortion as the basis of parody and also as the critique of
conventional morality in this brief account of The Lime Twig.
In this novel, the conflict with inimical forces which affects
Hencher initially, then Margaret and Michael Banks later, and
finally the world of conventional morality generally, is in effect
seen to be a struggle with the innermost, disruptive fantasies which
lurk behind the impoverished lives of the central characters.  The
violence and the fatal outcome of Larry and the fantasies of Michael are
both contained and dramatized in the horse as a literal focus of
intrigue and a symbolic embodiment of Michael's most secret desires.

Given the implicit presence of crimes and intrigue, murder and
violence, the novel is both a thriller and a detective story.  Both
conventions of writing are distinguishable one from the other;
however they are often interrelated:

> A mystery story . . . is simply one in which a mysterious
> circumstance crying for solution is presented to certain
> characters — and to the reader . . . But detection of the
> reason for the mysterious circumstance is the basis of the
> story and provides its thread of action, whether it be an
> actual detective story or not. [18]

Fundamentally, a detective story contains a crime, a detective,
the process of unravelling the crime which founds the  sequential
narrative, and a criminal who is unmasked at the climax on which the
story ends.  From this prescription it is evident that The Lime Twig
is both a thriller and a detective story.  Hencher is killed in
mysterious cricumstances;  Margaret is abducted, beaten and raped;
Cowles is brutally murdered;  a horse is stolen and disguised and
entered for a famous race.  A sports' columnist, not directly
involved in any of the novel's action, expresses his suspicions
and asserts his desire to solve the mystery surrounding the horse
and Banks' involvement:  his is the voice of detection.  Actual

policemen appear rarely, but the novel ends with detectives beginning
an investigation into the 'particulars' of the crime.    Perhaps it is
at this point that the traditional detective story would have begun,
with the discovery of Hencher's body.    The discovery of the body
is the pre-condition for a conventional murder story.    We may
suspect that this novel's intentions are different.    The detectives
are seen to search for clues in petty details:

> . . . they inspected the hinges, the type of nail used,
> made note of a dead wasp caught on a green splinter . . .
> The straw would have to be sifted through a screen.[19]

But we suspect also, after the prior effectiveness of Larry's world
and its total divorce from the criteria of the conventional world
and its morality, that the so-called forces of evil have already
triumphed over those that represent conventional law and order.    The
least the police can do, in conjunction with the reader through his
conventional expectations, is to continue to hunt for clues, even if
none will be forthcoming.    The quest for evidence belongs to
different conventions of the novel.    Furthermore, it is precisely
those conventions which this novel disrupts through parody.    Hencher
as first-person narrator, Slyter as pseudo-detective and voice of a
commonsense reality, and the police of the final pages are all stereotypical figures who prove ineffectual in the face of the inimical
forces that are comprehensible only superficially on the level of
crime and intrigue on which these figures function.    A closer
reading of the novel on the level of its symbolic structure and its
recurring and interrelated motifs will allow us to understand these
forces, the manner by which they are dramatized and infused with the
literal level of plot, and finally the psychological and moral
preoccupations they indicate.

In order to situate any reading of the novel in terms of symbols
and motifs, I must refer briefly to the expectations aroused by
the prologue and also place a statement by the author in the context
of The Lime Twig which may enable a clarification of the intricate
connections between symbols, motifs, and psychological preoccupations
which, in Hawkes's work, provide the structure of narrative and the more
far-reaching consequences of that work's parody. Crucial here is the
extent to which motifs, symbols, and their emphatic recurrence are
symptomatic of an intention not only to indicate the attempts to
encapsulate psychological issues themselves, but also to carry the
parody of conventional novelistic forms to a more disturbingly
condemning level. In this novel, the intention is apparently to
parody the soporific plot of the conventional detective-thriller, its
stereotypical, easy-going narrative moving from enigma through to
revelation, and its reliance on the denotative surface of the text
with its consequent absence of psychological depth. The novel enables
the reader to enter the connoted hidden world of the unconscious by
offering ,firstly, a mode of recuperation of the later sections in
the form of a first-person narrative of realism, which also provides
a conventional rationale for the ensuing exposure and enactment of
inimical forces from the unconscious desires of Banks and his
wife; and,secondly,    the possibility of verbal coherence through
symbols and motifs which themselves function as a critique of the
conventional, formulaic simplicity of the thriller and detective
genres. For, despite the structure of stereotypes on which the
novel is founded, profound inroads are made into the denotative
surface whereby symbolic embodiment of unconscious desires,and the
ambivalent dimensions enabled through recurring motifs, serve to fracture
the soporific nature of the stereotype plot sequence. The novel is

thus a profound critique of levels of impoverishment, both in the
view of the lives of the characters established in the prologue,
and in the stereotype of the detective-thriller genre, with its naive
realism.

The prologue characterizes Hencher as the voice of an historical
perspective which, as I suggested above, lends a certain plausibility
to the ensuing drama, by creating the norms of realism and its
cognate intelligibility through association with the reader's
normative empirical response to his daily life-world. He describes
an urban landscape of desolation and loneliness in war-ravaged
London. The emphasis on the loneliness of Hencher's life, especially
after the death of his mother, and the consequent fantasizing which
fills his life, founds an expectation wholly bound up with the Dreary
Station existence. The rhetoric of first-person narration, and the
stark realism of these particular pages, entice the reader into
sympathetic identification with Hencher's view of this desolate city-
scape, especially in its reduced focus on the surrounds of Violent
Lane and Dreary Station. Hencher directly confronts the reader with
the situation which he wishes to emphasize:

> Or perhaps you yourself were once the lonely lodger . . .
> A lodger is a man who does not forget the cold drafts,
> the snow on the window ledge, the feel of his knees at
> night, the taste of a mutton chop in a room in which he
> held his head all night. (p.4-5)

The narrator's first-hand experience of such an existence leaves
a vacuum which needs to be filled with the escape into dream.
Early in the narrative, the reader's attention is focused on the
fantasy possibilities which (for Hencher) surround 'the gilded
cherubim' which is 'big as horses that fly off the top of the Dreary

Station itself' (p.7).   This is the first association of horses
with flights of fantasy and escape from the boredom and impoverishment of existence.   The reference itself foreshadows the symbolic
interpretation of involvement with Rock Castle, the stolen race-
horse, itself emblematic of the embodiment of the unconscious
desires of Michael Banks.

The initial pages of the novel not only establish the connection
between daily impoverished lives and the necessary recourse to fantasy,
but also enable a natural association between the symbolic and
literal levels of the narrative.   Hencher, a man of affection with
a potential for devotion, is committed to 'helping' his new land-
lord and his wife transcend their impoverishment.   Hencher functions
as a catalyst who effectively sets in motion the involvement in
intrigue and the release and enactment of unconscious desires.   He
bridges the present-time of the plot and the recent past, referring
to real history in a realism which is the most powerful force of
recuperation in the novel.   The expectation of rational explanation is founded in this prologue, but its plausibility is increasingly rescinded as the symbolic level impinges disruptively on the
thriller-detective plot.

The mode of establishing expectations from conventional sources
is intensified in the traditional elements of characterization
which follow the normative descriptions of Hencher's life.   The
Banks themselves are portrayed in similar fashion.   The boring
repetitions of Margaret Banks's week centres around the 'daring'
excursion to the shops on Wednesdays, and, while she is away,
Michael reveals his extreme sexual frustration:

> Now he is standing next to their bed — the
> bed of ordinary down and ticking and body
> scent, with the course of dreams mapped on the
> coverlet. (p.31)

The very ordinariness of his home is linked with the plain
ordinary wife whose principal nightmare is to find him gone and
who fears the 'horrible touch of the barber's lips' (p.65), or
being in the dark where 'men with numbers wrapped round their
fingers would feel her legs'(p.68).   She is characterized by a
general fear of life and especially of anything which may disrupt
the quotidian routine of existence.   Margaret describes herself
significantly as 'plain, only a girl who could cook, clean, sing
a little' (p.66).   Once Michael has left with Hencher to become
involved in the horse-stealing intrigue, she becomes the epitome
of loneliness,conversing with her cat about her fears for Michael.
Her conventionality and simplicity portray her as 'a girl with a
band on her finger and poor handwriting, and there was no other
world for her' (pp.69-70).   However, below this surface is a more
disquieting world contained in her fantasies:  she dreams of
children tied on railway tracks and sees 'the sparks hitting the
pale heads and feet' (p.71).   For her the divorce between violent
fantasy and banal existence is complete.   We are prepared for her
pathetic response to the fatal beating by Thick and the rape by
Larry:

> She was Bank's wife by law, she was Margaret, and
> if the men ever did get hold of her and go at her
> with their truncheons ar knives or knuckles, she
> would still be merely Margaret with a dress and a
> brown shoe. . . (p.70)

Her response to the violence in chapter six is naturalized for the
reader by our established expectations of her complete inability
to react other than through her banal view of life.   What happens

to her is 'violence that seemed not meant for her'; for 'she knew
there was enormous penalty for what they had done to her' (p.125),
and,although she tells herself it was to be expected, 'it was something done to abducted girls, that's all', yet in rationalizing
the brutality of the assault she declares that 'it was something
they couldn't even show in films' (p.126). Her response is
symptomatic of her inability to have any immediate physical relation
to others. Her banality enables her to mitigate those brutal acts,
and indicates the extent of her impoverishment in relation to
physical sensations.

The traditional elements of realistic character portrayal both
in the figure of Hencher, and in that of Margaret, are powerful
forces of recuperation which enable the reader to account for the
actions of Michael in both orgy and intrigue, within the terms of
realism established in the first-person narrative with which the
novel begins. The structure of the narrative is founded on the
relationship between verbal and psychological coherence through
the ambivalent oscillation between realism and the dramatization
of the symbolic fantasy-desires of the protagonist, Michael.
The conditions for fantasy are established through realism with
the recurring images of fog, mist, steam, and even the smell of
dampness. These descriptive elements become symbolic embodiments
of states of ambiguity when associated with the nether world of
surreptitious violence initially related to the gangland world,
yet subsequently associated with the enactment of Michael's
unconscious desires. The symbolic focus and the element which
fuses the real world of crime with the fantasy world is the horse
itself.

Just as we are informed that Margaret's own worst dream 'was one
day to find [Michael] gone', so, in like manner, Michael's 'own
worst dream, and best, was of a horse which was itself the flesh
of all violent dreams' (p.33).   Through Hencher, he is within
reach, literally, of possessing the horse of his dreams in the
flesh, and this event is firmly located in time, a Wednesday, which
nevertheless will be like no other Wednesday.   It is described as
'only a time slipped off its cycle with hours and darkness never
to be accounted for' (p.49).   The latent mystery and consequential
violence which surround the horse 'in the flesh' point to the
dramatization of disruption effected by the collision between
unconscious desires and the desires of the 'visible world'.   The
horse is harmless as a figment in Michael's fantasy.   Once it
literally enters his life through Hencher, it causes the disruption
not only of his banal existence with Margaret, but of life itself.
The stallion becomes the symbol of hitherto suppressed violence, a
force which Hencher has unwittingly released on the level of plot.
In this respect, we may acknowledge the relevance of the following
assertion:

> Once released to find objectification in the race horse,
> Banks' fantasies take over his life — he literally
> experiences the dream.   His unconscious desires find
> fulfilment in his new dream-defined reality but entrance
> to his dream world costs him his life. [20]

The inimical force contained in the fantasy is irrevocably
associated with the image of the horse whose power to drive 'down
the hoof to splinter in a single crash one plank of that empty
Dreary Station floor' (p.33) is also symptomatic of Michael's
wish for sexual force and dominance.   Not only can the horse
function as an enabling focus for the illusion of sexual power,

but it is also able to symbolize the potential for the violent
destruction of the dreariness and boredom of this daily existence.
Rock Castle, the race-horse, does lead him to the utter fulfilment
of all his sexual fantasies during the orgiastic night on the eve
of the race, and, as a central unifying image in the novel, leads
Hencher, Michael, Margaret, as well as Cowles, and a little girl,
to their death through involvement with the intrigue.  Hencher's
death (killed by the horse itself) is the first indication of the
force of violence, the almost mythic power which the horse embodies.
Michael's death, a self-willed act of defiance, is engineered by
the protagonist only after he has become fully conscious of the
power he has unleashed.  The horse finally becomes the instrument
of his death-wish:

> Michael fails to realize that his obsession to smash
> his loneliness and thus clear the way for escape into
> his dream world amounts to his death warrant, for
> without his routine reality he ceases to exist.  The
> dull life with ordinary, timid Margaret is Michael
> Banks; take away that life and he is destroyed.[21]

He becomes so involved in the world of gangsters, drugs, sex, and
gambling where their laws of life and death are totally alien to
his habitual way of life that he ceases to have an identity as such,
and both he and Margaret become pawns in someone elses' plot.  It
is as witness to the apparently senseless killing of a child by the
local policeman, the traditional emblem of law and order, that Michael
is provoked through indignation into positive action.  The principal
moral dimension of the novel in terms of character and plot is made
explicit at this point.  Michael emerges as a potential hero, and
the horse is once again the instrument through which he can act.

The horse, then, as an image of sexual power and violent, destructive
potential is the apparent motivation for the plot as well as the
unifying symbol lending coherence to psychological concerns.  It
fuses the ongoing narrative of intrigue and the thematic preoccupations of the novel, and is associated one way or another with
each character and their fate.  The horse is the most significant
and destructive lime twig in the work, entrapping those who are
attracted to it:  through the conscious enactment of unconscious
desires, they become ensnared, like birds 'stuck fast' to the lime.
Michael, for instance, is trapped by his involvement with Rock Castle,
and further limed by the sexual offerings of Sybilline, the arch-
temptress, who enables him to transcend, albeit momentarily, the
shortcomings of his habitual sex-life.

Towards the end of the novel, at the point where Michael realizes
that he is finally alone, allusion is made to the mate of the oven
tit first encountered in the previous chapter.  For, we are informed,
'even two oven tits may be snared and separated in such a dawn'
(p.159).  The allusion to the novel's title emphasizes the centrality of a set of recurring motifs which enable structural coherence
to be achieved.  The coherence functions on a thematic level.  For
both Margaret and Michael are separately ensnared in the gangland
world.

I have already briefly mentioned the recurring images of fog, mist,
dampness, even rain, which create a mood of dreariness.  More
significantly, these images enable a unifying motif:  symbolic
of the fact that it is never clear initially what precisely happens
in a novel whose basic plot is founded on a sequence of events (as
in the thriller), the motif of mist is at the same time a powerful

reference to the murky dream-world of fantasy.  A clichéd
atmosphere for the thriller, where what happens is withheld until
the end, fog or mist blurs any clear distinction between the
realism of the horse-stealing intrigue and the dream-world of
Michael's darkest desires.  Motifs of entrapment, of power and
powerlessness, the blurring of information and the denial of a
clear distinction between the symbolic exposure of psychological
concerns and the realism of plot, and finally the spanning, far-
reaching symbolic and actual image of the horse, all fulfil the
intention of finding a narrative structure which may enable both
verbal and psychological coherence through recurring motifs and
images.  The undermining of a linear, sequential narrative indicates
Hawkes abiding critique of the bounds of realism.

So far I have concentrated on the psychological concerns, the motifs
and the symbolic interpretation, and those modes of recuperation,
founded in Hencher's narrative which enable a certain type of
reading based in realism to establish the false expectations necessary
for the effective strategy of parody.  The parodic intentions of
The Lime Twig are seen to be related also to aspects other than
that of technique per se.  The novel wishes to dramatize elements
of psychology (those hidden complex motives for action) which would
not be available in the more simplistic plot of the formulaic
thriller.  Finally, the novel intends to extend the critique of
traditional expectations to include a moral perspective.  Destruction
is relocated in the apparent innocence of victims, and the daily,
conventional world is portrayed as the harbinger of repression, a
state effected in this novel by the utter impoverishment of existence
resulting in the actual destructive potential, itself prefigured in
the fantasies of Michael and Margaret Banks.  The novel problem-

atizes precisely what the reader conventionally brings to his
active engagement with the text, and the need to re-align sympathies
stem from the concern in the novel with both literary form and
normative morality as impoverished conventions.

More evidently, Sidney Slyter's sports-column bears witness to
the gulf between the banal surface reality well documented by
Hencher in the prologue, and the more disturbing and psychologically
profound order of experience in the main text of the novel.
Slyter's comments act as a 'chorus' on the novel. Written in
colloquial journalese, a style which itself contrasts markedly
with the often elevated prose of the main text, these sections
evince a frustrating search for facts and clues. Slyter's quest
for the truth, like the quests of the police in the closing pages,
and the reader throughout, is denied because it is founded on a
false rationale, and because he, like the police, is powerless in
a world as apparently autonomous as that of Larry and his gang.
Structurally, these sections do enhance the element of the thriller-
detective genre and they do offer an important amount of circumstantial realism in a world of racing and gambling.

Be that as it may, Slyter is more than just an impotent commentator
on the novel's inherent mysteries. The kind of consciousness which
his opinions and demands invoke is a powerful example of the latent
evil in the 'visible world'. His curiosity, 'his callow optimism,
his lower middle-class English ego, his tasteless rhetoric, his
vaguely obscene excitement in the presence of violence' as Hawkes
himself claims,[22] allow Slyter to be the embodiment of all that is
morally distasteful and degrading in the world of so-called conventional morality. The evil and violence of Larry appears noble in

the light of Slyter's evident characteristics.   Moreover, as a
commentator, he is very unreliable, not only because of the
perverse nature of his character, but more especially because of
his apparent inability to penetrate below the mere surface appearance of events.   Thus when he comments confidently on the forthcoming action, the reader must be suspicious of his shallow knowledge:
deeper psychological truths and motivations are beyond his ken.
Initially, one suspects Slyter's role to be another strategy in the
process of disruption of the expectations of suspense (seemingly
pre-empting the sequence of events), but his inability to do more
than scratch the surface, so to speak, demands that the reader carry
on his role and search for a more satisfying explanation.   The
implicit critique of Slyter's shallowness is further enhanced by
the reader's privileged insights into the unconscious desires of the
main protagonists through motifs, symbols, or direct comment from
an implied author of particular states of consciousness.

The sports-column sections indulge in the realism first witnessed
in Hencher's narrative, and,through Slyter's questioning tone, his
obsessive, self-opinionated view-point, the reader is coerced into
maintaining an ambivalent response to the novel as a whole.   The
continual presence of realism and the rationale of Slyter's search
for the truth practically misleads the reader into judging the main
body of the text in terms dictated by the conventions of realism, and
especially the realism of the detective genre.   The intentions of
parody are seen to be emphasized in this fundamental structural and
thematic technique whereby the failure of Slyter's realism and his
cognate search for truth is implicitly contained in the difference
between what 'Sidney Slyter says . . .' and what the text of the
novel itself evokes.   The reader's sympathies and conventional

responses are sharply examined in a novel which conspires through devious tactics to mislead one into a simplistic cause-and-effect argumentation.

Through demonstrating the banality and callowness of conventional reality, described by Hencher and exemplified in the character of Slyter, Hawkes has demonstrated precisely what that reality conceals. He has achieved his avowed aim:

> . . . constantly to test in the sharpest way possible
> the range of our human sympathies and constantly to
> destroy mere surface morality.[23]

It is normative conventional morality which is seen to be destructive, and that untraditional assertion is evident in Slyter's presence in the novel, in the recourse to the violent enactment of fantasies, and significantly in the divorce between Margaret's banal, routine life and her violent and repressed dreams. The scenes in which she is beaten and finally raped are perhaps the sharpest examination of the reader's response.

Thick's explosion of violence is recuperated by her situation in the plot and by her role as helpless victim. In fact, she has attempted to escape captivity and is being punished. The actual violence of his assault is muted through her strangely inadequate response: she is distanced from her pain, as if incapable of registering the physical reality. Her reactions are a symptom of her simple, ordinary mind. She sees herself as others would from her banal, daily experience and is aware that this violation of her modesty would shame her in the eyes of her neighbours. The only way she can even begin to understand the horror of the assault is to recall the contents of her worst nightmares: swimming in the petrol tank of a lorry or 'watching three rubber dolls smartly burning' (p.132). For her, the order of experience in her dream-world is very divorced from that of daylight reality: at least on waking, reassurance of normality would return. But this particular situation _is_ of the order of her nightmares; it _is_ her present reality, and this she finds difficult to come to terms with. Her situation as helpless, lonely victim is stressed through her own thoughts, and the brutality is held at a distance. The scene is not sadistic in that pain is not conveyed.[24] But how much sympathy can we feel for Margaret, especially as a conventional helpless victim? Only a limited sympathy is felt because of the strange inadequacies of her response in a novel which is filled with examples of inadequate response (Hencher, Slyter, Margaret, the police at the end, and perhaps the unsuspecting reader). If sympathy is called for initially, then a clearer understanding of the ambiguity inherent in the psychology of victim-victimizer relation-ships, symbolized by Thick and his captive, is demanded in the end. For just as Michael is finally a victim of his unconscious desires, so his wife in the end fulfils her violent and erotic fantasies. The rape-scene is given a plausible cause by the intentional temporal disjunction between the events of chapters six and seven: Larry seeks revenge for Michael's sexual exploits which are described in chapter seven. Hawkes has therefore technically enabled the reader to face his response to the brutality without recourse to any immediate, rational explanation on the level of plot.

The Lime Twig, through the device of parody, seems to entertain the possibility of conventional realism and yet at the same time offers the means through which to transcend the formal limitations of that convention. The critique of form is grounded in a particular genre, and this in itself enables a more specific problematizing of techniques, expectations, and stereotypes which themselves symbolize a more far-reaching questioning of thematic expectations. Hawkes's use of parody as a means of disruption and criticism is aimed at the restrictions of the conventional novel (the soporific plot of the thriller in this instance) and also the limitations of conventional morality. I must in the end agree with one critic who has asserted that:

> Not only freeing Hawkes from the limits of realism, this distortion of probability helps him investigate the deeper psychological truths which flourish beneath surface reality and beyond the dictates of rationality.[25]

(iv)  Claude Simon, <u>Le Vent</u>.

In this chapter, John Fowles's <u>The French Lieutenant's Woman</u> has
been described above as a critique of the conventional Victorian
novel and its ambient society on which it founded its content and
from whose implicit ideology it developed an abiding aesthetic.
This novel was seen to define itself historically in terms of pastiche,
parody, and self-conscious articulation of the underlying assumptions
of a given convention.   In the end, the realistic mode of writing was
seen to be endorsed while an existential, post-nineteenth century
wisdom was invoked as the means to effect a modernization of
consciousness dramatized in both character interaction and moments
of lucid, self-conscious narration.   John Hawkes's <u>The Lime Twig</u>
has been described as parodying a well-defined and popular genre
whose model derives from similar sources as that of Fowles's novel,
that is to say, conventional realism, though realism of a different kind.
Hawkes's novel enables the
/techniques and expectations of a stereotype form of the detective
thriller to be rendered problematical;  and this was seen to extend,
in its claims for disruption and criticism, to a questioning of
conventional morality and to the investigation of deeper psychological
truths.

Claude Simon's novel, <u>Le Vent</u> (1957), is also grounded in the
intentional disruption of conventional realist writing, but in this
case the work in question is a more fundamental and over-arching
critique of the underlying aesthetic and philosophical assumptions of
the very idea of realism in narrative fiction.   The novel, <u>Le Vent</u>,
casts serious doubt on what I have defined in this study as the
normative logic of narrative (especially in terms of causal sequences
in plot, and the notion of verisimilitude).   The text focuses on the

relationship between language and 'truth', whereby a profound
scepticism is built into the whole rationale of mimesis.    For here,
History is best understood as homologous with story (as the French
word 'histoire' clearly implies), where the interference of interpretation on the gloss of veracity further complicates the relationship between rhetoric, the art of persuasion, and the claims of
epistemology, the narrator's assertions of knowledge.    In Le Vent,
the attempts to tell the story of Montès through the variety of
sources at the narrator's disposal dramatize the failure of
conventional storytelling in terms of its commensurate epistemological
certainty.    In what follows, I shall discuss Le Vent with emphasis
on its implicit criticism of the novel and on its attempts to found
an enabling poetics which would indicate the extent of this particular
work's modernity.

The subtitle and the subsequent quotation from Valéry function
as initial guides to the reader.    The narrative intends to be a
'tentative de restitution d'un retable baroque'.    Firstly it is
both an attempt at restoration, and also a tentative venture
implying hesitancy, experiment, and incompletion.    The activity of
restoring old masters is a painstaking and costly process and may
well result in a certain falsification, a loss of the texture of
the original.    The 'retable baroque' invokes the ritual, the
ceremony and the apparent mystery in religious art combined with the
incongruous exaggerated complexity of rich design and apparent formlessness characteristic of baroque architecture.    Formally distinct
boundary lines are blurred, and the illusion of movement and disorder
is created through an apparent dispersal of elements.    The baroque
is the art form which only offers us  'the tension of transience'.[26]

Nothing is self-contained and complete.    The invocation of baroque
art establishes the claims for structure in a work which implicitly
demands that it be read as a tentative reconstitution of something
which has been abandoned to the whims and destruction of passing time.
Moreover, the reference to the twin menace of order and disorder is
related to the claims for structure on the one hand and the predictions
of its inevitable failure on the other.    The difficulty is dramatized in the novel of 'remaining between the extremes of utter
dispersion and implausible compactness'.[27]    The notion of reconstitution, or reconstruction is also seen to be an attempt to understand and consequently to control;   the narrator is seen to search
compulsively for the logic of events, and the fragmentation in the
actual narrative of Le Vent is partially explained and naturalized
by interpreting its vagaries as the result of the vacillating
consciousness of the narrator.

In Le Vent, traditional narrative sources are abundantly available:
evidence is compiled from hearsay, local gossip, eye-witness,
the personal acquaintance, albeit brief, of the narrator with Montès,
and the latter's own assertions in recalled conversations with the
narrator.    The key concepts which enable a transformation of these
sources into the orderly structure of narrative are underlined on the
first page of the novel: 'raconter', 'inventer', 'essayer de déduire
ou d'expliquer';   and these activities, commensurable with the
imposition of an approximate logic, may enable a satisfying order to
replace the disorder of what amounts to, 'cette connaissance fragmentaire, incomplète'.[28]    The process of orderly reconstruction is
undermined from the outset when the notary is seen to be a major
source of information about Montès:  he is manifestly unreliable

because of the bounds of his viewpoint which is restricted to the
judgment of people in terms of wealth, interest, and property,
terms befitting his role as legal advisor.    In the face of unreliable
information and the overwhelming urge to seek the truth, the narrator
is forced to recreate imaginatively only what might have been the
case.    The reader is offered what amounts to a slogan for the
theoretical assumptions which this work dramatizes in its failure
to produce a story of a conventional type.    Significantly, the
following lines are parenthetically evoked by the reference to 'cette
histoire' and the need to find 'une approximative logique' to remedy
the hazardous deductions based on fragmentary and incomplete knowledge.    The motivation for story-telling is claimed to be founded
in 'notre appétit de logique':

> . . . et maintenant, maintenant que tout est fini,
> tenter de rapporter, de reconstituer ce qui s'est
> passé, c'est un peu comme si on essayait de recoller
> les débris dispersés, incomplets, d'un miroir,
> s'efforçant maladroitement de les réajuster, n'ob-
> tenant qu'un résultat incohérent, dérisoire, idiot,
> où peut-être seul notre esprit, ou plutôt notre orgueil,
> nous enjoint sous peine de folie et en dépit de toute
> évidence de trouver à tout prix une suite logique de
> causes et d'effets...(p.10)

The tentative aspects of this venture, the urge towards the
conventional rationality of cause and effect, and the consequent
structure of logical sequence in narrative is prefigured in the
hesitations and questionings, the implicit epistemological doubt
underlying the accumulation of 'facts', and the continual digressions
into parentheses.    The narrator's role in his quest for the order
of narrative is two-fold:   he is seen to be a reconstitutor who
aims to organize information and 'facts', while at the same time
he questions the inference and doubts the very status of those 'facts'.

These apparently contradictory roles enable a doubt about the
successful outcome of reconstitution to be felt continually by the
reader.   The oscillations of the narrator undermine the reader's
response in terms of expectations which are perpetually being
established only to be swiftly disrupted.   The problem is initially
one of intelligibility, and, at this level, Le Vent can be described
as a fusion of literature and criticism in its implicit questioning
of precisely how a story may be written, especially when it is
firmly based in a process of historical investigation.   In order
to discuss this further, I shall outline the extent of the work's
realism and locate precisely how the aesthetic discourse about the
novel is fused with the attempts of a narrator to produce a work
of traditional realism.

Barthes's notion of the enigma, to which I refered in Part Two
above, offers a starting-point.   For, as in Sarrasine, a character
is the central focus for a narrative.   Who is the old man? is the
primary, motivating question for the tale about Sarrasine and Zambinella.
The question of who the Notary and the narrator are discussing in
the first pages of Le Vent creates a similar motivation.   Montès,
like the old man in Sarrasine, functions as the enigma not only for
the reader but also for the narrator, and for the small-town community
from which he seeks the information on which to base his story.
Montès is also a catalyst who sets in motion, unwittingly, the
intrigues in which he becomes involved fatalistically.   It is the
presence of the enigma in the character of Montès which founds,
primarily, the realistic novel of intrigue and misfortune which
Le Vent attempts to be.   In this respect, the work continually
manifests elements of realism which are only seen to function

negatively when placed alongside a second conception of the novel
with which it is in dialectical tension.   This second conception
is based on the conscious, intentional manipulation of the underlying assumptions of the first type of novel, whereby through the
dramatization of the manner by which the text is constructed,
criticism is effected.

Loubère, in her recent study of Simon's novels, states the case
about realism in **Le Vent** succinctly:

> An accumulation of carefully observed details and
> gestures authenticates the lives of all the characters
> and animates the heterogeneous, noisy population —
> policemen, street vendors, gypsies, children — in
> the windy, dusty streets of the town.29

Significantly, the narrator, a grammar school teacher, is a researcher
into local history, and spends time studying local romanesque chapels.
A level of plausibility (essential to realism) is attained by his
local interests and his knowledge of the area.   There is an
obsessive sense of place, environment, and nature, and the narrator
urgently quests for a complete, almost naturalistic portrait in which
to give substance to the presence of Montès in the area and in the
lives of its inhabitants.   This world of south-west France is well
documented in relation to the season:

> . . . la population (celle qui ne va à la mer que
> quelques dimanches d'été et le quinze août, par
> pleins tramways, dès le matin, avec les paniers
> à provisions, s'asseyant sur le sable tout près de
> l'eau, les hommes déballant leur attirail de pêche,
> les femmes aux visages fatigués . . .) . . . (p.229)

This kind of information about the seasonal customs of the local
people re-inforces a circumstantial realism which facilitates
the authentication of the presence of popular myth, especially
when it is about Montès.   The whole text may be described as a

diary, albeit fragmentary, a chronicle of the events concerning
Montès and his effect on the region.   A sustained documentary
realism brings the text to its close, where the chaotic movement
of life and its noises is interfused with the incessant cycle of
seasons and its weather patterns.

The presence of the wind unifies various levels on which the
novel may be understood.   As part of the novel's realism,
descriptions of the wind, both in its effect (the swirling dust,
the rubbish, and its potential for dispersion), and in the frequent
allusion to the 'noise' it causes, enable the evocation of a hostile
and barren landscape.   In many respects, and especially in terms of
symbolism, the wind is a central focus.   The narrator often refers
to the mistaken noises that are frequently only the wind:   'rien,
sinon le long chuintement du vent dans les pins comme le bruit même
de temps épuisé, harassé' (p.35).   These lines are the first
figurative reference of wind to time, and the inferences are those
of destruction.   In fact, the cycle of seasons is the temporal
focus for the process of nature, its moments of fecundity, its
predictable period of decaying.   Likewise, the wind rages in full
force, or dies completely and is replaced by a still, oppressive
heat (cf. pp.228-229).   This ceaseless 'va-et-vient' of seasons
and nature is the epitome of the menace of order to which the
quotation from Valéry refers.   Disorder is evident in the effects
this process has on man and his environment, and the destructive
potential of the wind and of time itself is seen in this novel to
be similar harbingers of man's disorder.

The varied pace and force of the wind is symptomatic of a general
dispersal on a formal and epistemological level.   The uncertainty

of memory-fragments, and the unreliability of available sources of
information precipitate an ongoing dispersion of scenes and
episodes, and this principal feature of the work's apparent
structural incoherence is further underlined by the eruption into
the text of moments of obsessive descriptive detail.  The narrator's
overwhelming intention is to 'faire vrai', to substantiate his
narrative with as many instances of authentic representation of the
'real world'.  The rage to describe is indicated in the repetition
of 'exactement' and then qualified by a less certain 'as if' (comme
si . . .), and finally reduced to a 'perhaps it was simply . . .',
or even to a positive assertion that all has been invented by the
narrator.  The cycle from certainty to doubt returns to the
assertive represention of the world in its descriptive state,
'adjectived', and thus traditionally knowable in its completed,
fixed description.[30]  Yet, the tentative nature of the work of
restitution will allow nothing to remain fixed or certain.  Just
as the wind disperses the objects of man's world at random, so the
contents of the impotent memory of the narrator are seen to be
affected by time's destructive work.

Fragments of memory, half-remembered conversations, fabricated
local myths, all these elements serve to undermine the search for
truth.  As I suggested above, the whole narrative, Le Vent, is
comprehensible in terms of the frustrated musings of a narrator
imagining, visualizing, speculating what may have been the case,
and thus it stands as a pre-text which offers the reader a mélange
of 'facts' and suppositions which require him to (re-)write the
text in order to attain the linear, rational order of a conventional
narrative.  The enigma which begins with the necessity to discover

precisely who Montès is  now extends to the whole work in its underlying thematic and aesthetic concerns.   The reality-effects are
held in suspension by the increasing scepticism of a reader who
must be disturbed by the fetishistic insistence on details concerning
characters, actions, and the 'real world'.   If we have not grasped
the point, the narrator will guide us now and again in our lesson
on the unreliability of memory as a basis for narrative:

> Seulement voyant, enregistrant sans en prendre tout à
> fait conscience, de sorte que le récit qu'il m'en fit
> fut sans doute lui-même faux, artificiel, comme est
> condamné à l'être tout récit des événements fait après
> coup, de par le fait même qu'à être racontés les
> événements, les détails, les menus faits, prennent un
> aspect solennel, important, que rien ne leur confère
> sur le moment . . . (p.49)

The status of facts is undermined by the epithet, 'menus' (petty),
and this is further undermined by the emphasis on the element of
exaggeration, embellishment in any re-telling.   Knowledge of the
past, the 'what happened' of history is distorted unavoidably by
interpretation.   The 'histoire' of Montès, even those events
retold by the protagonist himself, is seen to be dubious epistemologically, and concomitantly indicates the impossibility of
conventional realism.

The narrator's anxiety in his growing realisation of the inevitable
failure of any claims for realism and truth is contained in the
frequent oscillation between implausible omniscience and the self-
conscious assertions of pure supposition.   The bold attempts to
re-imagine Montès and his confrontation with Rose ('Et je me les
représente tous les deux, la façon dont cela arriva . . .(p.71)'),
coupled with frequently recurring assertions like  'et je n'avais
pas besoin qu'il me la décrivât pour l'imaginer (p.73)', collapse

into the doubts and uncertainties of tentative reconstitution.
The realism of 'tel qu'il est' is often problematized by the
doubt built into the text with the recurrance of 'ou plutôt',
'ou encore', 'peut-être', and the agglomeration of synonyms,
alternative words and phrases, digressions into parentheses, and
all these predominant stylistic features are levelled to an equivalence contained in the 'as if' of simile.   In other words, the
excesses of writing undermine any attempt to state the case simply
as it was, and the equivalence of words and phrases signal an
explosion of the search for language as a means of representation.

The conventions of realism demand a relationship of writing to the
world whose rationale is grounded in the believability available
in verisimilitude.   The obsessive claims for stating (or visualizing)
events exactly as they were becomes problematical in a text which
offers the reader a proliferation of expressions, or interrogations
of cause.   'De sorte que' is a causal conjunction which typifies
the sometimes arbitrary linkage between sentences, paragraphs, or
even whole chapters (cf. p.40).   The search to substantiate a
causal explanation is seen to fail, just as any question of what
happened, the truth-factor of history  (or in this case Montès's
'histoire'), is never fully realized without the aid of imaginative
reconstruction and, consequently, inevitable falsification.   Our
appetite for logic is never satisfied because of the false expectations
which the rationality of a representational aesthetics has established.
The unknowability of Montès and the events that surrounded him is
primarily understood through the unreliability of the sources of
information: '. . . ce que peu à peu les gens avaient reconstitué
par bribes, fragments . . . (p.26)'.   How many times removed are the
facts about Montès?   How far is he a partial recreation through the

refractions of local gossip, hearsay, and further embellished by
the popular myths of a suspicious small-town community. Enigma
permits the full play of everyone's deprived imaginations. This
level of plausibility in Le Vent is often reiterated. The unsuspecting reader is trapped within these limited boundaries of
expectations which themselves stem from the rationale of realism.
For the unavailability of knowledge and certainty is not unrelated
to the impossibility of truth and 'reality' in any text. This may
be indicated in the stylistic anomalies and the very failure of
language to be a stable picture of the 'world'. At best, this
text in its unfinished state is symptomatic of the impossibility
of narrative to represent anything other than its profound and
intentional failure to be the representative language-construct
of an a priori reality.

The novel's cumulative realization of its inbuilt failure reaches
a point of clarity in chapter seven. Montès is described as both
an enigma and a catalyst, and the fascination he causes in the
local people exasperates any attempt to exceed the bounds of
supposition (cf. pp.106-7). The proliferation of questions in
these pages culminates in the invocation of the fact of historical
distance and its cognate falsification through hindsight and
interpretation, all of which contribute to the unknowability of
Montès. In spite of these rational and epistemological doubts,
the narrator continually pretends to have a viable status as chronicler of events and potential Balzacian novelist. Confident generalizations and appeals to common knowledge indicate the extent of the
narrator's quest for solidarity with a reader schooled on the conventions of nineteenth century fiction of the 'dear reader . . .' type.

Examples range from: 'car cela chacun le savait: cette fuite, cette vengeance de femme . . .(p.19),' relying on stereotypical situations, to the common knowledge-factor encapsulated in the often reiterated formula, 'une de ces sortes de . . .' or phrases like, 'cette similitude d'appartenir à cette espèce d'hommes (p.61),' evoking generalized 'truths', and even to more localized statements about the inhabitants which may well be common elsewhere and thereby establish a certain authenticity (i.e., 'ceux que l'on peut voir, le Samedi ou le Lundi . . .(p.104)'). The narrator also offers numerous generalizes of the stereotype, conventional differences of the sexes, and he is especially forthright on the nature of women: '. . . de cette disponibilité qui est comme l'essence même du genre féminin . . . (p.218)'. The use of demonstratives in the phrase 'like one of these (those) . . . ' is the signal of an all-wise authorial voice who is apparently able to typify the world. But the profound epistemological doubt and the commensurable problematizing of representation at the level of language undermine the claims of the narrator for the kind of authority founded on this model of realism with its predominant <u>gnomic code</u>.[31] In fact, these phrases may well stand as a pastiche of Balzac.

Realism is further enhanced in <u>Le Vent</u> in the elements of direct speech. Colloquialisms lend an authenticity to the fragments of conversation, and the intentional juxtaposition of conversational passages with the linguistic excesses of the narrator's musings serve to indicate the extent to which that 'magma'[32] called reality is reduced and simplified by people. All that remains in these unreliable sources of information is the generalized characteristic of any aspect of the traditional 'slice of life'. When the narrator attempts to flesh out these sparse fragments, the text's

digressions and convolutions are themselves a symptom of the
impossibility of his task.    The gestures towards realism will
always result in the posing of more far-reaching aesthetic and
epistemological questions.    Occasionally, a conventional narrative
sequence evolves, momentarily, leading from a once-upon-a-time
('tout d'abord . . .') through a succession of recounted events ('Et
il me raconta la suite . . .'), towards the finality, and fixity of
the end (the terminable 'enfin . . .') (cf. pp.121-125).    The novel
itself does move towards its close, evoking the stereotype of autumnal
ending, death, and the cessation of the apparently interminable voice
of the narrator.    But despite these gestures towards the conventional,
rational sequential structure of narrative, the text has largely
relied on the dictates of the narrator's ruminations and unreliable
reminiscences.    Disruption of traditional narrative logic, based on
the teleology of sequential events is in part intelligible through
the rhetorical and figurative use of the present participle.    Verbal-
izing the world in terms of the 'passé simple' enables the realist
novelist to express order, certainty and the fixity of the world
articulated and knowable in language.[33]    The present participle
however, indicates an indefinite state of fluidity, of ceaseless
becoming, where nothing is fixed or certain.    Even in an early work
like Le Vent (1957), questions about precisely what the narrator may
know about other minds and the events of the past  are indications of
the extent of the work's overarching critique of the implicit claims
of the novels of realism exemplified in the work of Balzac.

Suffice it to suggest, in conclusion, that Le Vent implicitly rejects
the well-constructed story,with its psychology based on nineteenth
century models of characters and its traditional cause and effect

rationale. For the multiplicity of possible viewpoints problematizes the question of perspective: representation is replaced
by interpretation, and the production of the whole text is an
interrogation of its own conditions of meaning. Le Vent dramatizes
its own poetics by continually questioning the representationalist
aesthetics of conventional realism and its cognate philosophical
substructure. The novel interrogates the bounds of the 'lisible,'
as Barthes defined it in S/Z (1970), and as a profound challenge to
our traditional sense of literature is seen to be a 'mise en scene
de l'écriture.' This is the extent of its modernity.

(v)  Conclusion

Discussion in this chapter has focused on the precise relationships
which selected works intentionally establish with conventions of the
novel.    All three writers oscillate between the limitations of
realism and the provocations of its critique.    The extent of the
disruptions of paradigms defines each work's essential difference.
Self-conscious, self-interpretive texts indicated the limits  of
their rejection of traditional paradigms in terms of defamiliarisation
through forms of parody, pastiche, and the play on expectations.
How far specific narratives are not recuperable within rational
schemes dictated by established forms may well be the indication of
the work's modernity, especially in Barthes's sense.[34]

Within the bounds of realism, Fowles's novel was described above in
terms of a self-conscious investigation into the historical and
deep-structural connections between conventions of writing, modality,
and specific codes of intelligibility commensurate with a given
social reality.    The novel staged a confrontation of modern and
nineteenth century consciousness and their cognate practice of
writing.    An existential, historical, and aesthetic critique was
effected within the bounds of realism.    Claude Simon's 'critical'
novel shifts our emphasis from modality and history (central to the
meaning of Fowles's novel) to the problematical relationship between
epistemology and rhetoric.    The narrator in Le Vent gestures
frequently towards a realism verging on a Zolaesque naturalism, and
yet these excesses of writing are undermined by the perpetual doubt
built into the claims for representation.    Hawkes's The Lime Twig
is a profound critique of levels of impoverishment.    The soporific
nature of a detective story, a surface-structural psychology, and a

middle-class morality founding a clearly defined good and evil
dichotomy, are deconstructed in a work that aims to examine sharply
the reader's expectations and sympathies through a thoroughgoing
exploitation of the possibilities available in parody. If a given
genre be the basis for this novel, its implicit rationality is
perpetually undermined.

The principal focus for the three selected texts has been the question
of how the novel may be historically redefined. Various traditional
paradigms were deconstructed in the quest for form: the logic of
narrative, the aesthetics of representation, normative morality
(founded on literary as well as social models), notions about the
self on which characters are based, all received different degrees
of emphasis in the three works. Parody, as a mode of aesthetic
foregrounding, defines a particular mode of historical consciousness.
The tradition of English parodistic novels has always allowed
'criticism' of the text's status as fiction to co-exist with realism
itself. Ostentatious narrators from Fielding and Sterne through
to the self-observing narrator of <u>The French Lieutenant's Woman</u>,
flaunt characteristic narrative devices and remind the reader that
the representation of reality is always necessarily a stylization.
By systematically drawing attention to the conditions of its own
artifice, such texts probe into 'the problematical relationship
between real-seeming artifice and reality.'[35]   For as Robert Alter
cogently explains:

> [In] a fully self-conscious novel . . . there is a
> consistent effort to convey to us a sense of the fictional
> world as an authorial construct set up against a back-
> ground of literary tradition and convention.[36]

In this respect, Fowles's notion/of parody is traditional, and functions
in two distinctive ways:  firstly, he uses what may be called 'local'
parody, whereby a number of authors and works are referred to, or
even imitated;  secondly, he uses a more 'general' parody of a
convention of realism, a narrative stance, and an attitude to the
reader.   In this, Fowles is clearly comparable with Hawkes and
Simon.   However, coming after the questions about the status of the
text raised by modernism itself, it seems no longer sufficient
merely to draw attention to the artificial nature of the text.   For
the whole question of authority and the claims for knowledge and
representation are the lessons of modernism which the novel cannot
entirely overlook.   These three novels which I have discussed
clearly demonstrate the position of each writer in relation to this
fundamental issue, if only because they are more explicitly parodic in
their different ways than other novels by the same writers.
In the more Subject-centred narrative of <u>Le Vent</u> (as opposed to the
effacement of such a strategy in his later works, which I described
in <u>part two</u> above), the restrictions inherent in the conventions of
nineteenth century Realism are dramatized through the consciousness
of a narrator who searches for the knowledge that may enable a well-
constructed story.   The novel is a profound record of the degree of
his failure.   Likewise, in the works of Fowles and Hawkes which
were discussed above, constrictions inherent in writing conventions
were related to the bounds of given worldviews, psychological
explanation, and accepted moral 'truths'.

These works are comprehensible on another level of self-consciousness.
For, all three works indulge in the use of author-figures as portraits
of the artist.   Fowles's impressario is also a lay-preacher, a

collector, and a magus; Simon's narrator is a failed realist
author in search of a protagonist; and Hawkes offers us the sly,
callow Sidney Slyter, his journalistic style and his failure to
solve the deeper mysteries.    Fowles's artist is a magician in
danger of overdetermining his characters;  Simon's author-surrogate
is self-critical and self-deluding;  and Hawkes's voice of quotidian
morality (Slyter) is undermined by the powerful, disruptive forces
released in the main plot.    Thus form is problematized at the level
of its production:  how may the novel end?  What constitutes a narrative text?  Can 'truth' be made available in writing?    Author-
surrogates attempt to solve such crucial questions in these novels.
The implicit conclusions they reach are contained in the fundamental
dissimilarities of the three works.    The aim of this chapter has not
been to outline these differences explicitly, for this in itself has
been a cumulative process of argument throughout this study.    Rather,
I have been concerned to describe the type of poetics inherent in
the marriage of narrative fiction and criticism which may enable the
founding of a more abstract typology of the precise historical status
of such works.    As Claudio Guillen rightly claims, 'the battleground
of much of modern poetics would be the writer's approach to the
"reality-principle".'[37]   Questions raised by 'modern' texts
demonstrate that the literary critic should beware of looking for
clearly defined properties of a category (parody in this instance)
in a work.    For that category would indeed have to be revised to
account for the apparent recalcitrance of the new work:

> ... the itineraryof genres can be regarded not as the
> evolution of independent norms, nor as the survival of
> timeless "structures," but as the history of changing
> theoretical systems.[38]

## CONCLUSION

The novels and stories of John Fowles are grounded in the self-conscious analysis of storytelling which itself relates narrative form to the events and the intelligibility of 'contingent reality'. These works also contain much overt discussion on pertinent questions about modern art and the function of the artist in the modern world. His novel The French Lieutenant's Woman effectively considers nineteenth century Realism in the light of recent thought about fictionality and the creation of character. Playing with 'the leisurely circumlocutions of nineteenth century rhetoric',[1] the author undermines (and perhaps partly envies) the epistemological and cultural self-confidence of which it is a symptom. The self-conscious postures which obtrude into the Victorian illusion serve to disable any positive theory of the novel. Prescription is avoided despite the abundance of 'discussion'. 'What matters is not a permanent paradigm for the novel, but the precarious moment by moment relationship with the reader.'[2] Thus for Fowles, the potential 'power' of narrative is effected by the seductive qualities of enigmatic stories. They function to involve the reader in the critical awareness of his world and the possible use of literature in that operation. In this respect, the existential crisis of free-will transcending the determinate plots of the social world finds analogies in the form of the novel. For, self-conscious exposure of artistic means coexists with a basic concern with realism in Fowles's works. They are historically comprehensible (and never more so than in his historical novel, The French Lieutenant's Woman) because of their implicit understanding of the problematic interplay between conventions of writing, the intellectual foundations of a society, models of reality, and the models of man on which literary characters are based.

Stable views of society and coherent, unified models of man are
absent from the modern world.  Man's loss of reality, for Fowles,
is reflected in the dehumanization and mathematical precision of
modern abstract art against which the artist Breasley tirades in
The Ebony Tower.  He coins the expression, 'ebony tower', to describe
such abstractionism.  Like the retreat into the 'ivory tower' of art
for art's sake before it, 'ebony tower' art shirks the artist's
necessary response to the major issues of his time.  His art-form
both risks nothing, because abstract art is now an orthodoxy, and
also serves to camouflage a hollow reality.  Thus, the clarity and
commitment of a realism which does not fear the principal issues of
history and society is Breasley's prescriptive solution.  Fowles's
work firmly endorses this view.  Furthermore, faced with the
commercialization of art in the modern world, the artist (and the
writer) needs to offer his work as a more profound mirror of the
'real self'.  In Daniel Martin (1977), the Hollywood movie and
television are modern forces which have served to atrophy a 'vital
psychic function':  the ability to imagine for oneself.  The pervasive
metaphors of scenario, script, role, and special effect are ironically
called upon in this novel.  But the surface lie of the cinema screen
can never achieve the private reality of the novel, for the camera
can never capture the 'true inner self'.  If the media have an
ominously stereotyping function, then the novel has a tendency towards
solipsism and 'a far greater capacity for retreat'.  As this novel
underlines, the novelist needs his private domain;  and from that
vantage point of exile, he may then break through the illusions
created by commercialised mass culture, and move away from onanism
into a more direct intercourse with the beleaguered public.[3]  The
choice is then a simple one for the modern writer:  in Lukács' words,

he needs to choose  'the great progressive literary traditions of
realism in preferance to formalistic experiment.'[4]   The nobility
of great art stands against the hollowness of pure abstract design.
For, as this most recent novel by John Fowles clearly demonstrates,
art and morality continue to be indivisible, and thus, for the
literary critic, the analysis of form will always be related to the
cognitive basis of the work.

Hawkes is also interested implicitly in the relationship between
formal paradigms for the novel and possible interpretations of
the world.   Often by placing the onus for 'truth' on the vagaries
of a single consciousness, Hawkes's conclusions, evident in the
formal problems, the dislocations of his works, are more disturbing
than those of Fowles.   For the kind of rationality that Fowles
prescribes for the 'elect' artist-figure is seen to be impossible
for Hawkes's artist surrogates, as rationality itself collapses
under the repressive forces of modern life.   Given their different
'philosophical' bases for the novel, it is no surprise to find
Hawkes rejecting conventional realism for historical reasons (although,
as I have argued, his works never wholly transcend such realism
because of their subjective relativism).   Hawkes equates realism in
this sense with 'pedestrian' thinking and 'pedestrian' techniques.
In answer to the claim that reality has changed so markedly since the
nineteenth century for instance, the author concludes:

> I suppose innumerable worlds have disappeared.   And
> given the loss or diminishing value of so much we
> accepted — gods, family, afterlife, etc. — and given
> all we know about our terrifying, destructive possibilities
> and the courage needed to affirm human potential, any kind
> of art or fiction that reflects the worn-out, dead, banal
> views is intolerable.[5]

The relationship between problems of the self and the problem of encapsulating this in an appropriate narrative form clearly emphasize Hawkes's twin preoccupations: a psychology which transcends the 'old stable ego' model of characterization, and a commensurate form which aims to combine novelistic and poetic methods grounded in the use of language as itself a resonant structural phenomenon. Foregrounding the repressed self at the same time as reconstructing the possible narrative basis for the novel are both part of Hawkes's desire to reject 'worn out, dead, banal views'.

Claude Simon's narrative texts are primarily reflections on their own composition. The self-reflexion of the text is enhanced by the unfinished quality of these novels, conceptualizing the image of the writer as 'fabricant', modulating and enumerating the possibilities available for a narrative. The effect is one of a 'texte non corrigé', which seems to correct itself as it produces more text. The notion of 'work in progress' is born out not only by the tentative nature of any one text with its repetitions and fragmentations, but also by a technique of assemblage grounded in the use of 'old pieces' from previous novels. This collage technique, akin to much modern abstract art, gives the fragmentary look to a highly structured text.[6] This artisanal work of writing, a text hewn from the very fragments of other 'texts', is figuratively described in the term, 'bricolage', coined by Lévi-Strauss,[7] and connoting the rearrangement of fragments into a new, structured whole. It encapsulates the notions of inventiveness and dramatic tension which characterize Simon's works. More recently, the author has talked in terms of the 'texte sauvage' which he attributes especially to Triptyque: 'une espèce de bouillie, avec des répétitions.'[8]

This insistence on the productive, yet never completed or 'produced', aspect of his works is precisely that creative movement of language which I described above.  For Simon, the novel is no longer the story of the adventure of an exemplary hero, but rather the story of the very adventure of writing as it constitutes itself.  The text is a mosaic of traces of other texts captured in the present moment of its writing, as the novel is seen to be unable, intentionally to transcend the bounds of its own status as language.  'Le présent de l'écriture' is  'a complex moment of replacement and supplementarity.  The "present of writing" is . . . a process of reinscription of the traces of the past within a space which in turn will provide the "material" for another "present", a space which is open not closed.'[9]  This permits a complexity and a pluri-dimensionality to exist as the novel generates itself through its own writing, through the self-conscious play on language at its moment of production.  Even in the earlier novels where the 'memory-thesis' could be applied, the notion of collage was seen to be symptomatic of a fragmentation in our knowledge of the self;  for, as memory was seen to try to bring together the traces of a past identity in La Route des Flandres and Le Palace, for instance, narrative form constituted nothing other than an unstable 'bricolage' of the self.

The analyses of the narrative basis of the novel have deconstructed the works of Fowles, Hawkes, and Simon in order to lay bare the implicit philosophical and aesthetic presuppositions on which these works may well be grounded.  Whatever interpretative procedures came into operation, what related each of them was a persistent search for the inner coherence of a work, a coherence which can never

be fully intelligible if structure is not finally related to a
logic of content which is precisely the social and historical
character of that work. Jameson would want to go further and
establish a genuine 'dialectical criticism' based purely on the
categories which each individual work invokes:

> to the degree that each work is the end result of
> a kind of inner logic or development in its own
> content, it evolves its own categories and dictates
> the specific terms of its own interpretation.[10]

The bounds of formalistic analysis in the realist texts of Fowles's
novels, and the success of such a methodology with Simon's narrative
fiction, largely endorse this view. However, precisely at the point
where the logic of content becomes the abstract historical character
of a work, specific terms of reference give way to the common
problematics of an era. The differences between the works of the
three writers in question are partially belied by their different
responses (but responses all the same) to what Benoist has called
the general 'coupûre épistémologique', the 'diffraction du sujet',[11]
and to what Jameson has characterized in existential terms as
experience being no longer whole.[12] John Fowles's work has moved
from the diagnosis of contemporary society with the sociological
argument of roles and masks, to the more epistemological (and
narrational) problem of 'whole sight' in Daniel Martin. Fowles's
concern with fictionality both in the world and in the novel undermines the authority of the literary text and the consciousness of
its narrator. The vagaries of the partly psychotic narrative
perspective in Hawkes's novels reach a point of extreme introversion
in his latest novel, Travesty (1976), where the work relies purely
on the single vacillating consciousness to effect a perplexing
'travesty' on the conventional expectations of authority and knowledge

in the realist novel.   Simon's novels are more thoroughly critiques
of the knowledge status of literary texts.   The later works play
on the reader's need to recuperate them into more conventionally
rational schemes.   These novels offer a fundamental critique of
the more naive claims of realism.   For, as Culler rightly suggests:

> In place of the novel as mimesis we have the novel
> as a structure which plays with different modes of
> ordering and enables the reader to understand how
> he makes sense of the world.[13]

The fundamental problematics surrounding the post-Modernist novel
are commensurate with the feeling, articulated in the philosophy
of social science in terms of real social causes, that the subject,
or consciousness is  'a kind of construction rather than a stable
substance . . . a locus of relationships rather than an ego in the
older sense.'[14]   Fowles's work seems to be grounded in a contradiction,
insofar as he recognizes this problematic of society yet persists in
a belief in 'authenticity' in man's actions.   Both Hawkes and Simon
consistently recognize the historical impossibility of basing their
work on a stable notion of consciousness.   Thus, as consciousness
and the self are conventionally (and by definition) the most
referential aspect of literature, then the works of Hawkes and Simon
are more militantly critical of literary realism.   Fowles's
humanism places him in opposition to the intellectual history which
encompasses the epistemology of French Structuralism and the ideological character of the nouveau roman and its more radical version
in Tel Quel.   In Foucault's words:

> De nos jours, et Nietzsche là encore indique de loin le
> point d'inflexion, ce n'est pas tellement l'absence ou
> la mort de Dieu qui est affirmée mais la fin de l'homme . . .

> Plus que la mort de Dieu, — ou plutôt dans le sillage
> de cette mort et selon une corrélation profonde avec elle,
> ce qu'annonce la pensée de Nietzsche, c'est la fin de son
> meurtrier; c'est l'éclatement du visage de l'homme dans
> le rire, et le retour des masques. . .15

This statement clearly characterizes what Foucault calls the
'épistème moderne',[16] whereby the certainties of a nineteenth
century model of reality are no longer viable in the twentieth
century. For, insofar as belief systems are called into question,
so the literature reinforces the more general doubts. Fowles's
philosophical presuppositions are intelligible within the modern
'épistème', especially in his play on masks, and his preoccupation
with fictionality. But, despite this, he maintains a belief in
the final pre-eminence of a transcendental signifier as the text
relates meaningfully to the world. The most extreme critique of
this position derives from French Structuralism and indicates the
difference between Simon's and Fowles's aesthetic. For as Jameson
states, referring to Julia Kristeva, the proposal is 'to replace
the older metaphysical notions of literary form with that of the
text as a self-generating mechanism, as a perpetual process of
textual production.'[17] This is not to say that Structuralism does
not bring a fundamental internal contradiction to the study of
literature. For, indeed, if the onus is placed on the presence of
the sign as a relational concept, and also if there is no transcendental signified, then, as Jameson rightly claims (following Derrida),
the very concept of sign must be abandoned. 'Sign' has always been
understood by its status as sign-of, and signifier by its reference
to a signified.[18] The structuralist method that resolves this
inherent contradiction for literature is Barthes's codal model in S/Z.
The very notion that the Subject is only partially knowable in terms
of relationality, a notion which, despite the denial of the primacy

of the Cartesian and Sartrean _cogito_, remains functional to
structuralism and to functionalist sociology, still requires the
idea of reference, even if the status of the knowledge acquired
is held in perpetual doubt.

Despite the claims for the complete non-referentiality of the text
in the aesthetics of _Tel Quel_, Barthes has shown that not only is
the text a web of codes, intentional or not, but also the reader
himself is characterized as a cipher of codes and expectations.
The play on recuperation in Simon's _Leçon de Choses_ (1975) relies
for its effectiveness on the rational expectations of the reader.
This operation largely relates literature to literary tradition and
conventions.  Texts which tend more towards realism (Fowles's works,
Hawkes's most recent texts especially, but also his earlier, more
surrealistic works, and Simon's works especially from _Le Vent_ to
_Histoire_) effect a critical relationship to the world in terms of
demystification.  Deriving from the lessons of Marx and Freud, such
works emphasize that 'true reality is never what is manifest on the
surface, and that the nature of truth may be measured by the degree
to which it eludes you.'[19]

The logic of narrative, as distinct from the 'logique du récit' of
French structural analysis, needs, as this study has argued, to
conceptualize the intelligibility of the literary text in terms of
the reading of character, structure, and self-consciousness.  The
logic of content dictates the structure of the compositional whole,
and gives form its historical character.  For as Adorno has claimed:

> no authentic work of art and no true philosophy,
> according to their very meaning, has ever exhausted
> itself in itself alone, in its being-in-itself.  They
> have always stood in relation to the actual life-process
> of society from which they distinguished themselves.[20]

Given this conception of the relationship between literature and the world, an enabling analysis of the literary text would want to transcend what Jameson has called 'that sterile and static opposition between formalism and a sociological or historical use of literature between which we have so often been asked to choose.'[21] The lessons of the methodological critique in this study endorse this view.

The most programmatically subversive form of writing of the nouveau roman and Tel Quel, as exemplified in this instance in the work of Claude Simon, seems to be continually and explicitly concerned with the kind of novel it is no longer possible to write. The fetishistic preoccupation with describing the world in Simon's narrative fiction always portrays a necessary sense of failure, as the proliferation of interpretations of reality throughout history undermine the very stability of any interpretation, and as the thinking Subject upon which those models of the world depended for their legitimation are cast in doubt. Although Fowles's texts do not go as far as totally subverting the realist aesthetic to account for the status of fiction in our apprehension of the world, they do acknowledge the impossibility of ever going beyond the masque as a metaphor. Hawkes, however, clearly manipulates the unreliability of a narrator to effect a subversion of the normative process of narration. In each of these instances, the logic of narrative testifies to the claim that what is 'real' is always but one interpretation. For as Philippe Sollers claims:

> la notion de réalité . . . est déclaré réel,
> dans des circonstances historiques données . ..
> et le langage d'une société, ses mythes, est ce
> qu'elle décide être sa réalité.22

Naive realism may well have affirmed the <u>appearance</u> of the world,
its observable structures, as 'reality'.  It may even have, in a
more sophisticated stage, affirmed the primacy of sensory perception
as a reliable mirror in which to reflect the world.  But it is
difficult, if not indeed untenable, to support such a 'prescientific'
view of the depiction of 'reality'.  Fowles, Hawkes, and Simon offer
different degrees of a critique of such a naive position.  Their
works are replete with the problems underlying attempts to understand
the world on the part of characters and narrators.  Simon's works
finally reject  such epistemological enquiry, and carry  the argument
to its next phase, as they attempt to construct the 'self-generating'
text.

If the critic searches for the underlying logic of narrative in a
novel, he would then avoid the foreclosing assumptions of any naive
relationship between the literary text and the world.  The complex
sets of relationships between the logic of content and the formal
structure of a work need to be carefully understood in order to
relocate History in a formalistic methodology.  As Fowler has rightly
asserted, 'we can reasonably postulate that structures in the text
correlate with systems of experience and values transcending the
individual work.'[23]  The analysis of narrative structure offers a
formal point of entry for the interpretive activity of the critic.
Furthermore, the critic should describe the principles of coherence
on which any work is grounded in relation to both its historical moment
and the fundamental conventions without which (and often against which)
it would be unintelligible.  I would concur with Jameson when he
claims that the apparently incommensurable 'demands of synchronic
analysis and historical awareness, of structure and self-consciousness,

language and history, can be reconciled'.[24]   In this respect, the
notion of fragmentation, for instance, must be understood historically
as a symptom of social life.   For, literature does not just passively
reflect this, it offers the ideological character of the fundamental
problematic of an era.   Thus, in the light of the questioning of
the status and authority of the literary text in the Modernism of the
late nineteenth and early twentieth century, the principal concern of
the post-Modernist novel is to redefine the bounds of narrative
coherence in order to account for the changing 'realities' of the
world and the more perplexing questions about the role and status of
literature.

In this study, the diversity of aesthetic claims for the novel has
been matched by a diversity of theoretical positions in order to
offer a basis for a comparative study of recent narrative fiction.
If the novels of Fowles, Hawkes, and Simon have common archetypes
in history, it must also be clearly stated that the literary
histories of each of their national literatures deviate from their
common starting-point.   While this would account for the persistent
realist-aesthetic in the post-war English novel, the experimental
eclecticism of many American novels, and the linguistic and
epistemological disruptions of the French nouveau roman, it may
never obviate the need for more thoroughgoing theoretical perspectives
on the possibilities for the narrative basis of the post-Modernist
novel.

## NOTES AND REFERENCES

### Preface

1. John Lucas in a review of John J. Richetti, Defoe's
   Narratives: Situations and Structures, Oxford University
   Press (London, 1975), and of John Halperin (ed.) The Theory
   of the Novel: New Essays, Oxford University Press (London,
   1974), published in Literature and History, 6 (Autumn 1977),
   p.258.

2. Ralph Freedman, The Lyrical Novel, Princeton University
   Press (Princeton, New Jersey, 1963, reprinted 1971), p.17.

3. Gabriel Josipovici, The World and the Book, Paladin
   (St. Albans, 1973), p.xiv.

4. Fredric Jameson, The Prison-House of Language, Princeton
   University Press (Princeton, New Jersey, 1972), p.136.

5. Fredric Jameson, 'The Ideology of the Text,' Salmagundi
   31-32 (Fall, 1975 - Winter 1976), p.219.

6. Fredric Jameson, The Prison-House of Language, op. cit., p.146.

7. Two recent books which offer different perspectives on this
   issue are Gabriel Josipovici, The Lessons of Modernism,
   MacMillan (London, 1977), and David Lodge, The Modes of
   Modern Writing: Metaphor, Metonymy and the Typology of
   Modern Literature, Edward Arnold (London, 1977).

8. J-M. Benoist, La Révolution Structurale, Bernard Grasset
   (Paris, 1975), p.25.

9. Ulrich Weisstein, Comparative Literature and Literary Theory,
   Indiana University Press (Bloomington and London, 1973), p.70.

10. Fredric Jameson, Marxism and Form, Twentieth Century
    Dialectical Theories of Literature, Princeton University
    Press (Princeton, New Jersey, 1974), p.374.

11. Malcolm Bradbury, The Novel Today, Fontana (Glasgow, 1977),
    Introduction, p.10.

12. Ibid., p.14.

PART ONE: INTRODUCTION

1. Cited in Culler, Structuralist Poetics: Structuralism, Linguistics and the Study of Literature, Fontana (Glasgow, 1976), p.235.

2. Vladimir Propp, Morphology of the Folk Tale, University of Texas Press (Austin, 1973).

3. Cf. 'L'Analyse Structurale du Récit', in Communications, 8 (1966). Also, for their particular approach to character, see the work of A.J. Greimas.

4. A cogent critique of the reductionism of this mode of character analysis may be found in S. Chatman, 'On the Formalist-Structuralist theory of Character', in the Journal of Literary Semantics, 1 (1972), p.57ff.

5. Barthes, S/Z, p.9. quoted by Chatman, loc. cit., p.79.

6. Clearly, what underlines Barthes's considerable achievement in S/Z is his enabling historical method of analysis.

7. Cf. G. Genette, 'Vraisemblable et Motivation' in Communications 11, (1968), reprinted in Figures II, Seuil (Paris, 1969).

8. Barthes, 'L'effet de réel', in Communications 11, (1968), pp.84-9. P. Hamon, 'Statut semiologique du personnage' in Poétique du Récit, Barthes et al., Seuil (Paris, 1977).

9. A counter-argument may be found in D. Spearman, The Novel and Society, Routledge and Kegan Paul (London, 1966).

10. D.H. Lawrence, 'Letter to Edward Garnett, 5 June 1914', in Selected Literary Criticism, edited by A. Beal, Heinemann, (London, reprinted 1967).

11. See Richardou's analysis of character names in Pour une théorie du nouveau roman, Seuil (Paris, 1971), p.234ff.

12. W.C. Booth, The Rhetoric of Fiction, University of Chicago Press (Chicago, 1970).

13. Barthes, S/Z, p.211.

14. Jean-Marie Benoist, La Révolution Structurale, Bernard Grasset (Paris, 1975), p.59.

15. Fredric Jameson, 'The Ideology of the Text', loc. cit., p.217.

16. Ibid.

17. P. Berger, B. Berger, and H. Kellner, The Homeless Mind, Penguin (Harmondsworth, 1973), pp.73-74.

18. Ibid., p.86.

19. Ibid., p.18.

20. Ibid., p.37.

21. A term coined by Lévi-Strauss, and one which takes on an increasingly crucial significance in this study, as problems of the self relate to problems of narrative form in the post-modernist novel.  Cf. Lévi-Strauss, La Pensée Sauvage, Plon (Paris, 1962), especially chapter one.

22. The Homeless Mind, op. cit., p.90.

23. T.W. Adorno, 'Society', translated from the German by F. Jameson in Salmagundi, 10-11 (1969-1970), p.151.

24. The Homeless Mind, op. cit., p.99.

25. Ibid., p.102.

26. A. Dawe, 'The Two Sociologies', in Sociological Perspectives, edited by K. Thompson and J. Tunstall, Penguin (Harmondsworth, reprinted 1976), pp.542-554.

27. Ibid., p.551.

28. E.g. Colin Fletcher, The Person in the Sight of Sociology, Routledge and Kegan Paul (London, 1975).

29. Dawe, op. cit., p.553.

30. Martin Hollis, Models of Man, Philosophical thoughts on Social Action, Cambridge University Press (London, 1977), p.12.

31. Ibid., p.69.

32. E. Goffman, The Presentation of Self in Everyday Life, Doubleday (New York, 1959); Relations in Public, Penguin (Harmondsworth, 1971); Frame Analysis, Penguin (Harmondsworth, 1974).

33. Hollis, op. cit., p.89.

34. Ibid.

35. Ibid., p.3.

36. Ibid., p.106.

37. Adorno, 'Society', loc. cit., p.146.

38. Ibid., p.147.

39. Ibid., p.148.

40. Ibid.

41. Cf. H. Marcuse, One Dimensional Man, Abacus (London, 1972).

42. R. Dahrendorf, Homo Sociologicus, Routledge & Kegan Paul (London, 1973), p.38.

43. Ibid., p.40.

44. Ibid., p.56.

45. J. Culler, _Saussure_, Fontana (London, 1976), p.78.

46. Quoted by Culler, _Saussure_, op. cit., p.78.

47. Given the aforementioned characterization of modern society, and man's socially-caused reduction to one-dimensionality and self-anonymization, then the plea for 'authenticity' may well be seen to be no more than a futile romantic gesture.   In this respect, T.W. Adorno's _The Jargon of Authenticity_, Routledge & Kegan Paul (London, 1973) offers a powerful counter-argument to that of the existentialism which, in this instance, derives from Kierkegaard and is manifest in such recent German thinkers as Buber, Jaspers, and Heidegger. Adorno argues that, 'this theory has become a mystification of the actual processes of domination' (Trent Schroyer in the forward, p.viii).

48. H.  Marcuse, _Eros and Civilization_, Abacus (London, 1973), p.143.

49. S. Freud, _Civilization and its Discontents_, _Collected Works_, XXI, Hogarth Press (London, 1930), p.130.

50. Cf. Marcuse, _One Dimensional Man_, op. cit.

51. Ibid.

52. Cf. T. Tanner, _City of Words, American Fiction 1950-1970_, Jonathan Cape (London, 1971), p.421.

53. Ibid.

54. Culler, _Saussure_, op. cit., p.78.

CHAPTER ONE

1. S.R. Giles, _The Problem of Action in Modern Drama_, Unpublished Doctoral thesis,(University of East Anglia, 1976,) p.197.

2. John Fowles, _The Aristos_, Pan Books (London, 1968), p.42.

3. Ibid., p.43.

4. Ibid., p.175.

5. Ibid., p.164.

6. Ibid., p.211, and p.213.

7. Ibid., p.199.

8. _The Collector_, Pan Books (London, 1965), p.42.

9.  Ibid., p.218.

10. Ibid., p.10.

11. Ibid., p.217.

12. Ibid., p.218.

13. F. Karl, A Reader's Guide to the Contemporary English Novel, Thames and Hudson (London, 1963), p.356.

14. John Fowles in Counterpoint (ed.) R. Newquist, Simon and Schuster (New York, 1964), p.225.

15. W.J. Palmer, The Fiction of John Fowles, University of Missouri Press (Columbia, 1975), p.32.

16. Quoted by Palmer, op. cit., p.33.

17. A revised edition of The Magus has recently been published. References will be made to the original version (1966) except where otherwise stated.

18. Palmer, op. cit., p.59.

19. The Magus, Pan Books (London, 1966), p.372.

20. The Magus, A Revised Version, Jonathan Cape (London, 1977), foreword by John Fowles, p.10.

21. The Magus, A Revised Version, p.409.

22. Ibid., p.627.

23. Bradbury, Possibilities, Essays on the State of the Novel, Oxford University Press (London, 1973), p.261.

24. The French Lieutenant's Woman, Panther (London, 1970), p.181.

25. Ibid., p.399.

26. A Kennedy, The Protean Self, Dramatic Action in Contemporary Fiction, MacMillan (London, 1974), p.258.

27. The Magus, A Revised Version, p.386.

28. Ibid.

29. Ibid., p.132.

30. Ibid., p.405.

31. Ibid., p.404.

32. Ibid., pp.347-8.

33. The French Lieutenant's Woman, p.87.

34. <u>The Magus, A Revised Version</u>, p.569.

35. <u>The Ebony Tower</u>, Jonathan Cape (London, 1974), p.93.

36. Ibid., p.108.

37. Ibid., p.232.

38. Ibid., p.210.

39. Ibid., p.215.

40. Edited text of an interview on the B.B.C. 'Book Programme', reprinted in <u>The Listener</u>, 31 October, 1974.

41. <u>Daniel Martin</u>, Jonathan Cape (London, 1977), pp.72-73. All subsequent references will be in parenthesis following the quotation.

42. <u>Harpers and Queen</u> (October, 1977), p.151.


CHAPTER TWO

1. John Hawkes, interview reprinted in <u>The Contemporary Writer</u>, (Interviews with sixteen novelists and poets), edited by L.S. Dembo and C.N. Pondrom, University of Wisconsin Press (Wisconsin, 1972), p.4.

2. <u>The Beetle Leg</u>, New Directions (New York, 1951), p.129.

3. Ibid.

4. <u>The Cannibal</u>, New Directions (New York, 1949), p.20.

5. <u>The Beetle Leg</u>, p.8.

6. John Hawkes, <u>Notes on 'The Wild Goose Chase'</u>, reprinted in <u>Studies in 'Second Skin'</u>, edited by J. Graham, Charles E. Merril Studies (Columbus, 1971), p.22.

7. John Hawkes, 'Notes on writing a novel', in <u>TriQuarterly</u>, 30 (Spring, 1974), p.117.

8. Printed in full in 'Notes on writing a novel', loq. cit., pp.118-119.

9. Ibid., p.119.

10. 'I'm trying to hold in balance poetic and novelistic methods (Hawkes).' Cf. <u>The Contemporary Writer</u>, op. cit., p.11.

11. Cf. Hawkes's comments in 'Flannery O'Connor's Devil', <u>The Sewanee Review</u>, LXX, 3 (Summer, 1962), pp.395-407.

12. John Kuehl, <u>John Hawkes and the Craft of Conflict</u>, Rutgers University Press (New Jersey, 1975), p.86.

13. Ibid., p.96.

14. E. Kraus, 'Psychic sores in search of compassion: Hawkes' Death, Sleep and the Traveller', in Critique, Studies in Modern Fiction, XVII, 3, (1976), p.52.

15. L.K. Boutrois, 'Parody in Hawkes' The Lime Twig', in Critique, Studies in Modern Fiction, XV, 2 (1973), p.55.

16. Tanner, City of Words, op. cit., p.16.

17. 'John Hawkes: Interview' in Kuehl, op. cit., p.162.

18. 'John Hawkes: Interview', reprinted in The Contemporary Writer, op. cit., p.5.

19. R. Scholes, 'A Conversation on The Blood Oranges', Novel, 5 No. 3 (Spring, 1972), p.203.

20. Charivari, in Lunar Landscapes, Stories and Short Novels, Chatto and Windus (London, 1970), p.53.

21. Ibid., p.85.

22. Cf. Charivari, pp.131-132.

23. N.O. Brown, Life Against Death, Vintage Books (New York, 1959), p.10.

24. Freud, Civilization and its Discontents, op. cit., editor's introduction.

25. H. Marcuse, Eros and Civilization, op. cit., p.24.

26. Charivari, p.55.

27. The Lime Twig, New Directions (New York, 1961), p.33.

28. Ibid., p.132.

29. Ibid., p.30.

30. Ibid., p.31.

31. Hawkes, Notes on 'The Wild Goose Chase', loq. cit., p.22.

32. The Blood Oranges, New Directions (New York, 1971), p.204.

33. Ibid., p.207.

34. Kuehl, op. cit., p.9.

35. Ibid., p.20.

36. Hawkes, 'Notes on writing a novel', loq. cit., p.112.

37. Kraus, loq. cit., p.50.

38. Ibid.

39. The Cannibal, p.131.

40. Ibid., p.54.

41. Ibid., p.55.

42. The Lime Twig, p.170.

43. E. Rovit, 'The fiction of John Hawkes: An Introductory View.' Modern Fiction Studies, XI, No. 2, (Summer, 1964), p.158.

44. Tanner, op. cit., p.226.

45. Second Skin, Chatto and Windus (London, 1966), p.19.

46. Ibid., p.1.

47. Ibid., p.67.

48. Ibid., p.9.

49. Ibid., p.33.

50. F. Busch, Hawkes: A Guide to his Fictions, Syracuse University Press (New York, 1973), p.122.

51. Cf. the stage directions preceding the short play, The Questions by John Hawkes in The Innocent Party, Four Short Plays, Chatto and Windus (London, 1967).

52. The Blood Oranges,p.3.

53. Ibid., p.11.

54. Ibid., p.14.

55. Ibid., p.146.

56. Ibid., p.93.

57. Ibid., p.96.

58. Ibid., p.65.

59. Ibid., p.25.

60. Ibid., p.34.

61. Hawkes, Notes on 'The Wild Goose Chase', loq. cit., p.22.

62. Death, Sleep and the Traveller, Chatto and Windus (London, 1975), p.74.

63. Cf. Ibid., pp.164-167.

64. Ibid., p.164.

65. Ibid.

66. Ibid., p.179.

67. Ibid.

68. This claim is made by D. Greiner in his paper, 'Death, Sleep and the Traveller: John Hawkes's return to terror,' Critique, Studies in Modern Fiction, XVIII, No. 3 (1976), p.35.

69. Death, Sleep and the Traveller, p.2.

70. Ibid., p.8.

71. Ibid., p.9.

72. Ibid., pp.137-138.

73. Ibid.

74. Ibid., p.37.

75. Ibid., p.74.

76. Ibid., p.90.

77. The author's reply, in R. Yarborough, 'Hawkes's Second Skin', Mosaic, VIII/1 (Fall, 1974), p.73.

78. Death, Sleep and the Traveller, p.143.

79. Cf. the idea of the writer serving 'as his own angleworm', whereby for Hawkes, 'the sharper the barb with which he fishes himself out of the blackness, the better.' Notes on 'The Wild Goose Chase', loq. cit., p.23.

80. Travesty, Chatto and Windus (London, 1976), p.67.

81. Ibid., Cf. p.90, and p.102.

82. Ibid., p.97.

83. Ibid., p.110.

84. Ibid., p.121.

85. Hawkes, 'Notes on writing a novel', loq. cit., p.113.

CHAPTER THREE

1. Le Palace, Menthuen Educational (London, 1972), p.158.

2. Quoted from Dictionnaire Larousse at the beginning of Le Palace.

3. Le Palace, p.131.

4. Gérard Roubichou, Lecture de L'Herbe de Claude Simon, L'Age d'Homme (Lausanne, 1976).

5. _Le Sacre du Printemps_, Calmann-Lévy (Paris, 1954), p.272.

6. _L'Herbe_, Éditions de Minuit (Paris, 1958), p.122.

7. Ibid., p.211.

8. Where detailed reference will be made to the recent and illuminating study of Simon's _L'Herbe_ by Gérard Roubichou, op. cit.

9. _L'Herbe_, p.146.

10. E.g. _La Route des Flandres_, Éditions de Minuit (Paris, 1960), p.119; _Histoire_, Editions de Minuit (Paris, 1967), p.193.

11. Aspects of theatre and 'spectacle' are discussed in relation to modes of representation in Simon's work by F. Van Rossum-Guyon in _Claude Simon/Colloque de Cerisy_, (ed.) Jean Ricardou, 10/18 (Paris, 1975), pp.88-106, and I shall have further and more detailed recourse to these ideas in my comments on 'structure' in _Part Two_ below.

12. Cf. the opening pages of _Leçon de choses_, Éditions de Minuit (Paris, 1975).

13. E.g. _La Bataille de Pharsale_, Éditions de Minuit (Paris, 1971), p.159.

14. J. Sturrock, _The French New Novel_, Oxford University Press (London, 1969), p.68.

15. _Le Palace_, p.22.

16. Ibid.

17. _Le Vent, Tentative de Restitution d'un Retable Baroque_, Éditions de Minuit (Paris, 1957), p.99.

18. _L'Herbe_, p.203.

19. Ibid., p.203.

20. _Leçon de Choses_, p.9.

21. _Histoire_, p.367.

22. _La Bataille de Pharsale_, p.267.

23. _Les Corps Conducteurs_, Éditions de Minuit (Paris, 1971), p.93.

24. _La Route des Flandres_, p.314.

25. Ibid., p.263.

26. Ibid., p.253.

27. Ibid., p.265.

28. Ibid.

29. L'Herbe, p.144 and p.145.

30. Cf. L. Janvier, Une Parole Exigeante, Éditions de Minuit (Paris, 1964), p.89.

31. La Route des Flandres, p.37.

32. Ibid., p.35.

33. Cf. La Route des Flandres, pp.42-43.

34. Ibid.

35. J.A.E. Loubère, The Novels of Claude Simon, Cornell University Press (Ithaca and London, 1975), pp.64-65.

36. E.g. Le Vent, pp.146-147.

37. Ibid., p.9.

38. La Corde Raide, Éditions de Minuit (Paris, 1947), p.73.

39. Ibid., p.175.

40. Cf. Bernard Williams, Problems of the Self: Philosophical Papers, (1956-1972), Cambridge University Press (London, 1973), p.3 and p.12.

41. Histoire, p.319.

42. Ibid., p.356.

43. Ibid.

44. Loubère, op. cit., p.130.

45. Ibid., p.131, where the author quotes Merleau-Ponty from Phénoménologie de la Perception, Gallimard (Paris, 1945).

46. Loubère, op. cit., p.132.

47. Olga Bernal's words quoted by Claude Simon in 'La fiction mot à mot,' Nouveau Roman/Hier, Aujourd'hui, Vol. 2: Pratique, 10/18 (Paris, 1972), p.84.

48. Le Palace, pp.109-110.

49. L'Herbe, pp.99-100.

50. E.g., La Route des Flandres, p.85, p.106; Le Palace, p.94, p.122.

51. La Route des Flandres, p.296.

52. Ibid., p.313.

53. Loubère, op. cit., p.73.

54. Ibid., p.196.

55. Ibid., p.196.

56. Even the conventional burden placed on the names of characters
as assurance of solid substance (personality) is itself often
undermined.   A recent example can be found in Leçon de Choses,
p.172:
      'Il crie Estelle écoutez-moi!   Estelle, Élodie,
      Émilie, Élisabeth, Hélène, Sylvie, Gilberte,
      Édith, Odette.'
Here, once again, the text comments on the repetitive cycle
of behaviour — the often repeated coupling in this instance —
whereby the same act attributed to a host of actors renders
stereotypical the act itself and belies the individuality
accorded to the actor.


## PART ONE:   CONCLUSION

1. Hawkes, 'Notes on writing a novel', loq. cit., p.113.

2. Leo Lowenthal, Literature and the Image of Man, Studies in
   European Drama and the Novel 1600-1900, Beacon Press (Boston,
   1957; reprinted 1966), p.xi.

3. Erich Heller, The Disinherited Mind, Essays in Modern German
   Literature and Thought, Farrar Strauss (New York, 1957);
   reprinted by Penguin (Harmondsworth, 1961), p.211.


## PART TWO:   INTRODUCTION

1. The seminal examples of this methodology are collected in
   Communications, 8 (1966), entitled, 'L'Analyse structurale
   du recit.'

2. Fowler, Linguistics and the Novel, Menthuen(London, 1977), p.123.

3. Kermode, The Sense of an Ending: Studies in the Theory of
   Fiction, Oxford University Press (London, 1967), p.36.

4. Ibid., p.46.

5. Barthes, Critique et Vérité, Seuil (Paris, 1966), p.65.

6. Kermode, op. cit., p.138.

7. F. de Saussure, Cours de Linguistique générale, edited by
   Tullio de Mauro, Payot (Paris, 1973); originally published
   posthumously in 1916.

8. Culler, Structuralist Poetics, op. cit., especially Part One.
   Furthermore, there is a developing area of research which
   approaches stylistics and structural analysis through actual
   linguistic phenomena in the surface structure of the text.
   Fowler's Linguistics and the Novel is a useful introduction,
   and contains a selected bibliography.

9. Propp, Morphology of the Folktale, op. cit. Lévi-Strauss, Anthropologie Structurale, Plon (Paris, 1958); La Pensée Sauvage, Plon (Paris, 1962).

10. Jameson, 'The Ideology of the Text', loq. cit., p.219.

11. A Good example of this method may be found in S. Chatman, 'New ways of analysing narrative structure,' Language and Style, 2, (1969), pp.3-36.

12. R. Weimann, Structure and Society in Literary History, Studies in the History and Theory of Historical Criticism, Lawrence and Wishart (London, 1977), p.5.

13. Ibid.

14. Ibid., p.157.

15. Ibid., p.168.

16. Gérard Genette, 'Frontières du récit', in Communications, 8 (1966), p.152: '... l'aspect singulier, artificiel et problématique de l'acte narratif.'

17. Richard Howard, Foreword to the English translation, S/Z, Jonathan Cape (London, 1975).

18. Barthes, S/Z, Seuil (Paris, 1970), p.27.

19. Culler, op. cit., p.262.

20. S. Heath, The Nouveau Roman : A Study in the Practice of Writing, Elek (London, 1972), passim.

21. R. Fowler, 'The Referential Code and Narrative Authority', Language and Style, 10 (Summer, 1977), pp.129-62.

22. Ibid.

23. Especially in the works which mark the progressive development of this tradition: Lubbock, The Craft of Fiction (London, 1921); Schorer's essay, 'Technique as Discovery', Hudson Review, 1 (Spring, 1948), pp.67-87; and Wayne Booth's The Rhetoric of Fiction, University of Chicago Press (Chicago, 1961).

24. Booth, A Rhetoric of Irony, University of Chicago Press (Chicago, 1974), p.172, and Culler, Flaubert, The Uses of Uncertainty, Elek, (London, 1974).

25. Communications, 8 (1966), pp.159-163.

26. Especially in the seminal work of Lukács, The Theory of the Novel, Merlin Press (London, 1971); originally published in 1920.

27. Weimann, op. cit., p.8.

CHAPTER FOUR

1. John Fowles, foreword, The Magus: A Revised Version (1977), p.6.

2. The Magus (1965), p.60.

3. Bradbury, Possibilities, op. cit., pp.260-261.

4. The Magus: A Revised Version (1977), p.371.

5. The Magus (1965), p.502.

6. John Fowles, in The Ebony Tower (1974), p.120.

7. The French Lieutenant's Woman, p.50.

8. Ibid.

9. Fiedler, Love and Death in the American Novel, Jonathan Cape (London, 1967).

10. Ibid., p.152.

11. Ronald Binns, 'John Fowles: Radical Romancer', Critical Quarterly,15, 4 (Winter, 1973). This paper offers a reasoned account of the first three novels grounded in Fiedler's analysis of the Gothic and Romance traditions.

12. R. Scholes, 'The Orgiastic Fiction of John Fowles', The Hollins Critic, VI, No. 5 (December, 1969), p.1.

13. The Magus (1965), p.399.

14. Ibid., p.416.

15. The French Lieutenant's Woman, p.399.

16. The Magus (1965), p.60.

17. For a detailed discussion of spatial imagery see Palmer, The Fiction of John Fowles, op. cit., pp.80-98. My comments above partly derive from Palmer's analysis.

18. Daniel Martin (1977), p.371.

19. Ibid., p.7.

20. Ibid., p.99.

21. Ibid., p.529.

22. Ibid., p.551.

23. Ibid., p.558.

24. The Aristos, p.165.

-348-

25. Ibid.

26. The Ebony Tower, p.217.

27. Ibid., p.91.

28. Published in Afterwords, Novelists on their Novels (ed.)
    T. McCormack, Harper and Row (New York, 1969), pp.161-175.

29. Ibid., pp.161-162.

30. Ibid., p.161.

31. The French Lieutenant's Woman, p.13.

32. Ibid.

33. Afterwords, op. cit., p.172.

34. C.G. Jung, Collected Works, Vol. IX, Part 1, translated by
    R.F.C. Hall, Routledge and Kegan Paul (London, 1959;
    reprinted 1971), p.27.

35. Ibid., pp.26-27.

36. Ibid., p.29.

37. The Aristos, pp.85-103.

38. The French Lieutenant's Woman, p.84.

39. The Magus (1965), p.473.

40. The Ebony Tower, p.297.

41. Daniel Martin, pp.463-464.

42. The Magus: A Revised Version, p.235.

43. 'A sort of Exile in Lyme Regis' in London Magazine, 10,
    No. 12 (March, 1971), p.43.

44. L. Sage, 'John Fowles' in The New Review, I, No. 7 (October,
    1974), p.37.

45. The French Lieutenant's Woman, p.208.

46. Daniel Martin, p.563.

47. B. Hardy, Tellers and Listeners, The Athlone Press (London,
    1975), Preface (vii).

48. The Magus (1965), pp.214-215.

49. Daniel Martin, p.172.

50. Ibid.

51. Ibid., p.644.

52. The Magus (1965), p.100.

53. Daniel Martin, p.59.

54. The Magus (1965).

55. The Sense of an Ending, op. cit., p.133.

56. For a further discussion of these issues and their specific relations to structure in the first three novels, see Dwight Eddins, 'John Fowles: Existence as Authorship', Contemporary Literature, XVII, No. 2 (Spring, 1976).

57. The Ebony Tower, p.177.

58. Daniel Martin, p.62.

59. Ibid., p.644.


CHAPTER FIVE

1. John Hawkes: Interview reprinted in The Contemporary Writer, edited by L.S. Dembo and C.N. Pondrom, loq. cit., p.11.

2. Ibid.

3. F. Busch, Hawkes: A Guide to his Fictions, op. cit., p.23.

4. The Cannibal, p.105.

5. Ibid., p.12.

6. Ibid., p.85.

7. Ibid.

8. Ibid., p.86.

9. Ibid., p.90.

10. Ibid., p.57.

11. Ibid., p.94.

12. Ibid., p.183.

13. In Kuehl, John Hawkes and the Craft of Conflict, op. cit., p.177.

14. The Lime Twig, p.7.

15. Busch, op. cit., p.101.

16. R. Scholes, The Fabulators, Oxford University Press (London, 1967), p.91.

17. _The Lime Twig_, p.159.

18. Ibid., p.160.

19. Ibid., p.170.

20. _The Blood Oranges_, p.15.

21. Ibid., p.271.

22. For a detailed account of images and motifs, and the manner by which scenes are 'related thematically and imagistically' Cf. J.V. Knapp, 'Hawkes' _The Blood Oranges_: A sensual new Jerusalem' in _Critique: Studies in Modern Fiction_, XVII, No. 3 (1976).

23. _Death, Sleep and the Traveller_, p.52.

24. Hawkes, _Notes on 'The Wild Goose Chase'_, reprinted in _Studies in 'Second Skin'_, edited by J. Graham, loc. cit.,p.22.

25. Kuehl, op. cit., p.20.

26. Ibid., p.181.

27. Cf. P. Thompson, _The Grotesque_, Menthuen (London, 1972), passim.

28. Wolfgang Kayser, _The Grotesque in Art and Literature_, translated by Ulrich Weissten, Indiana University Press (Bloomington, 1963), p.181ff.

29. Ibid., p.185.

30. Ibid., p.186.

31. Ibid., p.184.

32. _The Blood Oranges_, p.15.

33. Ibid., p.25.

34. R. Scholes, 'A Conversation on _The Blood Oranges_ between John Hawkes and Robert Scholes', _Novel_ 5, No. 3 (Spring, 1972), p.202.

35. _The Blood Oranges_, p.3.

36. _Second Skin_, p.33.

37. Ibid., p.149.

38. A. Guerard, 'The Light and the Dark Affirmation', in _Studies in 'Second Skin'_, op. cit., p.100.

39. _Second Skin_, p.1.

40. Ibid.

41. Ibid., p.37ff.

42. Ibid., p.162.

43. Ibid., p.3.

44. Ibid., p.5.

45. Ibid., p.4.

46. Ibid., p.210.

47. Ibid., p.48.

48. Hawkes, 'Notes on writing a novel', in TriQuarterly, 30 (Spring, 1974), p.111.

49. Ibid., p.125.

50. Second Skin, p.173.

51. N. Lavers, 'The Structure of Second Skin', Novel 5, No. 3 (Spring, 1972), p.209.

52. Second Skin, p.70.

53. Ibid., p.199.

54. Ibid., p.105.

55. Ibid., p.48.

56. This brief analysis of colour imagery is indebted to D. Greiner's perceptive comments on the topic. For a more detailed discussion within the bounds of his thesis, Cf. Comic Terror: The Novels of John Hawkes, Memphis State University Press (Memphis, 1973), pp.188-199.

57. Hawkes's written response to the paper by R. Imhoff, 'On Second Skin', Mosaic, VIII, 1 (Fall, 1974), p.61.

58. R. Imhoff, 'On Second Skin', loq. cit.

59. Hawkes, Interview reprinted in The Contemporary Writer, op. cit., p.11.

60. Quoted by Imhoff, loq. cit., p.52.

61. Ibid., p.53.

62. Ibid.

63. Ibid.

64. Quoted by Imhoff, loq. cit., pp.56-57.

65. Ibid., p.59.

66. Hawkes's words in Kuehl, op. cit., p.182.

67. Kuehl, op. cit., p.30.

68. D. Dunn, 'John Hawkes', Profile 11, The New Review, 1,
    No. 12 (April, 1975), p.28.


CHAPTER SIX

1. In French Structuralist literary theory, as I have shown
   above, there is an enabling distinction between fiction
   and narration, that is, the element of story (histoire)
   and its telling (discours).  Cf. the essays by Barthes,
   Todorov, and Genette in Communications 8 (1966).

2. Gérard Roubichou, Lecture de L'Herbe de Claude Simon,
   L'Age d'Homme (Lausanne, 1976).

3. The notion of 'the practice of writing' has been extensively
   analyzed in relation to the nouveau roman by Stephen Heath
   in The Nouveau Roman: A Study in the Practice of Writing,
   Elek (London, 1972).

4. John Sturrock, The French New Novel, op. cit., p.68: 'L'Herbe,
   where Louise, the narrator ...'; and Vivian Mercier, The
   New Novel (From Queneau to Pinget), Farrar, Strauss (New York,
   1971), p.300: ' ... instead of being told a story by an
   observer, we are experiencing events directly through the
   consciousness of the protagonist ...'.

5. L'Herbe, pp.124-125.

6. Roubichou, op. cit., p.83.

7. L'Herbe, pp.106-107.

8. Simon, quoted in Roubichou, op. cit., pp.129-130.

9. Roubichou, p.122.

10. Jiménez-Fajardo, Claude Simon, Twayne Publishers (Boston,
    1975), p.18.

11. La Route des Flandres, p.41.

12. Le Vent, p.10.

13. Sturrock, op. cit., p.51.

14. Heinrich Wölfflin, Renaissance and Baroque, translated by
    K. Simon, Collins (London, 1964), p.31.

15. Ibid., p.62.

16. Walter Benjamin, quoted in Jameson, Marxism and Form, op.
    cit., p.73.

17. <u>Histoire</u>, p.273.

18. David Carroll, 'Diachrony and Synchrony in <u>Histoire</u>', MLN, 92, No. 4 (May, 1977), p.821.

19. Jiménez-Fejardo, op. cit., p.32.

20. **Cf.** David Carroll, loq. cit., for a fully developed argument along these lines, where he used the notions of synchrony and diachrony to discuss the structure of <u>Histoire</u>.

21. Barthes, in <u>Communications</u>, 8 (1966), p.12.

22. <u>Histoire</u>, p.356.

23. Ibid., p.41.

24. Cf. Roubichou, op. cit., p.169.

25. Jean Ricardou, 'La Bataille de la Phase', in <u>Pour une theorie du Nouveau Roman</u>, Seuil (Paris, 1971), p.120.

26. Roubichou, p.172.

27. Cf. Ibid., p.202.

28. Jiménez-Fajardo, op. cit., p.65.

29. Claude Simon, 'La fiction mot a mot', in <u>Nouveau Roman/ Hier, Aujourd'hui</u>, 2 Pratiques, (ed.) Jean Ricardou and Françoise Van Rossum-Guyon, 10/18 (Paris, 1972), pp.88-89.

30. Ibid., pp.92-93.

31. François Jost, 'Les Aventures du lecteur', in <u>Poétique</u> 29, (Février, 1977).

32. E.g. <u>Le Vent</u>, p.10; <u>La Route des Flandres</u>, p.72.

33. <u>Leçon de Choses</u>, pp.10-11.

34. Ibid., p.11.

35. Jost, loq. cit., p.81.

36. Ibid., p.82.

37. Ibid., p.83.

38. Ibid., p.84.

39. Barthes, 'L'effet de réel', <u>Communications</u>, 11 (1968), pp.84-9.

40. Jost, loq. cit., p.89.

41. Loubère, <u>The Novels of Claude Simon</u>, op. cit., p.45.

42. Sturrock, op. cit., p.47.

43. La Route des Flandres, p.184.

44. Roubichou, op. cit., p.306.

45. Sturrock, p.101.

46. Jameson, Marxism and Form, op. cit., pp.201-2.

47. Cf. note 8 above.

48. A. Pugh, 'Claude Simon: the narrator and his double',
    Twentieth Century Studies, 6 (December, 1971), p.39.

49. 'Claude Simon, A la Question', in Colloque de Cerisy, op.
    cit., p.409.

50. Ibid., p.410.

51. Sturrock, op. cit., p.58 and p.94.

52. Cf. Ricardou, 'La Bataille de la Phrase', loq. cit., on
    word-play in La Bataille de Pharsale; and Heath, The
    Nouveau Roman, op. cit., pp.172-8 on the erotic word-
    play in La Route des Flandres.

53. Orion Aveugle, Editions Skira (Paris, 1970), introduction.

54. Roubichou, op. cit., pp.209-10.

55. Cf. Entretiens: Claude Simon, (ed.) M. Seguier, Rodoz
    (Paris, 1972), p.122ff, which gives examples of such
    'word-images' from La Route des Flandres, pp.257-292,
    and from La Bataille de Pharsale, pp.211-247.

56. La Route des Flandres, pp.183-5.

57. Ricardou, loq. cit., pp.129-130.

58. Simon, 'La fiction mot à mot', loq. cit., p.73.

59. La Route des Flandres, p.13.

60. Jameson, op. cit., p.397.

61. Jiménez-Fajardo, Claude Simon, op. cit., p.175.

62. E.g. Les Corps Conducteurs pp.164-5;  pp.62-3;  and pp.93-99.

63. J-M. Benoist, La Révolution Structurale, op. cit., p.58.

64. Le Vent, p.102.

65. Cf. the proliferation of 'comme si';  'peut-être';  'ou
    plutôt';  'peut-être aussi parce que';  'peut-être même
    pas';  'tout même';  and, 'à peu près comme'.  These
    scrupulous, yet ironic, expressions are symptomatic of
    the perpetual inadequacy of language, and narrative, to
    represent the world.  For further discussion see, B. Pinguad,
    'Sur la Route des Flandres', Les Temp Modernes, 16 (1960-61),
    p.1031.

66. Loubère, op. cit., p.171.

67. 'Claude Simon, A la Question', loq. cit., p.422.

68. Ibid., p.419.

69. The sequences which make up this composition are schematically explained in Jiménez-Fajardo, Claude Simon, p.185.

70. Loubère, op. cit., p.219.

71. F. Van Rossum-Guyon in Claude Simon : Colloque de Cerisy, p.103.

72. Benoist, op. cit., p.57.


PART TWO : CONCLUSION

1. This notion derives from Roland Barthes's paper, 'L'effet de réel', Communications, 11 (1968), pp.84-9.


PART THREE : CHAPTER SEVEN

1. Claudio Guillen, Literature as System, Essays toward the Theory of Literary History, Princeton University Press (Princeton, New Jersey, 1971), p.61.

2. Tzvetan Todorov, Introduction à la Littérature Fantastique, Seuil (Paris, 1970); see especially 1. 'les genres littéraires'.

3. Kermode, 'Novel and Narrative', in Halperin (ed) The Theory of the Novel, op. cit., p.174.

4. R. Fowler (ed)., A Dictionary of Modern Critical Terms, Routledge and Kegan Paul (London, 1973), p.138.

5. Culler, Structuralist Poetics, op. cit., p.152.

6. Bergonzi, The Situation of the Novel, Macmillan (London, 1970); reprinted by Pelican (Harmondsworth, 1972), pp.25-6.

7. Ibid., p.29.

8. Alter, Partial Magic, The Novel as Self-Conscious Genre, The University of California Press (London, 1975), p.158.

9. Erich Auerbach, Mimesis, The Representation of Reality in Western Literature, Princeton University Press (Princeton, New Jersey, 1953; reprinted, 1974), p.518.

10. John Fowles, The French Lieutenant's Woman, Panther (London, 1970), p.7. All subsequent references will be indicated in parenthesis following the quotation.

11. W.J. Palmer in The Fiction of John Fowles, op. cit., pp.25-9, gives a detailed account of the epigraphs and quotations in this novel.

12. The plight of the aristocracy in nineteenth century industrial England is well documented in Victorian literature.

13. Fowles differentiates this 'historical romance' from the convention of such a genre, which often looked back to a period of, say, sixty years with nostalgia and hindsight. Fowles differs from this by a complex interweaving of styles of writing, modes of consciousness, and historical situations, which, as I have argued, effect both nostalgia and relief for what has been lost. A more conventional novel with an historical perspective would be, say, George Eliot's Felix Holt (1866). A more recent example is Lampedusa's The Leopard (1958), which is largely set in the Sicily of the 1860s. This also uses the wisdom of hindsight to judge the past and the present, but without the more complex, aesthetic implications of Fowles's novel.

14. To use Auerbach's definition here, Cf. note 9 above.

15. In Notes on 'The Wild Goose Chase', reprinted in Studies in Second Skin, edited by J. Graham, op. cit.

16. Quoted by Boutrous, 'Parody in Hawkes' The Lime Twig, Critique 15, No. 2 (1973), p.49.

17. That is, in the more formulaic thrillers of the Sherlock Holmes type, and its many imitators. There have been more ambitious thrillers which play on multiple perspectives (those by Hammett, and Chandler, for instance).
In making claims about the suspense-detective story, my aim is to offer the ideal model from which Hawkes deviates.

18. Quoted in Boutrous, loq. cit., p.52.

19. John Hawkes, The Lime Twig, New Directions (New York, 1961), p.174. All subsequent references will be indicated in parenthesis following the quotations.

20. D. Greiner, Comic Terror: The Novels of John Hawkes, op. cit. p.128.

21. Ibid.

22. Hawkes, Interview reprinted in The Contemporary Writer, edited by L.S. Dembo and C.N. Pondrom, p.12.

23. Ibid., p.5.

24. Scholes, The Fabulators, pp.79-94.

25. Greiner, op. cit., p.127.

26. H. Wölfflin, Renaissance and Baroque, op. cit., p.62.

27. Jiménez-Fajardo, Claude Simon, op. cit., p.18.

28. Claude Simon, Le Vent, Éditions de Minuit (Paris, 1957), p.9.
All subsequent references will be indicated in parenthesis
following the quotation.

29. Loubère, The Novels of Claude Simon, op. cit., p.71.

30. Barthes, S/Z (1970), p.83.

31. Which Barthes defines in S/Z as crucial to the cultural
vraisemblance of any era.

32. A word coined by Simon to refer to reality as both massive
and unknowable, but also as a thick, doughy substance.

33. Barthes, Le Degré zéro de l'écriture, Seuil (Paris, 1953;
reprinted, 1972), pp.26-27.

34. Barthes S/Z (1970). His distinction between the 'classical'
and the 'modern', the lisible and the scriptible, is
important here.

35. Alter, Partial Magic: The Novel as Self-Conscious Genre,
op. cit., pp.x-xi.

36. Ibid.

37. Guillen, Literature as System, op. cit., p.65.

38. Ibid., p.134.

CONCLUSION

1. L. Sage, 'John Fowles' in The New Review, 1, No. 7
(October, 1974), p.34.

2. Ibid.

3. Daniel Martin, pp.306-310.

4. Lukács, quoted in Daniel Martin, p.559.

5. Hawkes's words in Kuehl, John Hawkes and the Craft of
Conflict, op. cit., p.183.

6. The author has said that perhaps the whole idea of
fragmentation of the 'fictional' was established by
Cubism in painting, with its play on continuity and
discontinuity — why not the novel? — Cf. 'Claude
Simon, A la Question', in Colloque de Cerisy, op. cit.,
p.414.

7. C. Lévi-Strauss, La Pensée Sauvage, Plon (Paris, 1962),
chapter one, where the idea of 'bricolage' refers to
the workings of the primitive mind.

8. 'Claude Simon, A la Question', loq. cit., p.427.

9. David Carroll, 'Diachrony and Synchrony in Histoire',
MLN, 92, No. 4 (May, 1977), p.805.

10. F. Jameson, Marxism and Form, op. cit., p.333.

11. J-M. Benoist, La Révolution Structurale, op. cit.,
especially chapter 1.

12. Jameson, Marxism and Form, xvii.

13. Culler, Structuralist Poetics, op. cit., p.238.

14. Jameson, referring to Denis Roche, in The Prison House
of Language, p.138.

15. M. Foucault, Les Mots et les choses, Une Archéologie des
Sciences Humaines, Gallimard (Paris, 1966), pp.396-7.

16. Ibid., p.397.

17. Jameson, The Prison House of Language, op. cit., p.182.

18. Ibid.,pp.185-186.

19. Jameson, quoting Lévi-Strauss in translation, ibid., p.142.

20. T.W. Adorno in Critical Sociology, (ed.) P. Connerton, Penguin
(Harmondsworth, 1976), p.263.

21. Jameson, Marxism and Form, p.331.

22. P. Sollers, Logiques, Seuil (Paris, 1968), p.236.

23. R. Fowler, Linguistics and the Novel, op. cit., p.128.

24. F. Jameson, The Prison House of Language, p.216.

BIBLIOGRAPHY

(i) PRIMARY SOURCES

John Fowles:

The Collector, Jonathan Cape (London, 1963),
reprinted by Pan Books (London, 1965)
The Aristos, Jonathan Cape (London, 1965),
revised edition, Pan Books (London, 1968).
The Magus, Jonathan Cape (London, 1966),
reprinted by Pan Books (London, 1968).
The French Lieutenant's Woman, Jonathan Cape
(London, 1969), reprinted Panther Books
(London, 1970).
The Magus, A Revised Version, Jonathan Cape
(London, 1977).
Daniel Martin, Jonathan Cape (London, 1977).
The Ebony Tower, Jonathan Cape (London, 1974).

John Hawkes:

The Cannibal, New Directions (New York, 1949,
reprinted, 1962).
The Beetle Leg, New Directions (New York, 1951).
The Lime Twig, New Directions (New York, 1961).
Second Skin, New Directions (New York, 1964),
first published in Great Britain by Chatto and
Windus (London, 1966).
Lunar Landscapes, Stories and Short Novels
1949-1963, Chatto and Windus (London, 1970).
The Blood Oranges, New Directions (New York,
1977).
Death, Sleep and the Traveller, Chatto and
Windus (London, 1975).
Travesty, Chatto and Windus (London, 1976).

Claude Simon:

Le Tricheur, Éditions du Sagittaire (Paris,
1945).
La Corde raide, Les Editions de Minuit (Paris,
1947).
Gulliver, Calmann-Lévy (Paris, 1952).
Le Sacre du printemps, Calmann-Lévy (Paris, 1954).
Le Vent, Tentative de Restitution d'un Retable
Baroque, Les Editions de Minuit (Paris, 1957).
L'Herbe, Les Editions de Minuit (Paris, 1958).
La Route des Flandres, Les Editions de Minuit
(Paris, 1960).
Le Palace, Les Editions de Minuit (Paris, 1962);
published by Methuen Educational (London, 1972).
Histoire, Les Editions de Minuit (Paris, 1967).
La Bataille de Pharsale, Les Editions de Minuit
(Paris, 1969).
Orion Aveugle, Editions Skira (Paris, 1970).
Les Corps Conducteurs, Les Editions de Minuit
(Paris, 1971).
Triptyque, Les Editions de Minuit (Paris, 1973).
Leçon de Choses, Les Editions de Minuit (Paris, 1975).

(ii) SECONDARY SOURCES

Adorno, T.W.,  The Jargon of Authenticity, Routledge and
              Kegan Paul (London, 1973)
              'Society', in Salmagundi, 10-11 (1969-70),
              pp.144-53, translated from the German by
              F.R. Jameson

Alter, R.,  Partial Magic, The Novel as Self-Conscious
            Genre, University of California Press
            (London, 1975)

Auerbach, E.,  Mimesis, The Representation of Reality in
               Western Literature, Princeton University
               Press (Princeton, New Jersey, 1953,
               reprinted 1974)

Barthes, R.,  Le Degré zéro de l'écriture, Seuil (Paris,
              1953, and 1972)
              Critique et Vérité, Seuil (Paris, 1966)
              'L'effet de reel', in Communications 11
              (1968)
              S/Z, Seuil (Paris, 1970)

Barthes, R., et. al.,  'L'Analyse Structurale du Récit', in Communications
                       8 (1966)
                       Poétique du Récit, Seuil (Paris, 1977)

Benjamin, W.,  Illuminations, Fontana (Glasgow, 1977)

Benoist, J-M.,  La Révolution structurale, Bernard Grasset
                (Paris, 1975)

Berger, P. and
Luckmann, T.,  The Social Construction of Reality, A Treatise
               in the Sociology of Knowledge, Penguin
               (Harmondsworth, 1967, and 1973)

Berger, P.,
Berger, B., and
Kellner, H.,  The Homeless Mind, Modernization and
              Consciousness, Penguin (Harmondsworth,
              1973)

Bergonzi, B.,  The Situation of the Novel, Macmillan (London,
               1970); reprinted by Pelican (Harmondsworth,
               1972).

Binns, R.,  'John Fowles: Radical Romancer', Critical
            Quarterly, 15, 4 (Winter, 1973).

Booth, W.C.,  The Rhetoric of Fiction, University of Chicago
              Press (Chicago, 1961 and 1970)
              A Rhetoric of Irony, University of Chicago
              Press (Chicago, 1974)

Boutrous, L.K.,  'Parody in Hawkes' The Lime Twig', Critique,
                 Studies in Modern Fiction, XV., No. 2 (1973),
                 pp. 49-56.

Bradbury, Malcolm, — Possibilities, Essays on the State of the Novel, Oxford University Press (London, 1973)

Bradbury, Malcolm, (ed.) — The Novel Today, Contemporary Writers on Modern Fiction, Fontana (Glasgow, 1977)

Brown, N.O., — Life Against Death, Vintage Books (New York, 1959)

Busch, F., — Hawkes, A Guide to his Fictions, Syracuse University Press (New York, 1973)

Carroll, D., — 'Diachrony and Synchrony in Histoire', in Modern Languages Notes (MLN), 92, No. 4 (May, 1977)

Chatman, S., — 'On the Formalist-Structuralist Theory of Character', in the Journal of Literary Semantics, 1 (1972).

Connerton, P., (ed.), — Critical Sociology, Penguin (Harmondsworth, 1976)

Culler, J., — Structuralist Poetics. Structuralism, Linguistics, and the Study of Literature, Routledge and Kegan Paul (London, 1975) Saussure, Fontana (Glasgow, 1976)

Dahrendorf, R., — Homo Sociologicus, Routledge and Kegan Paul (London, 1973)

Dawe, A., — 'The Two Sociologies', in Sociological Perspectives, edited by Thompson, K., and Tunstall, J., Penguin (Harmondsworth, 1976), pp.542-54

Dembo, L.S., and Pondrom, C.N., (ed.), — The Contemporary Writer, (Interviews with sixteen novelists and poets), University of Wisconsin Press (Wisconsin, 1972); interview with John Hawkes was originally published in Wisconsin Studies in Contemporary Literature, (now, Contemporary Literature), VI, 2 (Summer, 1965)

Dunn, D., — 'Profile 11 : John Hawkes', in the New Review, 1, No. 12 (April, 1975)

Eddins, D., — 'John Fowles : Existence as Authorship', in Contemporary Literature, XVII, No. 2 (Spring, 1976)

Federman, R., (ed.), — Surfiction, Fiction Now and Tomorrow, Swallow Press (Chicago, 1975)

Fiedler, L., — Love and Death in the American Novel, Jonathan Cape (London, 1967)

Fletcher, C.,        The Person in the Sight of Sociology,
                     Routledge and Kegan Paul (London, 1975)

Fletcher, J.,        Claude Simon and Fiction Now, Calder and
                     Boyars (London, 1975)

Foucault, M.,        Les Mots et les Choses, Une Archéologie
                     des Sciences Humaines, Gallimard (Paris,
                     1966)

Fowler, R., (ed.),   A Dictionary of Modern Critical Terms,
                     Routledge and Kegan Paul (London, 1973)

Fowler, R.,          Linguistics and the Novel, Methuen (London,
                     1977)
                     'The Referential Code and Narrative Authority',
                     in Language and Style, 10, No. 3 (Summer,
                     1977), pp.129-62

Fowles, J.,          'Notes on an Unfinished Novel', in
                     Afterwords (ed.) McCormack, T., Harper and
                     Row (New York, 1969)

Freedman, R.,        The Lyrical Novel, Princeton University
                     Press (Princeton,New Jersey, 1963 and 1971)

Freud, S.,           Civilization and its Discontents, Collected
                     Works, Vol. XXI, 1927-1931, Hogarth Press
                     (London, 1930)

Giles, S.,           The Problem of Action in Modern Drama,
                     Unpublished Ph.D. thesis, University of
                     East Anglia (Norwich, 1977)

Goffman, E.,         The Presentation of Self in Everyday Life,
                     Doubleday (New York, 1959)
                     Relations in Public, Penguin (Harmondsworth,
                     1971)
                     Frame Analysis, Penguin (Harmondsworth, 1974)

Graham, J., (ed.),   Studies in 'Second Skin', Charles E. Merril
                     Studies (Columbus, 1971)

Greiner, D.,         Comic Terror : The Novels of John Hawkes,
                     Memphis State University Press (Memphis,
                     1973)

Guillen, C.,         Literature as System, essays toward the theory
                     of literary history, Princeton University
                     Press (Princeton, New Jersey, 1971)

Halperin, J., (ed.), The Theory of the Novel, New Essays, Oxford
                     University Press (New York and London, 1974)

Halpern, D.,         'A Sort of Exile in Lyme Regis', in the
                     London Magazine, 20, No. 12 (March, 1971)

Hamon, Ph.,             'Statut Sémiologique du Personnage', in
                        Poétique du Récit, Barthes, R., et. al.,
                        Seuil (Paris, 1977)

Hardy, B.,              Tellers and Listeners, The Athlone Press
                        (London, 1975)

Hawkes, J.,             'Flannery O'Connor's Devil', The Sewanee
                        Review, LXX, 3 (July-Sept., 1962)
                        'Notes on Writing a Novel', in TriQuarterly,
                        30 (Spring, 1974) pp.109-26

Heath, S.,              The Nouveau Roman, A Study in the Practice
                        of Writing, Elek (London, 1972)

Heller, E.,             The Disinherited Mind, Essays in Modern
                        German Literature and Thought, Farrar
                        Strauss (New York, 1957), reprinted
                        Penguin (Harmondsworth, 1961)

Hollis, M.,             Models of Man, Philosophical thoughts on
                        Social Action, Cambridge University Press
                        (London, 1977)

Imhoff, R.,             'On Second Skin', in Mosaic, VIII/1 (Fall,
                        1974)

Iser, W.,               The Implied Reader, Patterns of Communication
                        in Prose Fiction from Bunyan to Beckett,
                        John Hopkins University Press (Baltimore,
                        1975)

Jameson, F.,            Marxism and Form, Twentieth Century Dialectical
                        Theories of Literature, Princeton University
                        Press (Princeton, New Jersey, 1971)
                        The Prison-House of Language, A Critical
                        Account of Structuralism and Russian Formalism,
                        Princeton University Press (Princeton, New
                        Jersey, 1972 and 1974)
                        'The Ideology of the Text', in Salmagundi,
                        No. 31-32 (Fall, 1975-Winter, 1976), pp.204-46

Janvier, L.,            Une Parole Exigeante, Les Editions de Minuit
                        (Paris, 1964)

Jiménez-Fajardo, S.,    Claude Simon, Twayne Publishers (Boston, 1975)

Josipovici, G.,         The World and the Book, A Study of Modern Fiction,
                        Paladin (St. Albans, 1973)

Josipovici, G., (ed.),  The Modern English Novel, the reader, the
                        writer and the work, Open Books (London, 1976)
                        The Lessons of Modernism, and other Essays,
                        MacMillan (London, 1977)

Jost, F.,               Introduction to Comparative Literature,
                        Pegasus (Indianapolis and New York, 1974)
                        'Les aventures du lecteur', in Poétique,
                        29 (Février, 1977)

Jung, C.G.,         Collected Works, XI, Part 1, translated
by R.F.C. Hull, Routledge and Kegan Paul
(London, 1959 and 1971)

Karl, F.R.,        A Reader's Guide to the Contemporary
English Novel, Thames and Hudson (London,
1963, revised, 1972)

Kayser, W.,        The Grotesque in Art and Literature, translated by Ulrich Weissten, Indiana University
Press (Bloomington, 1963)

Kennedy, A.,       The Protean Self, Dramatic Action in
Contemporary Fiction, MacMillan (London,
1974)

Kermode, F.,       The Sense of an Ending:  Studies in the
theory of Fiction, Oxford University
Press (London, 1967)
Modern Essays, Fontana (London, 1971)

Kingsley, M.,      'John Fowles : Collector's Piece', in
Harper and Queen (October, 1977)

Knapp, J.V.,       'Hawkes' The Blood Oranges : A Sensual New
Jerusalem', in Critique, Studies in Modern
Fiction, XVII, No. 3 (1976)

Kraus, E.,        'Psychic sores in search of compassion :
Hawkes' Death, Sleep and the Traveller',
in Critique, Studies in Modern Fiction,
XVII, No. 3 (1976)

Kuehl, J.,        John Hawkes and the Craft of Conflict,
Rutgers University Press (New Jersey, 1975)

Lavers, N.,        'The Structure of Second Skin', in Novel
5, No. 3 (Spring, 1972)

Lawrence, D.H.,    Selected Literary Criticism, (ed.), Beal,
A., Heinemann, (London, 1956)

Lévi-Strauss, C.,  Anthropologie Structurale, Plon (Paris, 1958)
La Pensée Sauvage, Plon (Paris, 1962)

Lodge, D.,        The Modes of Modern Writing : Metaphor,
Metonymy and the typology of Modern
Literature, Edward Arnold (London, 1977)

Loubère, J.A.E.,   The Novels of Claude Simon, Cornell University
Press (Ithaca and London, 1975)

Lowenthal, Leo,    Literature and the Image of Man, Studies in
European Drama and the Novel 1600-1900,
Beacon Press (Boston, 1957; reprinted 1966)

Lukács, G.,  The Theory of the Novel : A historico-
philosophical essay on the forms of
great epic literature, Merlin Press
(London, 1971; originally published in
German in Berlin, 1920)

Mandelbaum, M.,  History, Man and Reason, A Study in Nineteenth Century Thought, John Hopkins
(London, 1971)

Marcuse, H.,  One Dimensional Man, Abacus (London, 1972)
Eros and Civilization, A Philosophical
Inquiry into Freud, Abacus (London, 1973);
first published by The Beacon Press (Boston,
1955)

Macquarrie, J.,  Existentialism, Penguin (Harmondsworth,
1973)

McCormack, T., (ed.),  Afterwords, Novelists on their Novels,
Harper and Row (New York, 1969)

Mercier, V.,  The New Novel from Queneau to Pinget,
Farrar, Strauss (New York, 1971)

Miller, J.H.,  The Disappearance of God, Five Nineteenth-
Century Writers, Schocken Books (New York,
1963)

Newquist, R., (ed.),  Counterpoint, Simon and Schuster (New York,
1964)

Palmer, W.J.,  The Fiction of John Fowles, Tradition, Art,
and the Loneliness of Selfhood, University
of Missouri Press (Columbia, 1975)

Pingaud, B.,  'Sur La Route des Flandres', in Les Temps
Modernes, 16 (1960-61), pp.1026-37

Propp, V.,  Morphology of the Folktale, University of
Texas Press (Austin, 1973)

Pugh, A.,  'Claude Simon : the narrator and his double',
in Twentieth Century Studies, 6 (December,
1971)

Ricardou, J.,  Problèmes du Nouveau Roman, Seuil (Paris,
1967)
Pour Une Théorie du Nouveau Roman, Seuil
(Paris, 1971)
(ed.), Claude Simon/Colloque de Cerisy,
10/18 (Paris, 1975)

Ricardou, J., and  Nouveau Roman: Hier, Aujourd'hui, 2 vols.
Van Rossum-Guyon, F.,  10/18 (Paris, 1972)

| | |
|---|---|
| Robinson, R., | 'Giving the reader a choice: A conversation with John Fowles', in The Listener (31 October, 1974) |
| Roubichou, G., | Lecture de L'Herbe de Claude Simon, L'Age de l'homme (Lausanne, 1976) |
| Rovit, E., | 'The Fiction of John Hawkes : An Introductory View', in Modern Fiction Studies, Xl, No. 2 (Summer, 1964) |
| Sage, L., | 'Profile 7 : John Fowles', The New Review, 1, No. 7 (October, 1974) |
| Saussure, F. de., | Cours de linguistique Générale, Payot (Paris, 1973; first published posthumously in 1913) |
| Scholes, R., | The Fabulators, Oxford University Press (London, 1967) 'The Orgiastic Fiction of John Fowles', in The Hollins Critic, VI, No. 5 (December, 1969) 'A Conversation on The Blood Oranges between John Hawkes and Robert Scholes, Novel, 5., No. 3 (Spring, 1972) |
| Scholes, R., and Kellogg, R., | The Nature of Narrative, Oxford University Press (New York, and London, 1966 and 1968) |
| Seguier, M., (ed.), | Entretiens : Claude Simon, Rodoz (Paris, 1972) |
| Simon, C., | 'La Fiction Mot à Mot', in Nouveau Roman : hier, aujourd'hui : 2 Pratiques, (ed.) Jean Ricardou, Françoise Van Rossum-Guyon, 10/18 (Paris, 1972) |
| Sollers, P., | Logiques, Seuil (Paris, 1968) |
| Spearman, D., | The Novel and Society, Routledge and Kegan Paul (London, 1966) |
| Sturrock, J., | The French New Novel, Oxford University Press (London, 1969) |
| Sykes, S., | 'Mise en abyme in the novels of Claude Simon', in Forum for Modern Language Studies, IX., No. 4 (October, 1973), pp.333-345 |
| Tanner, T., | City of words, American Fiction 1950-1970, Jonathan Cape (London, 1971) |
| Thompson, P., | The Grotesque, Methuen, critical idiom series (London, 1972) |

Todorov, T.,       Introduction à la Littérature Fantastique, Seuil (Paris, 1970) 'Les catégories du récit littéraire', in Communications 8 (1966)

Watt, I.,       The Rise of the Novel, Penguin (Harmondsworth, 1957)

Weimann, R.,       Structure and Society in Literary History, Studies in the History and Theory of Historical Criticism, Lawrence and Wishart (London, 1977)

Weisstein, U.,       Comparative Literature and Literary Theory, Indiana University Press (Bloomington and London, 1973)

Wellek, R., and Warren, A.,       Theory of Literature, Penguin (Harmondsworth, 1973; first published in the U.S.A., 1949)

Williams, B.,       Problems of the Self : Philosophical Papers, 1956-1972, Cambridge University Press (London, 1973)

Wölfflin, H.,       Renaissance and Baroque, translated by K. Simon, Collins (London, 1964)

Yarborough, R.,       'Hawkes's Second Skin', in Mosaic, VIII/1 (Fall, 1974)

# EPISTEMATA — Würzburger wissenschaftliche Schriften

*Reihe Literaturwissenschaft — Band 2 (1980)*

EITEL FRIEDRICH TIMM

WILLIAM BUTLER YEATS
UND FRIEDRICH NIETZSCHE

Verlag
Königshausen - Neumann

**Eitel F. Timm**

## WILLIAM BUTLER YEATS
## UND
## FRIEDRICH NIETZSCHE

*331 Seiten*

ISBN 3-88479-012-9

Die Nietzsche-Rezeption im angelsächsischen Kulturbereich ist Gegenstand zahlreicher und umfangreicher Untersuchungen, die in ihrer Tendenz den Höhepunkt des Nietzsche-Einflusses mit dem Beginn des Ersten Weltkrieges schon überschritten sehen. Die geistesgeschichtliche Entwicklung Englands um die Jahrhundertwende ist in der Forschung als wesentlicher Grund für die Nietzsche-Begeisterung angenommen worden und somit der Verfall der Nietzscheschen Gedanken mit dem Niedergang der evolutionistischen, sozialutopistischen und fortschrittsgläubigen Ideen als vorgezeichnet betrachtet worden. Am Beispiel des irischen Dichters W. B. Yeats kann gezeigt werden, daß eine Nietzsche-Rezeption entgegen zeitgenössischen Strömungen aus dem Geiste fortschrittskritischer, mystischer und leiblich-künstlerischer Weltsicht bis in die dreißiger Jahre möglich war. Zur Erhellung des vielschichtigen Funktionszusammenhanges zwischen den Yeats zugänglichen Nietzsche-Publikationen und der Entwicklung seiner Bildersprache enthält die Arbeit in großem Umfang unveröffentlichtes Material sowie in einem Anhang eine Liste mit den Nietzsche-Übersetzungen in Yeat's Bibliothek mit dem Verzeichnis der von Yeats vorgenommenen Markierungen. Zum Verständnis der Yeatsschen Geisteswelt liefert die vorliegende Untersuchung einen wichtigen Beitrag und weist dabei den Einfluß Nietzsches als wesentliches, unüberhörbares Element auf.

## Verlag Dr. Johannes Königshausen + Dr. Thomas Neumann

Elisabeth Danninger

# SIEBEN POLITISCHE GEDICHTE DER HS. B.L. HARLEY 2253

## Textausgabe und Kommentar

334 Seiten, kt., DM 42,–  ISBN 3-88479-007-2

In der vorliegenden Textausgabe wurden sieben der mittelenglischen politischen Gedichte der Hs. B.L. Harley 2253, die sowohl in sachlicher wie in sprachlicher Hinsicht oft Verständigungsschwierigkeiten bereiten, unter Zugrundelegung des Textes der Hs. und im Vergleich mit anderen Textausgaben und Anthologien kritisch ediert und sprachlich erläutert.

Im Einleitungsteil wird auf Datierungs- und Lokalisationsfragen der Hs., auf Fragen der literarhistorischen Einordnung mittelenglischer politischer Gedichte, auf die Autorenfrage und auf die Dialekte der einzelnen Gedichte eingegangen.

Arthur Bartle

# IDEOLOGEME IM AMERIKANISCHEN ROMAN DER SÜDSTAATEN

*A. Tates, THE FATHERS, R.P. Warrens ALL THE KING'S MEN, C. McCullers THE MEMBER OF THE WEDDING und Fl. O'Connors THE VIOLENT BEAR IT AWAY*

320 Seiten, kt., DM 38,80 – ISBN 3-88479-011-0

Der amerikanische Roman der Südstaaten gehört – eingebettet in die „Southern Renaissance" – mit zu den wichtigsten Aspekten amerikanischer Literatur. Die Studie untersucht an vier verschiedenen, neben Faulkner zentralen Autoren des amerikanischen Südens die Prägekraft übergreifender, im weitesten Sinne kultureller Erfahrungen dieser Region. Dem historisch-gesellschaftlichen Aspekt wird auf zweifache Weise Rechnung getragen: Einerseits schält sich die gemeinsame semantische Basisstruktur als Sinngebung einer *konkreten* Situation in den Südstaaten heraus. Andererseits wird offenbar, daß infolge geschichtlichen Wandels Basisideologeme geändert, neu akzentuiert oder teilweise gelöscht werden.

Neben dem Korpus fiktionaler Texte werden auch expositorische Arbeiten von Literaturwissenschaftlern, Soziologen, Historikern etc. über den amerikanischen Süden mit einbezogen.

Verlag Dr. Johannes Königshausen + Dr. Thomas Neumann

# EPISTEMATA

## Würzburger wissenschaftliche Schriften

*Reihe Literaturwissenschaft, Band I (1980)*

### Hermann Kurzke

## AUF DER SUCHE NACH DER VERLORENEN IRRATIONALITÄT

### Thomas Mann und der Konservatismus

196 Seiten, kt. — DM 36,80
ISBN 3-88479-000-5

Thomas Manns konservativ-nationalistische Parteinahme während des Ersten Weltkriegs, die sich vor allem in den *Betrachtungen eines Unpolitischen* (1918) niederschlug, wurde bisher meist als vorübergehender „Ausrutscher" eines sonst sozialdemokratischen Autors beurteilt. Die Untersuchung zeigt die fundamentale Tragweite der Kategorie Konservatismus für das gesamte Frühwerk und noch weit ins Spätwerk hinein. An Stelle des üblichen Entwicklungsschemas vom Ästheten zum demokratischen Antifaschisten entsteht das Bild eines im Herzen stets Konservativen, der nur unter dem Druck der Zeit zum „Wanderprediger der Demokratie" wurde, aber bei nachlassendem Druck sogleich wieder zu einem unpolitisch-ästhetizistischen Konservatismus neigte. Im Zentrum stehen Analysen der Begriffe „Leben", „Geist", „konservative Revolution", „Ironie" und „Ästhetizismus" sowie Interpretationen der *Betrachtungen eines Unpolitischen*, des *Zauberberg* und der Republikrede von 1922.

Hermann Kurzke ist auch Autor eines 1977 im S. Fischer Verlag erschienenen Berichts *Thomas Mann Forschung 1969-1976* und Herausgeber einer kommentierten Taschenbuch-Ausgabe der Essays Thomas Manns (mit Michael Mann).

Verlag Dr. Johannes Königshausen + Dr. Thomas Neumann